Motor Cruising

PETER CUMBERLIDGE

NAUTICAL

Published by Nautical Books
an imprint of
A & C Black (Publishers) Ltd
35 Bedford Row, London WC1R 4JH

© Peter Cumberlidge 1989

ISBN 0 7136 5810 X

A CIP catalogue record for this book is
available from the British Library.

Typeset by Pindar (Scotland) Ltd, Edinburgh
Printed and bound in Great Britain by
Butler and Tanner Ltd, Frome, Somerset

Acknowledgements

Some of the contents of this book first appeared in article form in *Motor Boat and Yachting*, and I am grateful to all the magazine staff for their help in putting together both my monthly columns and the longer features. I would particularly like to thank Tom Willis (the present Editor), Alan Harper (Deputy Editor), and Alex McMullen (the previous Editor) for all their guidance on the difficult matter of deciding which aspects of cruising and seamanship are most relevant to today's motor boat owners.

Various companies and individuals have provided photographs to help illustrate the book, for which my thanks are due to: Aquamarine Ltd; Martin Beasley of HPS Ltd; F Booker Marine; Corvette Cruisers Ltd; Ron Dummer; Fairline Boats PLC; Grand Banks Boat Showrooms; Paul Hadley Boat Sales; Hatteras Yacht Sales (UK) Ltd; Joan Hill of Cole Communications; Marine Projects Ltd; Motor Boat and Yachting; Natant Marine; Nautech Ltd; Robert and Eve Phillips; Navstar SA; Prout Catamarans Ltd; Sait Marine Ltd; Silva Yates (Plastics) Ltd; Andrew Shanks of Willoughby Stewart Associates; Shipmate Ltd; Simpson-Lawrence Ltd; Sunseeker International Ltd; Whisstocks Ltd; University of Dundee Satellite Station.

My thanks also to Jane Sandland and Mike Collins for drawing the originals for most of the diagrams and charts; Joyce Cumberlidge, for combing the text for errors; Dasher Briggs of Dartmouth, for tracking down the details of some of the older boats; and Peter Coles, for transforming a veritable assortment of material into this book.

Contents

Introduction

The late 1980s saw a rapid increase in the range and popularity of all types of motor boat, from sportsboats right up to the most sophisticated motor yachts. Although there has been a general trend towards planing boats and greater high speed performance, there are also some excellent new designs of displacement hull which are particularly well suited to comfortable cruising.

Motor cruising goes back a long way, before the days of turbo-charged diesels, Decca navigators and mod-con galleys, so it is perhaps surprising that more of the new wave of motor boats are not cruised more widely. There is sometimes a tendency among boat owners of an older school to dismiss planing motor yachts as flashy weekend toys, and yet they offer considerable potential for cruising which, in most cases, is sadly under-used.

Fast cruising speeds can contribute to safety, enabling you to dodge spells of bad weather and escape from trouble if conditions deteriorate unexpectedly. If you don't quite reach shelter in time, many planing hulls perform well at sea in quite heavy conditions, so long as they are adequately powered and you understand how to handle them. Electronic navigation equipment can take much of the stress out of passage-making, provided that you appreciate its limitations and are proficient in the basic principles of navigation.

The comforts and facilities aboard a modern motor yacht are often much better adapted to cruising out of the way places than were their counterparts of an earlier era. Extreme bad weather has to be avoided, of course, but most boats can be taken on much more ambitious expeditions than their owners realise.

At the same time, displacement boats have a lot in their favour when it comes to cruising; a more sea-kindly hull for when the going really gets difficult, greater fuel economy and simplicity of equipment, a more relaxed pace of travel, and a generous capacity for storing all the gear which cruising folk seem to accumulate over the years.

Whichever type of boat you prefer, this book is aimed at the new generation of boat owners as much as those who have been afloat for some time. Keeping this in mind, I have tried to make the seamanship aspects particularly relevant to the boats that many people will now be buying and using. I have not attempted to start from scratch, but have assumed a certain amount of prior knowledge and experience. Because the idea of actually going cruising provides the main focus for the book, I have tried to concentrate attention on the various skills and techniques which seem important to that end.

I have therefore been deliberately selective in the range of subjects covered. This partly reflects my own interests and knowledge, but it also takes into account the idea that most contemporary boat owners probably don't require to know every last detail about their craft in order to be able to enjoy going cruising. Because this book is intended to be a guide to using a boat rather than a boating manual, I hope that it will serve as a decision-making aid to prospective owners, a helpful companion for new owners, and a talking point for established owners.

One point worth underlining here is that I decided not to deal with any technical aspects of engines, transmissions or propellers, since there are good books available written by experts in these particular fields. I think it is also fair to say that a yacht owner these days does not need to be an amateur engineer to the same extent that he used to. There are certain parallels with the world of motoring, in which engines are now taken for granted and seem to do what is required of them almost all the time. Modern marine engines are highly reliable as well, so long as basic checks and servicing are attended to regularly.

I have laid emphasis on boat-handling and general seamanship and, in this respect, I hope that there will be much in the book to help anyone who aspires to the various RYA Motor Cruising certificates, or their equivalents in Europe and the USA.

In all of this I have tried to reinforce my belief that, although going to sea is never something to be taken lightly, any kind of boating should be fun first and foremost. The size of your trusty vessel matters hardly at all. The old adage 'the smaller the boat, the greater the fun' still seems to have a good deal of truth in it, and you sometimes come across owners of large expensive yachts who *used to* enjoy their boating but have somehow managed to complicate the whole business to the point where they experience more stress than pleasure.

Cruising, to my mind, is an especially enjoyable and rewarding occupation, for it's when a boat is nosing into unfamiliar territory that she really seems to come to life and give the greatest satisfaction. Nor do you have to be a hardened seafarer in order to go cruising. A series of short passages can take you a surprising distance if you have enough time to spare and are not averse to lingering in congenial places when indifferent weather makes it imprudent to put to sea.

It is my intention and hope that, by dipping into this book, a few more owners may be tempted to venture a little further from home. I will probably see you somewhere along the way.

Peter Cumberlidge
Llanfair Kilgeddin
1989

A Hatteras 40 under way off the east coast of America. Hatteras have been building boats in the States since 1959, when William Slane's original 41ft motor yacht was based on the then largest production GRP hull anywhere in the world. Today's Hatteras 40 cruises comfortably at about 22 knots with her twin Caterpillar 3208TA V diesels, which drive conventional shafts and 24in×26in four-blade props.

Chapter 1

Types of Motor Cruiser and their Uses

The prospective first-time buyer of a cruising motor boat is usually confronted with a bewildering array of choices. He has only to visit a broker, wander round a boat show, or browse through the yachting magazines to become aware of the enormous range of different types of craft available. To complicate matters further, the technical jargon can be somewhat daunting to the initiate, who has to grapple with terms such as deep-Vee, semi-displacement, hard-chine, outdrives and flying bridges.

One can begin to distinguish different motor boats by classifying them, apart from by size and cost, according to hull shape, type of engine installation and material of construction. To a certain extent these categories are interlinked: for example, some hull shapes are more readily built in GRP than steel or aluminium; and particular engine configurations are more or less appropriate for a given hull type and size. However, it will be useful to consider these three headings in turn and look at some of the possible options for each. I will try and highlight some of the advantages and disadvantages of these options, their relative costs, and the kind of boating for which they are most suitable.

Types of Hull

There are three basic types of motor boat hull design: displacement, planing and semi-displacement (sometimes known as semi-planing). Very simply, displacement hulls always travel *in* water, planing hulls effectively skim *across* the water, and semi-displacement hulls are a compromise and do both.

Displacement hulls

These are traditional in the sense that all boats used to have them, prior to the development of ultra-powerful yet compact marine engines, and before a better understanding of hydrodynamics and naval architecture led to a more common use of planing hulls. According to Archimedes' well known principle, any floating object displaces its own weight of water, and this is true of all boats whatever their hull form so long as they are static. When a *displacement hull* actually starts travelling in water, Archimedes' principle still holds, and you can

9

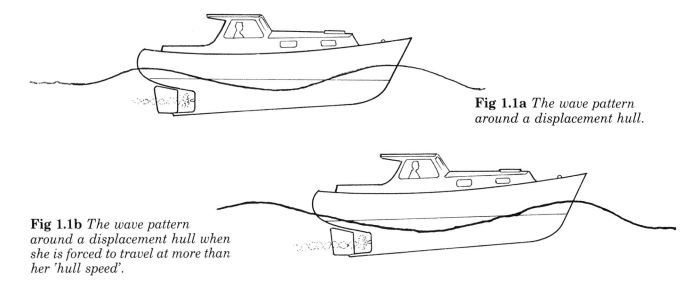

Fig 1.1a *The wave pattern around a displacement hull.*

Fig 1.1b *The wave pattern around a displacement hull when she is forced to travel at more than her 'hull speed'.*

visualise the boat's own weight of water being continually pushed out of the space which the hull is occupying and back to where the hull was just before. Constant pushing aside of the water sets up a wave pattern which moves along with the boat (Fig 1.1a).

As a displacement boat's speed increases, the length and height of these standing waves also increases until a point is reached when the hull is being supported by a single wave at the bow and another at the stern. The boat is then said to have reached her 'maximum' displacement speed, because the only way in which the hull can move any faster is by trying to climb over her own bow wave (see Fig 1.1b). Because this limiting position is determined by the maximum length of the standing waves, you can see that a displacement boat's maximum theoretical speed is closely related to her hull's waterline length.

In fact a hull's maximum displacement speed in knots is given approximately by the square root of the waterline length in feet multiplied by a factor of about 1.4. So a boat with a waterline length of 25ft will have a maximum displacement speed (or hull speed) of about 7 knots; a waterline length of 34ft will allow a maximum displacement speed of 8.2 knots. But what are the practical implications for actual performance? Perhaps the most important

is that the engine and propeller of any boat must be very carefully matched to her ability to be driven through the water and to her maximum displacement speed. A boat which is over-powered to the extent of being pushed beyond her maximum displacement speed will indeed begin to climb her own bow wave, tuck her stern right down in the trough and create a large and inefficient wash, while consuming a sharply increased amount of power to achieve a small speed increase.

Displacement boats of moderate size are thus inherently relatively slow. However, they require engines of much less power than planing or semi-displacement boats to run below hull speed, and are therefore, size for size, less expensive initially and more economical to run.

Another advantage of displacement hulls is that they are reckoned to be more seaworthy than planing boats in bad weather, having the advantage of curved 'wine glass' sections and deepish draught (Fig 1.2) compared with a planing hull's flatter and shallower bottom (Fig 1.3). These two factors make a displacement boat ride more easily than a planing hull *at displacement speeds*, and it wasn't too long ago that most planing boats were forced to slow down and come off the plane to prevent slamming in conditions kicked up by, say, a force 4–5 wind in

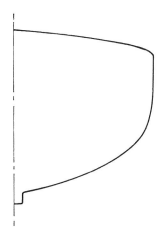

Fig 1.2 *The wine-glass sections of a displacement hull.*

Designed waterline
when the boat is at rest

15°

Chine

Rail

Fig 1.3 *Typical half-section of a planing hull.*

open water. But hull design is now so advanced that many production planing boats can hang onto their power in quite nasty conditions, and of course reach shelter more quickly than displacement boats. The seaworthiness debate is less clear-cut than it once was.

A classic example of a seaworthy displacement motor yacht is the genuine motor fishing vessel (MFV) type. These strongly built vessels are often fishing boat conversions with deep draught, a wide beam aft for stability, but a tucked-in canoe stern to minimise wash and make the hull easily driven.

A genuine MFV yacht makes a fine seaboat and a comfortable cruising home. Astra Volante is seen here anchored in the Mediterranean. (Photo: Robert and Eve Phillips)

Sari-Ann is a classic 58ft Silver motor yacht built in 1958. Powered by two 6LW 98hp Gardners, she cruises easily at 9 knots and uses only 4½ gallons of diesel per hour at this speed. Her fuel capacity of 350 gallons gives a working range of about 500 miles.

A Birchwood TS37 on Scotland's rugged west coast. The TS37 is a fast, comfortable boat which would normally cruise at around 22 knots, depending upon engine installation, but she can still keep up 15-18 knots in surprisingly rough water.

Other things being equal, narrow displacement hulls tend to be more easily driven than hulls with greater beam. Good examples are provided by some of the elegant motor yachts once built by traditional yards such as Thornycroft or Silver. Still readily available on the second-hand market, these vessels are long and narrow, able to slip through the water at 9 or 10 knots using a minimum of power and creating hardly any wash. By contrast, a modern Princess or Birchwood travelling at near her maximum displacement speed kicks up a considerable disturbance and looks most ungainly. However, one

The Pedro steel motor yachts are popular all over Europe. Built in the Netherlands by Pedro-Boot BV, they are usually fitted with single engines for simplicity and economy. This Pedro 33 is a nice size of boat, large enough to be comfortable and yet easily handled by a couple who know what they are doing. The aft deck steering position is pleasant in fine weather and useful when negotiating locks or marinas.

disadvantage of a narrow hull is its tendency to roll in any kind of beam sea.

There is now an attractive and workmanlike range of Dutch production displacement motor yachts on the European market. These boats are usually constructed in steel and often have a single diesel as a straightforward and economical engine installation. The Dutch are past-masters at building in steel and if I was thinking of buying a newish displacement motor yacht for cruising, I would be looking seriously at this type of boat. The popular Pedro 33 is a good example of the genre. She has the attraction of a good-sized aft cabin and a convenient outside helm position on the after-deck. With her traditional hull shape and generous displacement, she is a sturdy sea boat, can cruise economically

at 7 knots and has a maximum hull speed of about 8 knots.

A boat intended for cruising inland waterways will normally have a displacement hull, because speed limits on canals and rivers preclude the possibility of planing. Planing or semi-displacement boats tend to be unhappy at slow speeds; they often make an inordinate amount of wash when travelling off the plane and have poor directional stability at displacement speed. The traditional English canal boat has a displacement hull *par excellence*—long, narrow, usually built of steel, with a square or 'box' section and a flat bottom. Designed to cruise at only 4 or 5 knots in calm water, this kind of boat will generally be powered by a compact diesel engine of no more than about 30hp.

Cruising boats designed specially for the European waterways are much larger than the English narrow boats and you will come across two common styles of hull, both of displacement type. The first looks something like the popular 'waterbuses' of the Amsterdam canals. The beamy displacement hull has a round bilge but a very flat bottom, and the upperworks and roomy accommodation give the impression of a waterborne caravan. These boats are ideal for their intended purpose of gently meandering along the rivers and canals of France or Holland. You will see them advertised for hire in both these countries and on some English rivers. With their very shallow draught, however, they should not venture into exposed tidal waters.

The cruising barge is also a popular choice of boat for the European waterways. These workmanlike steel vessels are fashioned on the distinctive commercial barges but are shorter with not quite so much beam. The traditional wheelhouse is situated aft, and the accommodation is laid out where the cargo hold would be in a working barge.

Planing hulls

We have seen that displacement hulls have an effective maximum speed related to their waterline length, since it is this length which determines the extreme separation of the hull's bow and stern waves. A planing boat can escape from the constraints imposed by these waves by using a combination of extra engine power and clever hull design to develop vertical lift and thus climb partially clear of the water. The boat's maximum speed then ceases to be limited by her bow and stern waves, but is determined largely by her developed engine power, the water resistance of the hull, and the air resistance offered by the upperworks. In principle, a boat with a completely flat bottom would have the best planing performance, but such a hull would give itself and its occupants a very rough ride in any sort of sea. Therefore most planing hulls are V-shaped forward, so as to provide an efficient angle of attack to the water, with sections flattening out aft to gen-

Steel motor yachts are popular with the Dutch, who probably build the best steel boats in the world. Many have single engines for simplicity and economy, especially since the waterways dictate very modest cruising speeds most of the time.

14

erate the necessary lift when sufficient engine power is applied.

This hybrid hull shape is a sound practical compromise because it combines excellent shock absorbing qualities with an efficient planing surface, both where they are most needed. Such a hull is said, in the power-boating jargon, to have *variable deadrise*, referring to the angle between the athwartships plane of the hull and the horizontal. A hull with variable deadrise can also be said, rather unflatteringly, to have a warped bottom. Now you often come across the terms deep-Vee, medium-Vee and shallow-Vee applied to planing boats. These relative labels simply refer to the amount of deadrise in a particular hull. A pure deep-Vee hull has a fairly constant deadrise of 25°–30° along its length, a medium-Vee has about 20°, and a shallow-Vee anything less than 20°.

While displacement boats often have curved sections, planing boats generally have chine hulls, where there is a pronounced angle between topsides and bottom. Although one argument for chine hulls

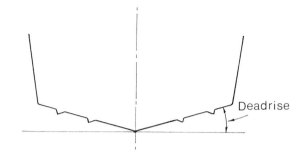

Fig 1.4 *Deadrise is the angle between the athwartships plane of the hull and the horizontal.*

is that they can be cheaper to construct than continuously curved hulls, the chine in a planing boat also forms a functional separation between the 'working' sections of the hull, normally immersed when under way, and the top part which is essentially a box containing the accommodation. In fact planing boats may have several chines, to direct water clear of the hull and reduce spray.

The Princess 35 is a popular cruising boat which can be seen in harbours and marinas all over the world. Her deep-Vee hull was designed by Bernard Olesinski and has integrally moulded spray rails. Speeds of up to 30 knots are possible, depending on the choice of engines. (Photo: Robert Chapman)

One of the important differences between displacement and planing hulls is that the latter depend largely on lift, and hence engine power, for their stability at sea and general ease of handling. Of itself, a Vee-shaped hull is not particularly stable in an athwartships (rolling) direction, either at rest or when travelling at displacement speeds. But once planing, such a hull will be considerably more resistant to rolling or heeling because a kind of self-levelling effect comes into play. If, for example, a high-speed planing boat heels to starboard, a greater area of planing surface is immersed on that side of the hull than on the port side; more lift is therefore generated on the starboard side and less on the port side, so the boat is forced upright again.

A planing boat's *directional stability* is minimal at displacement speeds because, if she has a keel at all, it is likely to be short, shallow, and not very effective until planing speed is reached. At low speed the bow is also immersed and this can help deflect the boat off course in one direction or another. At high speeds, however, the bow lifts clear of the water, even a short keel begins to work to advantage, and the drag of rudders and stern-gear tends to assist directional stability and make the boat easier to steer. As a rule, therefore, planing boats do not perform as well as displacement boats either where they are obliged to travel slowly, or at sea in such heavy weather that they are forced to slow down and come off the plane.

Another important factor affecting the performance of a planing hull is her fore-and-aft trim. Some boats are fitted with trim tabs at the stern, specially designed flaps (usually hydraulically operated) which work rather like those on the trailing edge of an aircraft wing. As these trim tabs are forced down into the stream of water just below the stern, they increase the lift right aft and help bring the hull nearly onto an even keel when planing. A boat which planes at too steep an angle is losing efficiency through water resistance. At too flat an angle it can be losing efficiency because more of the hull's length

The Nimbus 2100 is a well-built weekend cruiser with a lively turn of speed and good seakeeping qualities.

This Princess 412 is a versatile cruising boat with comfortable accommodation and cruising speeds up to 25 knots, depending upon engine installation. The radar and steaming light are mounted well up on the gantry and the davits make it straightforward to use the dinghy.

The Birchwood TS37 is large enough to be a comfortable cruising boat with good sea-keeping qualities, but not so large as to be too much of a handful in marinas and crowded harbours.

is actually in contact with the water and resistance is once again excessive.

The loading of a planing boat can easily affect her trim. While it is important for general seaworthiness not to carry too much weight forward, it is also not a good idea to load the stern down with spare anchors, coils of rope, cans of engine oil and other heavy bits and pieces. Moving some of your least-used gear forward can help flatten your boat's trim and reduce the speed at which she lifts onto the plane. The location of fuel and water tanks is also a critical determinant of trim. Although fuel tanks are often sited aft of the engines, there is something to be said for having water tanks forward of the boat's centre of gravity to compensate for this weight.

On the British and European markets there is now an impressive selection of production planing boats designed for fast cruising. Some of the most popular British-built boats are the Princesses, Birchwoods,

Fairlines, and Brooms. The picture above left shows a Princess 412, from the upper middle of the Princess range. With its three-cabin accommodation, twin diesel engines driving conventional shafts, and seaworthy deep-Vee hull, the 412 is a comfortable boat capable of ambitious cruising.

The picture above right shows a TS37, one of the most versatile boats from the Birchwood range, spacious for its length and with excellent sea-keeping qualities. One obvious difference in hull design between the Princess and the Birchwood is the way in which the hull chines are moulded. The Princess shown has flattish vertical topsides and the spray mouldings are largely confined to the bow area. The Birchwood has quite complex spray mouldings running well aft, a sophistication which adds to the cost of a hull but which helps return stray water back to the sea where it belongs, an important factor when the going gets rough.

A Fairline Corniche 31, designed by Bernard Olesinski. The Corniche is a high-performance sports yacht with a wide range of accommodation and engine options. Twin Volvo TAMD41s driving conventional shafts would give a top speed of around 30 knots.

A Broom 37 in the Firth of Clyde. Powered by twin Perkins diesels, this boat normally cruises at displacement speed and is comfortable, sea-kindly and easy to handle.

The Weymouth 32 has a sea-kindly semi-displacement hull, with a fine V-entry forward and round sections aft; she can be powered safely through surprisingly boisterous seas. Sapper 'A' normally cruises at 15-16 knots and has a maximum speed of about 22 knots.

Semi-displacement hulls

This is rather an elusive category because, in one sense, almost any planing hull can be said to have semi-displacement qualities, travelling as it must partly through the water even while skimming mostly over it. In practice, the term has come to refer to those heavier boats with relatively traditional lines which nevertheless, by virtue of their flattish aft sections, somewhat flared bow and adequate power, are able to generate a certain amount of lift and 'get-up-and-go'.

Good examples of this type are the 'Weymouth' and 'Humber' ranges of workmanlike cruising boat, both classes using one of the strong and well tried Nelson hulls which are so popular as pilot launches and fast workboats. The picture above shows a Weymouth 32, which has a deep-Vee bow running back to round-bilge sections midships and aft. This hull design has an excellent reputation for sea-keeping and the ability to hold onto power when the going gets rough. The curved sections give a more comfortable ride than a planing hull provides if conditions force you to throttle back to displacement speed. Because the deeper round bilge gives direc-

19

tional stability, handling at low speed is generally much better than you can expect from a more extreme planing hull. This type of semi-displacement boat is very versatile for cruising; I have taken a Weymouth 32 up narrow rivers and along some of the French waterways and she will amble along smoothly under one engine.

The Humber 34 shown below is a similar style of boat to the Weymouth 32, but with that little extra 'reach' in a sea and a bit more room below. The Humber 34 is built by F Booker Marine on a hull designed by John Askham and John A Bennett. Booker also built a Humber 35, a very practical

cruising boat with a roomy aft cabin and an outside helm position.

Another popular class of semi-displacement boat is the so-called 'trawler yacht', such as the Grand Banks 42 Classic shown opposite (below). In my view, the resemblance of these hulls to those of working trawlers is rather far-fetched, but this style of yacht is nevertheless highly functional and seaworthy for extended cruising. One point to bear in mind is that their draught is often much shallower than you might imagine. When the Grand Banks first came onto the British market in the early 1960s they were essentially conceived as displacement

The Humber 34 is a workmanlike semi-displacement motor yacht capable of fast passage-making in quite rough water. This boat is fitted with twin Sabre turbo-charged diesels of 150hp each. She cruises at 13 knots and has a maximum speed of 17 knots. With her 200 gallon fuel capacity, the safe working range is about 300 miles.

boats and usually fitted with a single diesel engine. More recently, most builders of trawler yachts have developed their hulls to allow semi-planing performance with more powerful twin engines. The basic underwater profile is similar to that of the Nelson type in that a fine Vee bow gives way to rounded sections aft; however, trawler yachts tend to have more beam and a flatter bottom which makes for greater lift at high speeds and rather more wash at displacement speeds.

These Danish fishing boats are true examples of MFV hulls, deep-draughted and seaworthy. The terms 'MFV' and 'trawler yacht' are often bandied about in sales literature these days, but often with considerable ad-man's licence.

The distinctive Grand Banks motor yachts are designed and built by American Marine Pte Ltd in Singapore. This Grand Banks 42 Classic is a practical cruising boat which provides comfortable accommodation for four in two spacious staterooms. Single or twin diesels can be fitted: the most economical option is the single Volvo TAMD41A, which gives up to 10 knots; twin Caterpillar 3208TAs will allow planing performance up to 20 knots.

A Corvette 32 anchored off the south coast of Spain. The Corvette is designed in the style of the so-called 'trawler yacht', although her semi-displacement hull is capable of speeds up to 22 knots when suitably powered. The faster versions are fitted with twin Volvo TAMD41A diesels of 200hp each. The accommodation is well arranged and the master cabin aft is comfortable and spacious.

One personal reservation I have about some trawler yachts is the considerable height and expanse of their wheelhouse and deck saloons compared with a relatively modest draught. Of course working trawlers often sport a large deckhouse and may also carry a fair amount of heavy gear aloft, but they have the advantage of a respectable amount of hull below the waterline. This is not to belittle the seagoing capability of trawler yachts or to suggest that they are in any way unstable, but it is important that an inexperienced buyer should not interpret the 'trawler' label too literally and imagine that his new vessel is capable of 'storm-force' endurance.

Some of the trawler yachts on the market are really quite compact and can make ideal cruising boats for, say, a couple and two youngsters. The smallest in the Grand Banks range is 32ft overall and there is an attractive and workmanlike competitor in the Corvette 32 (shown above).

Multi-hulls

Although catamaran and cathedral-hull workboats have been in use successfully for many years, it is still surprisingly uncommon for cruising motor boats to be based on a multihull. Catamarans in particular can be extremely power-efficient because, for a given size of boat, the wetted surface area of the hull and hence the water resistance can be relatively small.

Larger power catamarans can be very steady and seaworthy and are often used as high-speed, short-haul passenger ferries. In the motor yacht market, Prout Catamarans of Canvey Island manufacture an impressive-looking 'power cat' called the Panther 44 (shown opposite). This particular design amply demonstrates one of the more obvious advantages of a cruising multihull, the sheer volume of usable space that becomes available for accommodation. One of the features of the Panther 44 is her asymmetric hulls on which both 'inside' surfaces are

relatively flat while the outside surfaces are con-toured in much the same way as a monohull. This configuration gives a clean flow of water between the two hulls and also provides a high degree of directional stability.

It is sometimes a moot point whether catamaran hulls should be classed as planing or semi-displace-ment. Most cats have a fine bow entry and obtain some lift at planing speeds by a flattening of the midships and aft sections. Some of the faster work-boats have a slight 'step' in the bottom of each hull so that a kind of false stern-wave is generated to provide lift (Fig. 1.5). One slightly disconcerting characteristic of a catamaran is its unusual 'slith-ering' motion in a seaway. Multihull powerboats are undoubtedly very stable, in the sense that they don't roll or heel much, but if one hull is on the way up while the other is going down, you can experience an uneasy side-slipping which will confuse your stomach until you get used to this new motion.

The Prout Panther 44 Royale has an asymmetric cat-amaran hull powered by twin intercooled turbo-charged diesels. The cat hull is easily driven and fuel efficient; it also makes for extremely spacious accom-modation, especially in the saloon area.

Fig 1.5 *Some catamaran hulls have a slight step so that a false stern-wave generates extra lift.*

23

Which type of hull?

The type of boat which attracts you will be partly affected by the kind of cruising that you either prefer or are constrained to by circumstances, but it will also depend partly on your own temperament and general style of doing things. One of the most fascinating characteristics of cruising is that it means so many different things to different people, and this is brought home when you look around any yacht harbour and consider the great diversity of craft in which we collectively put to sea. Strangely enough, it is probably true that this diversity is even greater for motor boats than it is for sailing boats.

The experience of cruising in a traditional displacement boat is worlds apart, for example, from cutting along at 20 knots in a modern planing cruiser. Imagine, on the one hand, making a longish coastal passage in a converted MFV on a fine summer day. There is a light offshore breeze, a slight sparkling sea, and the motion of this deep-draught little ship is slow and predictable. Out on deck, you can enjoy the sun in relative peace and quiet, lulled by the gentle sibilance of the bow wave and the refined burble from the exhaust stack of the single Gardner engine. The galley is fully operational and lunch is taken 'alfresco', with siestas on deck in the afternoon. The MFV rumbles steadily on at 8 knots. Having left at 0900, she will have covered over 60 miles by the end of the afternoon, in a non-frantic, relaxing style.

Imagine the same trip made in a 36ft planing boat which can cruise easily at 20 knots, her power being supplied by twin 200hp, high-revving, turbo-charged diesels. If you leave at the same time in the morning, you will have covered 60 miles by midday and can be moored and tidied up at the same destination the MFV was bound for, but in good time for a relaxed lunch. You will have the whole afternoon ahead of you. The passage itself, however, will not have been so relaxing. However good the engine-room soundproofing, the incessant noise from the two monster power units will dominate the three hours for which you are under way. The exhausts do not burble

gently, but crackle in rather a threatening way, like the plant from some industrial works. If the sea is flat, you will manage a mid-morning coffee, but even that will go by the board if there is any sort of chop. It takes great persistence to work in the galley of a planing boat on the move; the unpredictable juddering of the hull can turn even a simple operation like spooning out sugar into a skilled task. Sunbathing may be possible if it is very warm and calm, but don't forget that you will be generating a good force 5 wind over the deck, in addition to what the weather may be supplying. It can be exhilarating up on a flying bridge, out in the fresh air and away from some of the noise, but even this can become tiring after the first couple of hours.

The question is, which of these two styles of cruising do you prefer? Is it better to travel gently or arrive quickly? Which gives you the most satisfaction—the steady and economical progress of displacement cruising or the sense of power and ability to eat up the miles which comes with a high-speed planing boat? The relative seaworthiness of the two types of hull is not, as we have seen, a straightforward issue. A strongly built and well-found MFV type is capable of withstanding some very nasty weather in the open sea and it would usually be the crew who would begin to weaken before the boat.

However, her modest cruising speed does leave a displacement boat more vulnerable than a planing boat to unexpected changes in weather, and she is also less able to make use of brief 'lulls'. On a passage of 70 miles, for example, our MFV needs a whole day of reasonable conditions. Her 400hp opposite number can take advantage of a fine morning and, even if worse weather is expected later, be safely tucked up before the deterioration. If a modern planing boat *is* caught short, her ability to take a dusting for a short period should not be underestimated, provided her machinery is all in good order. Reliable speed also enables passages to be contemplated where time is limited, as on weekends, and so can allow the boat to be used more freely. However, a fast cruising speed is of the essence. I have delivered under-powered planing boats which give the worst of both worlds, by keeping you at sea for longer than necessary and

The Freeman 27 (Photo: courtesy Motor Boat & Yachting)

The Channel Islands 22.

by preventing the hull from giving its best performance for lack of horsepower.

For smaller boats, say between 20ft and 27ft overall, the 'displacement versus planing' arguments for open water cruising can become blurred by the practical constraints on sea-going imposed by size alone. The picture above left shows one of the popular Freeman 27 cruisers which, although often seen on the Thames and other inland waterways, are quite capable of coastal passage-making in experienced or cautious hands. This last reservation is important because there is a definite limit on the sea conditions to which this type and size of boat should be exposed. The shallow-Vee hull is certainly capable of planing

in quiet water if suitably powered, but was not designed for driving at speed in heavy seas. The Freeman 27 is usually fitted with a single diesel of modest power, giving a displacement cruising speed of about 6 knots and a maximum of $7\frac{1}{2}$ knots. The spacious accommodation allows a family of four to cruise comfortably within the safe limits of the boat's sea-going ability.

On the other hand you have the Channel Islands 22 shown above right. This rugged little offshore boat has a sea-kindly semi-displacement hull and is quite suitable for extended coastal cruising if you are not too worried by the necessarily limited accommodation. A range of engine options provides

Two Sunseeker Tomahawk 37s powering across a calm Mediterranean. This high-performance sports boat has a spacious cockpit and a racing-type helm position with well braced co-pilots' seats. Designed for unashamed pleasure, the Tomahawk 37 has a large sunbed aft and a hydraulically operated bathing ladder which stows flush within the transom. The considerable power is supplied by twin Volvo diesels up to 200hp each, or twin Mercruiser petrol engines up to 370hp each.

various combinations of speed and economy.

The sea-going ability of the Channel Islands 22 is somewhat exceptional for this size of boat. First-time buyers should bear in mind that there are a good many displacement and planing motor cruisers of 27ft and under which, like the Freeman 27, are undoubtedly comfortable to live aboard and cruise in relatively sheltered waters, but which should only be used for open sea passages in quiet, settled weather, at least initially. Of course it is possible to become more ambitious about coastal cruising once you are completely familiar with your own boat, her engine(s) and her equipment, and once you have gained some local experience, either intentionally or unintentionally, of how she behaves in more boisterous conditions.

'Sports-cruisers' are a popular type of fast motor boat, many of which fall into the length range between about 22ft and 29ft. The genre also includes much bigger boats like the Sunseeker Tomahawk 37 (above), which is essentially a well-appointed and eye-catching fast funboat aimed squarely at the blue skies, warm seas, and bikini-draped cockpit market. However, the sophisticated Sunseeker hulls perform impressively in lively water and are readily capable of dealing with those short sharp seas which soon build up in a fresh breeze off Mediterranean coasts or on lakes. The smaller Sunseeker Portofinos have accommodation for two or three in the forecabin, and a couple can have great fun cruising this kind of boat wherever the weather is reliably warm and settled.

Chapter 2

Financial Aspects

If you are a prospective boat owner, there are four important questions which you need to address before seriously starting to search the magazines and brokers' lists for a suitable craft:

—Are you intending to buy new or second-hand?
—What level of total outlay can you realistically afford? Bear in mind that any budget will have to include: all purchase and survey costs; the basic price of the boat, plus any tax due; the cost of any proposed repairs (in the case of a second-hand boat), alterations or additional equipment; the likely annual cost of fuel, berthing, insurance and maintenance, which will depend not only on the size but also the type of boat that you buy.
—How will the purchase be financed and over what sort of period?
—Are you set on sole ownership, or are you interested in some form of boat-owning partnership or syndicate?

New versus Second-hand

The market in new or nearly new power boats has certain characteristics in common with the market in up-to-date cars. One of the most significant is that,

in real terms, the first owner of a modern production boat can usually expect a relatively steep depreciation over the first year or so of the boat's life. From the point of view of a buyer, this means that there will generally be a substantial difference between the new price of this year's boat, all fitted out and ready for sea, and the second-hand price of a similar, 'low mileage' boat a year or two old. Part of this gap reflects that rather intangible 'cost of newness', but part stems from the fact that even quite expensive items of 'extra' equipment fitted to a boat are apt to lose their individual value once she is being resold with all equipment included.

Another notable feature of the market is the growing trend for manufacturers to bring out frequent 'new models', which sometimes incorporate important design differences but which often add up to slightly restyled versions of the original. This process results in different 'generations' of a basic design of boat, with successively older models slotting into markedly lower price brackets on the second-hand market. For production boats, as with cars, you pay a premium both for newness and for owning a more or less current model. This trend is likely not only to continue, but to become even more accentuated as the recent growth in the market,

27

which gathered momentum in the mid-1980s, is gradually taken up. As this happens, the scope for new boat sales will become increasingly dependent on the creation of new lines of fashion.

This is good news for prospective buyers who are primarily interested in value-for-money and who are quite prepared to buy an 'older model' in sound condition if the price is right. On the other hand, it is an unfortunate fact nowadays that many GRP production boats are not being built with longevity in mind, so you will need to look very closely at any advertised craft which is more than about seven or eight years old. This is not to say that she is likely to be in imminent danger of falling to pieces, but there is always that niggling risk of osmosis in the hull, and a fair probability that many of the fixtures and fittings, which may not have been of the highest marine grade to start with, could now be suffering badly from prolonged exposure to sea air.

When considering the second-hand market, you should not restrict yourself to the comparatively recent strata of GRP production boats; remember that there are also plenty of more traditional wooden yachts still in sound condition and doing sterling service. The best examples of these might have emerged from their builders' sheds at any time between the 1930s and 1960s, and current prices of the larger yachts from the earlier part of this period compare favourably with those of today's powerful, high-speed cruising boats. Of course it is true that largish traditional yachts are apt to attract largish traditional maintenance bills, but they also use considerably less fuel per mile than their modern high-horsepower counterparts.

One of the main difficulties of buying a second-hand boat lies in accurately assessing the condition of her hull, machinery and equipment. An amazing amount of potential trouble can lurk unseen, just waiting for an inexperienced buyer to come along and claim it as his very own. If you find a boat which begins to interest you, it is important to inspect her thoroughly yourself, from stem to stern, before deciding to bring a surveyor onto the scene. Even if you are a relative novice about boats, you can still obtain a useful, overall idea of how well she has been

fitted out and looked after over the years. Take careful notes on anything that doesn't seem quite as it should, so that you can raise points with the surveyor at a later stage. By the same token, a surveyor's comments and report will make much more sense if you have first been over the boat yourself.

Look for a clean and well-organized engine space, as a first indication that the machinery has been methodically maintained under the present ownership: a tidy engineroom is usually a reliable hallmark of a caring engineer. If the boat is afloat and in commission, be sure to spend time listening to the engines running with their hatches or covers off, while watching carefully for oil or diesel leaks, or for signs of any water weeping from the cooling system. Check the instrument readings as soon as the engines are started and look for any appreciable fall in oil pressures as everything warms up. Listen for extra vibration and noises as the revs go up.

The next stage is to arrange a test run, probably with the owner but perhaps just with the broker. For this trip, it can be useful to have a nautically inclined friend along with you, not necessarily an expert but at least someone whose judgment and opinions you trust. Again, take careful notes for your eventual sessions with a surveyor, listing any item of equipment which doesn't appear to be working properly, such as windscreen wipers, bilge-pumps, autopilot, anchor winch and so on. Pay particular attention to the steering: does the system operate smoothly, or is there any stiffness or excessive play? Have the engine-space hatches removed for part of the trip, watching for leaks as before, but also looking for any excessive vibration when the engine is working under load. If you can do so safely, lay a hand on top of each gearbox, to check for any vibration which might be due to a shaft being either out of line or not quite straight.

Surveying a GRP hull is a specialist business, and some symptoms of structural stress or latent osmosis can be almost invisible to the untrained eye. However, before you commission a professional survey, and even while the boat is afloat, you can still inspect her topsides carefully for signs of cracks or major dents in the gelcoat. A hull which looks as if it has

Romara combines elegance, comfort and sea-kindliness in a style which is unsurpassed in these days of high-speed planing hulls. Built of teak on steel by Camper and Nicholson in 1934, Romara is still powered by her two original Gardner 68hp diesels. At her cruising speed of 10 knots, the 540 gallon fuel capacity gives a range of about 550 miles.

been in the wars may warn of a slapdash or less than competent owner. On the other hand, small and neatly executed gelcoat repairs may well be a sign that the owner is conscientious about his maintenance.

Professional surveys

A thorough, professional survey is undoubtedly a sound investment for anyone who finds himself suf-

ficiently interested in a particular second-hand boat to have ventured some form of offer to buy. It is not uncommon for a would-be purchaser to become so carried away with the prospect of owning his own boat, that he is tempted to push ahead with a quick transaction without the benefit of a third-party, professional opinion. This temptation must be strongly resisted. You should always remember that a surveyor's charges are relatively modest when set against most purchase prices, or when compared

Schalime II *was built in 1939 by Hornby and Co. of Wallasey. At just over 43ft overall, she has a beam of 10.7ft and a 4ft draught. Her twin Perkins 58hp diesels give her a comfortable and economical cruising speed of about 7 knots. There are still good examples of this style of boat on the second-hand market and, although the maintenance involves a significant commitment, these little ships are very satisfying to own and run.*

with the potential costs of a boat in worse condition than you had ever imagined possible.

On the other hand, you do need to be careful about choosing and instructing a surveyor. In principle, almost anyone may set up as a yacht surveyor, regardless of their qualifications or experience. It is therefore advisable that buyers should first get in touch with the relevant national professional association (see page 192). They will be able to advise on members located in any particular area, or to recommend those who have special expertise which might be required for a particular type of boat. It can be a good idea to talk with two or three surveyors, before deciding on one who seems both to know his business and with whom you think you will get on well.

The survey of a motor yacht should include not only the hull and structure of the vessel, but also all vital machinery and equipment. The steering gear often receives less attention than it deserves, and the whole linkage needs to be examined carefully for wear, or perhaps for bad engineering which may cause problems later. The engines themselves are clearly an important part of the survey, and so are such items as propellers and shafts, shaft brackets, all associated sterngear such as shaft and thrust bearings, stern glands, reduction gearboxes, and so on. What is the condition of the fuel and water tanks? Removing and replacing them can be a difficult and costly business. How about the pipework between fuel tanks and engines? Does this appear to be sound and neatly run, or does it wander around the engine space like so much spaghetti?

A survey report should cover the state of all sea-cocks in the hull, whether they serve the engines, heads, galley or cockpit drains. The installation of gas appliances is of critical importance, whether you are talking about cookers, cabin heaters, water heaters or fridges. Gas bottles should always be located outside the cabin, in a gas-tight locker with a drain overboard. Supply piping should be of high quality seamless copper, and the final connection to a gimballed stove ought to be made with a length of armoured, fire-proof, flexible pipe. The boat should also have a reliable gas detector.

The electrics represent a key area of a motor yacht's auxiliary and domestic equipment. The wiring itself should be of good quality and in sound condition, but the way in which the whole system is organized is also important. All cable runs about the ship should be clipped neatly to bulkheads, out of sight wherever possible, although easy to get at in case any lengths need replacing. You will of course prefer to see workmanlike junction-boxes rather than messy taped joints. All circuits should be properly protected, at least by a readily accessible fuse-box, but preferably by circuit-breakers, which are far more practical at sea than fuses. You will be interested in the condition of the batteries, because these heavy-duty types are expensive to replace.

There should be at least two bilge pumps aboard, one of them manual but both of adequate capacity. Two specific points for the surveyor to check are (a) the quality of the wiring to, and the general installation of, any electric bilge-pumps (there are plenty of Heath Robinson devices to be found masquerading as vital safety equipment), and (b) that all bilge

pumps are fitted with a filter or 'strum box' at the point at which they draw in their water. There are also various items of deck gear to bear in mind. For example, are the anchors and chain in good condition, large enough, and is the anchor winch up to the job? Are the cleats or bollards large enough and strongly bolted through the deck?

Problems with buying new

It is a mistake to believe that all the problems which you might associate with buying second-hand can be completely avoided by placing an order for a new boat, whether a stock or custom design. New kinds of problems arise, and it is not unknown for eager purchasers to be subject to late delivery, poor workmanship, or to discover that certain items of equipment on their dream boat do not work as they should. Manufacturers vary in their reputations for quality control and it is usually worth talking to recent new owners, preferably those who have just taken over a type of boat in which you are interested. Boat Shows are useful for viewing various boats in detail, but also for trying to get some idea of how various manufacturers are likely to treat customers after contracts have been signed.

Of course a certain give-and-take is required on both sides of the often delicate relationship between a customer and a boat-builder. Modern motor yachts are highly complex and it is hardly surprising that minor delays or faults sometimes occur. You as customer will need to be firm about insisting on the standard of workmanship, finish, and reliability that the manufacturer has led you to expect. At the same time, it is always helpful if customers appreciate some of the difficulties which builders can face, and are accommodating wherever possible.

Any new boat will need a shake-down period in which most defects can be brought to light and rectified. Engine trials are a key part of this process, and you should keep a very close eye on all aspects of the engines during their first few hours' running. Monitor all pressures, temperatures and charging rates frequently, but also examine the engines carefully while they are running under load, watching for oil, fuel or water leaks and checking for any excessive vibration, especially in the region of stern glands and gearboxes. It is wise to keep to a very modest cruising speed until you are sure that everything is functioning properly, gradually building up the revs over a period of time, in accordance with the manufacturer's running-in procedures.

There are two schools of thought about taking a new boat cruising. The first argues that a boat which has just been commissioned will be so prone to defects and so unfamiliar to her owner, that the first season should be spent in local waters, to allow everything on board to be gradually worked into sea-going trim. The second school insists that there is no better way to 'sort out' a new boat than to take her off on a cruise, so that all aspects of her equipment are tested under working conditions. I tend to subscribe to the second argument, with the proviso that it is vital to carry out thorough engine trials before embarking on a passage. The open sea in a freshening wind is no place to discover a diesel leak or an engine running hot.

Having said this, it makes good sense to plan any shake-down cruise in the expectation that not everything will run smoothly. Don't attempt too ambitious a schedule, and try to work out an itinerary that will allow you to call into harbours well provided with reliable engineers and electricians. It is a good idea to discuss your intentions with the manufacturers of your new boat and to come to some arrangement about what will happen if it is found that important warranty work needs to be carried out while you are away. If you are bound foreign, for example, it might be worth arranging your route so that it would be possible to call at one of the manufacturer's overseas agents in the event of any serious problems arising with the boat or her equipment—provided they actually can provide solutions on the spot.

The same kind of planned pessimism will be required on your first cruise with a second-hand boat, except that the question of maintaining contact with a manufacturer will not arise. However careful your winter programme of maintenance and fitting-out, you can always expect odd defects to turn up aboard

an unfamiliar boat in the course of a cruise. It is good policy to carry a wide selection of tools, spare parts, and plenty of nuts, bolts and screws, to help you cope with faults as they arise. Hope for the best by all means, but it is sound seamanship to suspect that things will rarely run according to plan, particularly where things mechanical are concerned; a prudent yachtsman will always try to make provision for those 'unexpected' breakdowns.

Costs involved in buying a boat

Anyone who has ever become the proud owner of any kind of cruising boat, will know that there is a considerable difference between an apparent purchase price and the total amount of money which somehow needs to be expended before the aforesaid trusty vessel has finally changed hands, found a safe berth and been made ready for sea in all respects. This mysterious budgetary phenomenon appears to apply more or less equally to new and second-hand craft, and it has perplexed generations of yachtsmen and their bank managers.

If you intend buying second-hand, you will begin to incur expenses as soon as you start travelling to look at boats. Perusing the classified ads in the yachting magazines doesn't cost much, but then you might spot a likely candidate at a reasonable looking price, moored on the other side of the country. You arrange to go and see her one weekend—it should after all, be an interesting trip. The boat isn't quite what you are after, but you get talking to her owner until quite late. You decide to stop the night at a hotel in a nearby village, enjoy a good dinner and return home the next day. A very pleasant jaunt but expensive if you repeat the process half-a-dozen times. Of course boat-hunting can be a very agreeable pastime in itself, and there are more than a few people exploring the creeks, rivers and boatyards around our coast on a more or less permanent basis.

Next comes the survey, but it is not uncommon for a prospective buyer to become sufficiently keen on a boat to have a survey carried out, and then be put

This Ocean Alexander is a distinctive motor yacht, built by the Ocean Marine Company Ltd in Taiwan and designed by Edwin Monk.

ff by a gloom-laden report of her defects. The whole process, including the settlement of a surveyor's account, will then have to be repeated the next time a suitable contender is discovered. Eventually, when you have found your boat, obtained an acceptable survey, negotiated a price and clinched the deal, you are then the proud owner of a vessel which may well be lying a considerable distance from where you intend to keep her, and which may or may not be seaworthy enough to undertake a passage to her new home port.

If she is currently moored at a boatyard or marina, you will usually become liable for berthing charges from the date of your title, unless you have come to a different arrangement with the previous owner. Before you finally agreed on a purchase price, you would no doubt have assessed how much work was necessary before your ship could be taken away, and carefully worked out how much this work would cost. When she is ready for sea, there will be a delivery element to build into your budget, whether you bring the boat home yourself, employ the services of a professional delivery crew, or even have her transported by low-loader. Cruising a boat home yourself over several weekends will involve marina charges or harbour dues for the 'pauses' between legs, as well as travelling expenses for your crew.

You may need to obtain certain basic items of gear before you can bring your boat safely home by sea; new lifejackets or flares, for example, and perhaps even warps, fenders or anchor chain. It might also be prudent to fit any major additional pieces of equipment sooner rather than later, e.g. a new VHF or maybe an autopilot. You will need charts and pilot books for a delivery trip, as well as the usual stores, tools and spares required for passage-making. The fuel tanks will have to be filled, an event which can result in a sizeable bill for large displacement yachts. And before you set off, is your new acquisition fully insured for the sea areas in which she will be travelling? When you arrive triumphant at your home port, the relentless berthing charges will begin their annual cycle.

Even if your boat has come straight from her builder's yard, don't expect to put your cheque book away as soon as the final part of the contract has been settled. New boats are often rather optimistically described by their manufacturers as 'ready to sail away', but are rarely to be found in such an ideal state. You should agree with the builder exactly what equipment is included as 'standard' and what is to be regarded as 'extra'. If you intend buying a boat abroad and bringing her back, make sure any additional taxes or import duties have been considered: this can represent a lot of money, especially if you have made no provision for it.

Financing your purchase

Many of the major yacht builders have a working arrangement with a particular finance company, in order to smooth the business of setting up marine mortgages or similar facilities for their customers. Marine mortgages used to be restricted to a very short term but five-year mortgages are now more common, with longer terms possible for preferred

customers who are purchasing at the more expensive end of the market. Most of the standard marine mortgages taken out for UK residents are conditional on the yacht being registered as a British Ship, a process which involves some expense. Any form of finance will require the yacht to be comprehensively insured for her full value, and a recent condition survey will be necessary for a second-hand vessel.

Even if a manufacturer does offer to arrange a mortgage through an associated finance company, it is important to make enquiries elsewhere, with a view to negotiating the best possible terms. It is a good idea to discuss the matter with your own bank at an early stage, since they may well come up with the most competitive facilities. If you are contemplating a purchase which is close to the edge of what you can comfortably afford, remember that certain items of a yacht's inventory consist of 'luxuries' whose purchase might reasonably be delayed for a year or two.

Joint ownership: partnerships and syndicates

Boat-owning partnerships and syndicates are becoming increasingly popular, partly because many yachtsmen are tending to look for greater cost-effectiveness in how these expensive assets are employed. Joint ownership can certainly represent a practical way of affording a larger or perhaps more modern boat than would otherwise be possible, at the same time as ensuring that she is kept busy during the season and that her annual costs are shared.

It is difficult to lay down guidelines for a successful joint ownership scheme, since many workable partnerships run on quite diverse lines. Some are based on agreements drawn up with great relish by solicitors, which specify the exact terms of the venture, the obligations and benefits attaching to each partner, and the boat's annual timetable of use. There are also many less formal arrangements, some of which work well and others being prone to various difficulties in the allocation of expenses, weekends of use or summer holiday periods. It is largely up to the individuals concerned to decide the degree of formality with which they feel comfortable, but it is wise for every partnership to have a written agreement which at least sets out each member's financial stake in the boat, their individual liabilities both for annual running costs and unexpected expenses, and a procedure for any party who wishes to dispose of his or her share.

Many yachtsmen could not contemplate joint ownership on any terms, simply because they regard a boat as a rather personal kind of possession which they'd feel unable to share with anyone else. Others would only consider it with a very good friend or a member of their family. Bear in mind, though, that the potential advantages of a partnership or syndicate are not simply financial. Partners who are keen on cruising reasonable distances will probably be able to organize rather more ambitious summer expeditions than a sole owner who has a similar ration of annual leave. Two partners can work out a cruise which involves one undertaking the outward leg and the other bringing the boat home. With more than two partners, you have even greater scope for cruising the boat quite long distances in separate legs.

Some important legal considerations

Clear title A prime consideration when you are proposing to buy a second-hand boat is that you first establish: (a) that the person offering the boat for sale is in fact her full legal owner, and (b) that the boat is free of all mortgages or other charges by banks or finance companies. On the first point, it will usually be easier to trace the title of a registered than an unregistered boat, since the Registrar should have had sight of the Bills of Sale on each occasion that she has changed hands.

On the second point, it is important for a would-be purchaser of a second-hand boat to appreciate the implications of either registered or unregistered mortgages. Now, any previous owner could have

taken out a mortgage either to pay for the boat, carry out substantial repairs or improvements, or perhaps even for an entirely unrelated purpose. If the boat was fully registered at the time and the funds were obtained through a bank or finance company, it is almost certain that the details would have been notified to the Registrar and the charge entered on the register as a *registered mortgage*.

Whether or not a mortgage is registered, it will attach to the boat until formally cleared, even if she subsequently changes hands. A buyer thus inherits any such charges, unless precise arrangements are made for the debt to be repaid to the mortgagee from the proceeds of the sale, or else transferred fully to the vendor. From a buyer's point of view, the only practical difference between registered and unregistered mortgages is that he will be able to find out about the former by making enquiries of the Registrar at the Port of Registry. Unregistered mortgages can be almost impossible to trace, so that final recourse for the buyer, in the event of an undisclosed charge coming to light, will depend largely upon the contract of sale with the vendor.

Contracting to buy a new craft A new motor yacht represents a substantial sum of money, both for the customer and for the builder, so it is crucial that both parties have identical and precise expectations of what is to be supplied, when and for how much. Misunderstandings over these deceptively simple questions form the basis of almost all disputes which arise over the sale of a new boat. It is therefore important that the purchaser and builder should agree and set down in detail the terms of the contract between them (see page 175).

Insolvency of the builder The late 1970s and early 1980s were difficult years for the marine trade: a good many boat builders ran into financial problems and were taken into receivership. Customers who had ordered boats and paid instalments found themselves in the unpleasant position of being unable to recover their money or to establish ownership of their part-completed vessel. Times have since improved and, at the time of writing, the European boat-building industry is relatively healthy and better managed than it ever has been. However, any buyer should at least consider the possibility of his builder going bankrupt.

The industry does not, unfortunately, maintain a guarantee fund to protect the customers of defaulting boat builders. There are really only three practical measures which a buyer can take to help safeguard his interest in a vessel which has not yet been completed or handed over to him. The first is to make careful enquiries about the builder's record, before entering into any serious negotiations. This will be a relatively easy matter in the case of the larger, established manufacturers, but more difficult where smaller, less well-known companies are concerned.

The second step is to draw up a precise contract with the builder before any money changes hands, preferably along the lines of a standard agreement such as that given on page 175. The terms of this agreement do not deal explicitly with the possible bankruptcy of a builder, although clauses 5 and 6 do cover the instance of a builder failing to proceed with the construction of the vessel with reasonable despatch, and with the purchaser's right of access to the vessel and the builder's premises. Clause 11 is the important term in the case of bankruptcy, and it states that: 'The craft and/or all materials and equipment purchased or appropriated from time to time by the Builders specifically for its construction (whether in their premises, water or elsewhere) shall become the property of the Purchaser upon the payment of the first instalment under this agreement or (if it be later) upon the date of the said purchase or appropriation ...' This leads to the third measure a buyer can take to secure his interests; that is, to identify and establish, at an early stage, all those items, especially the hull and engines, which the builder has already obtained or ordered for his boat. It can be seen that problems could especially arise where a first instalment has been paid, but various items which this money was intended to cover have either

not yet been delivered to the builder's premises or, if they have been delivered, cannot readily be traced back to the job in hand.

In practice, an appointed receiver will initially hold onto any assets which appear to belong to the builder or the company, including significant items such as complete or part-completed boats, hulls, engines, electronic equipment and so on. A customer caught up in this situation can only hope to recover that which can clearly be shown to 'belong' to him i.e. anything which the builder has bought or ordered on his behalf, against a paid instalment, rather than acquired for general stock.

All this is rather gloomy and the majority of new boat purchases proceed without any shadow of financial hiatus on either side. It is, however, a wise precaution for all i's to be dotted and t's crossed right from the outset. With any ambiguity thus cleared away, the relationship between builder and buyer is more likely to run smoothly to a mutually successful conclusion.

A Weymouth 32 cutting along at 15 knots off St Helier in the Channel Islands. This semi-displacement motor yacht is based on the sturdy Halmatic hull which has formed the basis of so many workboats and fast launches.

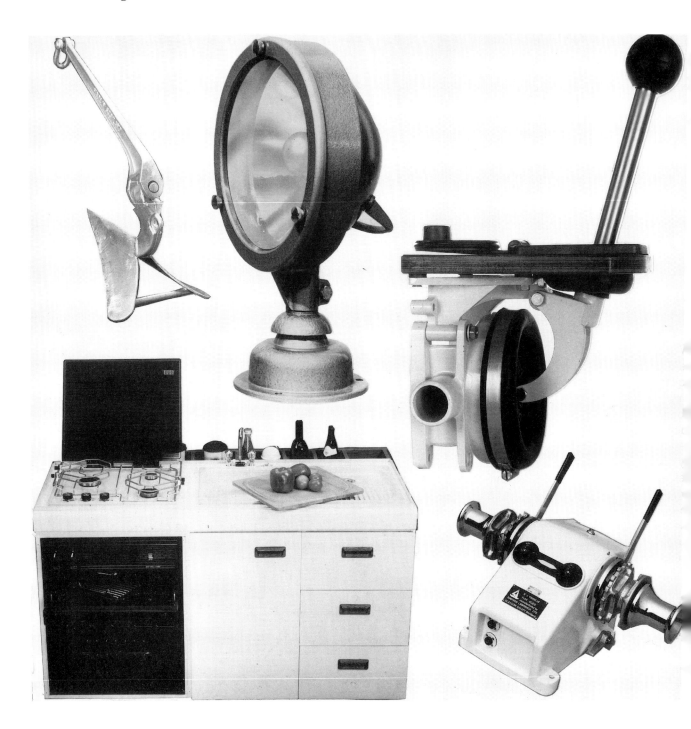

Chapter 3

Choosing Equipment

Whether you buy a new, a nearly new or a distinctly second-hand boat, the selection of 'extra' gear and equipment to go on board can occupy at least as much time (and a surprising amount of money) as thinking about the hull and the engines. In fact, most yachtsmen derive a great deal of satisfaction from the process of adding new items of gear to their boat year by year, so that she gradually becomes better and better suited to the kind of boating they like best. For the purposes of considering a reasonable selection from the huge range of boat equipment available, I will look at four different categories: domestic, deck gear, navigation and 'behind-the-scenes' equipment.

Domestic Equipment

This category of equipment is rather akin to the idea of making your house more comfortable and convenient. A few owners are somewhat spartan and prefer a minimum of mod cons, but if you are planning to make extended cruises with your boat, you will be living aboard her for long periods of time and there is therefore no reason for living any less comfortably than you would at home.

The galley

Most European production motor yachts use bottled gas for cooking. This is by far the most convenient fuel and is perfectly safe so long as the basic installation is sound and provided that you always follow two simple rules:

a) Always turn the gas off at the bottle when you are not using the cooker, especially overnight.

b) When lighting the gas, make a habit of always lighting the match *before* turning on the gas ring, so that no gas escapes into the boat unburned. Some boats use patent gas lighters in the galley, but some of these are more effective than others. If you have to wait for more than a second or two before the ring lights up, you risk accumulating a dangerous quantity of gas in the bilge over a period of time.

Given a choice, the use of bottled gas is best avoided aboard boats powered by petrol engines, since petrol vapour and butane or propane make a particularly explosive combination which probably more than doubles the risk of an accident. You might get away with a small quantity of stray petrol vapour, or a slight whiff of escaped gas, but a bit of both mixed together is a dangerous cocktail. Having said that, there are still plenty of boats around that have been cruising for years with a gas cooker and a petrol engine. If both are well installed and you are meticulous about avoiding spillage, you should not worry too much about buying such a boat second-hand and using her as she is.

A safer alternative to gas cooking for petrol-engined boats is to use a pressure paraffin stove, the modern versions of which are really quite sophisticated. The advantage of paraffin is purely one of safety, since it is not explosive. However, it is not all that easy to get hold of these days, and the burners need pre-heating when you light the stove, usually with methylated spirits (methanol). The American boat safety regulations are much stricter than they are in Europe and electric cooking is common aboard larger motor yachts in the States. I must say that I've no experience of this myself and have always imagined that you must need to turn on a generator, or have huge banks of batteries, to cope with the current drain. In principle, though, the system seems attractive from the point of view of safety and convenience, especially if you are cruising and are using the engines regularly in any case.

Refrigerators A galley fridge is practically standard equipment aboard even the smallest motor yacht these days and is definitely a great boon if you can find the space. Modern units are quiet and energy-efficient and are no problem at all to run so long as your auxiliary batteries have a reasonable capacity and you are running the engines every other day or so. If fitting a fridge yourself, make sure that you choose one which is large enough to hold everything you'd like to keep cool. Some of the very small yacht fridges are more trouble than they're worth, because all sorts of containers won't quite fit into them.

Some fridges can be run on either gas or electricity, the theory being that you use electricity while the engines are running and then switch over to gas in harbour. My own experience with this type of fridge, which may be untypical, is that the gas side of things seems prone to various niggling problems. You also have more gas pipe running around the ship, so I would generally prefer to stick to a battery-only unit.

Hot water Many motor yachts have two means of providing hot running water: (a) via the engine, by using a heat exchanger and a well-lagged hot-water tank, and; (b) using an instant gas heater, which can be mounted on a convenient bulkhead and lights up automatically whenever a hot water tap is turned on. There is much to be said for having both systems if space and budget allow. If, however, you have to choose, I would tend to go for the heat exchanger type. They are remarkably efficient, the water stays hot for a surprisingly long time after the engine is stopped, and of course the power is 'free', in the sense that the energy would otherwise be wasted by heating the cooling water that disappears over the side. Gas heaters normally work very well, but they need a carefully arranged flue to the deck and of course there is yet more gas piping to worry those of us with a nervous disposition.

One of the least considered aspects of a boat's water system is invariably the main tank capacity. Some production motor yachts have pitifully small water tanks and their owners are forever having to top up when they go cruising. Perhaps this is no great problem if you are in the habit of hopping from marina to marina, but it is a serious drawback if you like to escape to out-of-the-way anchorages. Self-sufficiency will become important and you will want to carry enough water for at least a week's not too miserly usage. Some of the larger ocean-going yachts have the luxury of a reverse-osmosis desalination plant to provide fresh water from sea water, but this equipment is both expensive and rather bulky and is not yet practical for the more modest sized production yachts.

Double drainers A double galley sink is highly practical aboard a boat, especially when you are passage-making. Washing-up can be safely left to drain in one of the sinks, which are also handy places to put mugs when you are making tea, coffee or soup.

Waste bin Few boat designers give serious thought to providing a proper waste bin in the galley.

one which is easy to use and has a decent capacity. The quantity of household rubbish that builds up from day to day is quite astounding. You take account of this in your kitchen as a matter of course, and yet there is all the more reason why a galley should incorporate a well-designed rubbish bin. The best and simplest system I have seen aboard a boat has a large plastic household gash bin (the type with a swinging lid) built into the galley area somewhere near the sink. All you normally see is the top of the bin, but the whole thing can be removed for washing and for replacing the plastic liners.

Ventilators   Some boats seem to have inadequate ventilation in both the galley and the heads, so it is worth considering whether your own accommodation could benefit from a better circulation of air. Efficient ventilation is good for the boat, her equipment and her crew, and it is preferable to err on the generous side when fitting either Dorade boxes or the more compact flat ventilators. Solar-powered vents seem to work quite well, but it is also a good idea to have several ports which can be left open in fine weather. A heads compartment really ought to have its own opening hatch.

Night lighting   For night passages, it is worth installing a low-wattage diffused red light both in the galley and at the chart table so that both can be used without ruining night vision. Engine instruments ought to be no brighter than necessary, as it is surprising how much total light a large bank of dials can give off.

The 'bathroom'

Modern production boats offer far more spacious and sophisticated facilities than the previous generation of yachtsman was brought up on. The 'heads' are generally much easier to use, with less of the complicated wheel valves and levers which once made their operation such a nightmare to the uninitiated. Shower units are now quite commonplace, although many are not all that simple to use in practice. I

think that the best type of shower is where the whole compartment can be wetted without any problem; those that depend on a small nylon curtain are very much a mixed blessing.

If you are installing a shower yourself, make sure that the outlet pump is a good heavy-duty unit fitted with a sturdy and easy-to-clean filter. I have been on numerous boats in which the shower outlet pump frequently became clogged with hair or bits of soap. If an unsuspecting crew member doesn't notice that the outlet is not working effectively, he can soon cause a major flood which can be the ruination of your saloon carpet!

The bathroom (it is difficult to know what else to call it these days) should have a reliably watertight locker in which toilet bags, toilet paper and other bits and pieces can be kept bone dry, however enthusiastic the person taking a shower may be. You need a reasonable sized wash basin, but not so large that your crew use vast quantities of water every time they wash their hands.

Cabin heating

Some form of cabin heating is functional and civilized on a boat, and a good installation can extend your cruising season considerably, especially in northern climes. Opinions differ greatly about which is the best kind of system to use. We actually have an anthracite stove on board and this keeps things cosy below even when the decks are covered with snow! Solid fuel gives off a very dry heat which is ideal for keeping condensation at bay, although you do have to be careful about how the stove is built in and where its flue is ducted. You also need a convenient coal bunker which is dry and easy to get at.

There are various diesel or paraffin burning hot-air systems on the market, which also give a dry heat with the advantage of being almost instantaneous to use. The exhaust for such installations is usually led to the stern, much higher up than the engine exhausts. It is advisable to fit the electrical control gear in its own special locker, which is both weatherproof and easily accessible for servicing.

With a multi-duct heater you can fit an outlet in your wet locker, so long as this small space is well ventilated and cannot overheat. One point to watch about hot-air systems is that they consume electricity at a fair rate. There is a high-wattage glow-plug to ignite the fuel initially, and then you are running two separate fans, to supply the combustion chamber with air and to carry the hot air round the boat.

Deck Gear

Anchors and anchor winches

Every cruising boat should carry at least two anchors of more than adequate weight, preferably of different patterns to cope with various types of bottom. I have always thought that the CQR makes the best general-purpose main anchor, because it performs well on a wide range of seabeds and is reasonably easy to manhandle and stow. For a second anchor I use a fisherman's which is no lighter than the CQR, and therefore serves as an alternative main anchor. The fisherman's anchor is more reliable than a CQR on a weedy or rocky bottom and we use it a great deal in these conditions. For years I have intended to carry a lighter CQR for temporary 'lunchtime' anchoring in quiet weather, and which would also be much easier to take out in the dinghy as a kedge, but I've never got around to doing so. The Bruce anchor certainly has something to recommend it as a kedge, but I have yet to be convinced that you can safely get away with using a significantly lighter Bruce than you would a CQR.

I prefer chain anchor cable to using chain with nylon, although there are plenty of yachtsmen who swear by their strong, elastic, nylon anchor warp. The sheer weight of chain seems to me to be a great plus point when it's really blowing hard, and yet nylon is undoubtedly good for absorbing snatch if you are anchored in a bit of a chop. The chain roller is an important item of deck equipment; the standard fittings aboard some production boats are rather too small and do not feed the chain easily as a result;

some have sharp edges that will quickly chafe through rope and galvanizing.

A sturdy anchor winch is well worth having on the foredeck, although I'd say that it is better to fit a good hand-operated winch than an electric or hydraulic one which is not really man enough for the job. Of the various power types available, electric winches are now the most common, being cheaper and easier to install, but hydraulic winches can generally provide more pulling power as well as greater reliability in the long term. However well weather-proofed an electric winch is said to be, it is only a matter of time before water finds its way into either the motor, the wiring or the switch. To my mind, hydraulics represent a much more robust engineering medium for the harsh environment of a foredeck. Having said that, the new designs of capstan winch, which are based on the same principle as sailing boat sheet winches, are very workmanlike. The electric versions can generate plenty of power when operated by hand, and although they are not exactly inexpensive, they seem to provide pretty good value as yacht equipment goes.

Dinghy davits

These are highly practical for cruising motor boats, not so much for their actual lifting power, but because they provide an ideal place to actually stow a dinghy so that it is ready for use, yet not taking up deck space. If you enjoy visiting natural anchorages you will use your dinghy a lot, so to be able to launch it easily in a few minutes is a great advantage.

Cleats and fairleads

We all have our own ideas about cleats and fairleads, but there has been an undoubted tendency in the past for builders to provide standard fittings which are on the small side. Picture the scene at a crowded visitors' pontoon or quay. You are moored alongside perhaps, with someone else alongside you. You will therefore need space on the foredeck to lead and make fast your head-rope, your bow spring possibly,

The workmanlike deck layout of the Grand Banks 42 Classic. Note the practical bin locker for fenders and warps, the sturdy windlass and the neat anchor stowage.

You don't often see a 'cat davit' these days, except on traditional MFV-type yachts. This highly practical piece of equipment is used for handling the main anchor aboard a boat whose anchor would normally be stowed on deck rather than in the hawse.

and your neighbour's forward breast rope. At least one of these lines may be doubled, giving two parts to be made fast. Ideally, one should be able to cast off any rope without disturbing any of the others.

Given the amount of time, effort and money which goes into designing, building, buying and running a boat, it seems crazy if the proud owner has to scrabble about trying to squeeze numerous warps onto a single cleat, or maybe two cleats, which are too small. A workmanlike foredeck ought to have two adequate sets of bollards and fairleads. But why not have a third set of bollards between the existing two, which could serve either side and avoid you having to double up unnecessarily? It is not as though substantial deck-fittings need look ugly these days. On the contrary, many of the modern designs are extremely elegant and only begin to appear ridiculous when they are clearly not solid enough. There's usually no problem about siting them so that you don't lose too much sunbathing space.

Amidships spring cleats really ought to be *de rigueur*, but why spoil the ship for a ha'porth of tar and only fit one each side? You will usually rig two springs so it is surely sensible to provide a cleat for each of them. Also bear in mind that, if someone comes alongside and you don't have enough proper fittings available for him to make fast to, then he is likely to secure to something else—a stanchion or part of your toerail. Good design often avoids the need for spring fairleads, if the cleats themselves are sited right at the deck edge, or on the outside of a toerail or tumblehome. However, you still see some new boats with their springs chafing because the cleats are neither in nor out and yet there are no fairleads. Fairleads at the stern *may* also be unnecessary if the aft cleats are sited at the extremities of the quarters and clear of stanchions, lifebelt holders and other encumbrances.

Hatches

The two most important features of hatches are that they should be completely waterproof, and strong enough to take the weight of a heavy crew member without risk of damage. This may sound obvious, yet leaky hatches are surprisingly common and some builders still fit rather flimsy ones, neglecting the rule that, on a boat, you shouldn't need to worry whether or not any part of the upperworks will take your weight safely; ideally, everything up on deck should be strong enough to be leapt upon!

Some designs of hatch have a 'vent' position for use when the boat is left on her mooring; the hatch is then not quite fully closed and yet is both rainproof and secure against vandals. This facility is well worth having, because the more ventilation you can arrange for your boat the better. Hatches should always be large enough to allow a large adult to scramble through in case of an emergency, such as fire down below.

The 'Couach' motor cruiser on the right of the picture is a rather dated design now, but was popular in France in the 1970s and early 1980s. The stern davits make a very useful stowage for the dinghy.

It is a nostalgic delight to come across a varnished clinker dinghy stowed on the aft deck of a large traditional motor yacht and handled with a proper pair of swinging davits.

Navigation lights

These ought to be as powerful and robust as possible. On a cruising boat you should consider the 25 watt units to be the minimum acceptable size. Even these have a nominal range of only two miles in good visibility, which is little enough if you are travelling at any speed. Nav lights need to be mounted where there is no risk of their being knocked, kicked, grabbed at as a handhold or used as an impromptu step; on boats which have a flying bridge, they are usually fixed on the outside of the bridge coaming so they are fairly high for maximum range, nicely out of the way, and yet easy to get at to change a bulb in a hurry.

It is important to have two reliable windscreen wipers on a cruising boat. I would regard these as rather too small and prefer straight-line wipers which cover most of the screen area. (Photo: Ron Dummer)

Windscreen wipers

These vital pieces of equipment should be given very careful consideration. I was always a great fan of rotating clear-view screens, although the general trend seems to have shifted to large, parallel-drive wipers. Whichever type you prefer, it is important to remember that wipers are not simply 'bad weather' items of equipment. On a planing boat they are used a great deal of the time, unless the sea is absolutely flat calm.

Rotating clear-view screens are highly practical in heavy weather.

Modern consoles are usually well laid out, but not all boats have a practical chart table. It is important to give careful thought to this vital working area if you are planning to make anything more than very short day passages. (Photo: Ron Dummer)

You ought to have two sets of wipers, even if the 'wrong side' of the windscreen is rather tricky to steer through in an emergency. At least you will have some kind of back-up, and a crew member can always keep watch while the helmsman steers from his side. Windscreen washers are a must on high-speed boats. On a bright summer day, perhaps with a force 3–4 blowing against a tide, the spray will be drying quickly and the windscreen can soon become smeared with salt.

Navigation Equipment

Nowadays, the selection of electronic navigation equipment seems to occupy a major place in the whole business of fitting out a boat. I deal with the question of choosing suitable navigation aids in Chapter 5, but it is perhaps important to emphasize here that many motor boats are highly over-provided with electronic goodies. If you so wish, it is perfectly feasible to embark on quite ambitious cruises with simply a good compass, an accurate log, and a reliable echo-sounder. Anyone arriving new to boating with a limited budget certainly shouldn't feel that they need to install all-singing all-dancing systems before they can get under way and start going places. If you have enough in the kitty for one major item of equipment, it is perhaps rather difficult to choose between a good radar set and a navigation system such as Decca or Loran. Much depends upon the type of cruising you plan to do, and also upon your general confidence as a navigator.

If I were *forced* to choose, I'd probably come down on the side of radar, since it gives you a rather magic facility which you cannot obtain in any other way. Most people can learn to navigate with reasonable accuracy, but to be able to 'see' in murky conditions is a real and welcome bonus. Even in good visibility, radar can provide a significant aid to coastal navigation, especially when making a landfall.

Video chart systems

Many of those involved in the marine electronics business, as well as some yachtsmen, envisage the day, in the not-too-distant future, when paper charts will become interesting relics of history. I wouldn't go quite that far myself, but there is no doubt that display technology is moving ahead in leaps and bounds. Video chart systems are now readily available at prices which are comparable with other items of electronic equipment and they will probably soon be seen as a matter of course alongside radar screens in motor boat wheelhouses. Most systems use tape cartridges to store a complete series of charts for a given cruising area, although the more recent developments are based on a laser disc, rather like a CD.

The software organizes the available displays into layers of increasing or decreasing scale. You begin with a small-scale index chart, select an area for enlargement using video 'cross-wires', and then gradually zoom in as far as the stored information allows. The system can also be interfaced with Decca, Loran or Sat-nav, so that your position appears as a

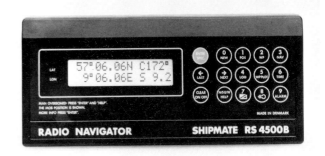

A radio navigator is now a standard item of equipment in a motor yacht's wheelhouse.

rather eerie moving target on the chart display. You can watch your boat approaching a coastline or working her way up a narrow river. You can also define waypoints using the video cross-wires. The navigation software will calculate true or magnetic courses between waypoints, show your position relative to a required track, and plot your actual track made good.

It is important to realise, however, that the electronic charts currently available do not yet contain anything like as much detail as Admiralty charts. Although the large-scale displays may seem quite accurate and life-like, they tend to be highly stylized and often do not discriminate between individual dangers, lumping them together within an all-embracing contour. Comparative beginners to boating should not be seduced into a false sense of security by thinking that navigation at sea is simply a matter of keeping a target on track, rather like some kind of computer game. At the moment, video chart displays fall into the category of an interesting navigation aid, but it would be misleading to believe that you can safely substitute your folios of real charts for a library of tape cassettes.

Electronic chart tables

These new devices are, in a sense, the high-tech substitutes for dividers and parallel rules. The system uses an electronically sensitive chart table onto which a standard Admiralty chart is clipped. There is a 'puck', rather like a sophisticated computer mouse, which can be located at any position on the chart by using its magnifying glass and cross-wires. As you move the puck over the chart, its position is displayed in latitude and longitude. You can also define waypoints and work out the bearing and distance between them.

The electronic chart table can be interfaced with a radio navigator or a sat-nav so that the puck is used either as a lat/long seeking device which gives you your present position on a standard chart, or as a means of entering waypoints into the navigation software. In many ways, I think that this kind of development may turn out to be more practical than video displays for use on a small boat. The navigator still has a traditional chart in front of him, which is both more detailed than a video chart and simpler to visualise. The electronics are simply helping with the error-prone task of transferring positions, bearings and distances.

Some clever developments are being made in the area of video displays, but it will be some time yet before mariners stop using 'real' charts. (Photo courtesy of Navstar SA)

Autopilots

An autopilot is now almost a standard fitting aboard all kinds of boat, but is especially valuable if you go cruising. A good autopilot can be equivalent to an extra crew member and take a lot of the fatigue out of passage-making. It is perhaps unusual to consider autopilots under the heading of navigation equipment, but they are increasingly being interfaced with position finders and even radar, so it can be helpful to think in terms of an integrated system. Even when used on its own, an accurate autopilot can be a great help to the navigator, who then has a fair idea of the course that has been steered over a given period of time. Inexperienced or inattentive helmsmen make the navigator's job very difficult because inaccurate helming can result in a considerable position error after a longish passage.

However, fast planing boats do not always respond well to autopilot steering, particularly in a following sea. The technology and engineering is becoming more sophisticated, but some of the older types of equipment do not react quickly enough to the violent

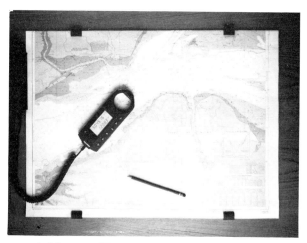

A Navstar Yeoman electronic chart table.

A *state-of-the-art navigatorium.*

changes of course that can occur, for example, when a boat is surfing down the face of even quite a modest wave. In such situations a skilled helmsman will probably turn in a more accurate course than the autopilot.

Where autopilots are interfaced with radio navigators, it is vital to check the reality of what is happening to your boat against what you believe your equipment is supposed to be doing. If you 'dial-a-course' on your autopilot, always check the main steering compass to make sure that you have actually come onto that course. If your navigator and autopilot are supposed to be guiding you towards a physical waypoint, such as a buoy or beacon, don't lose sight of what is actually happening around you. Will you pass the right side of the buoy, for example, or are you in danger of hitting it if your navigation has been rather too accurate? The risk of collision is

traditionally the most significant danger associated with autopilots, because watch-keepers tend to become less vigilant once 'George' has taken over the helm. Navigators can be susceptible to a similar syndrome, becoming so intent on dials and digits that they lose the ability to visualise where their boat is actually travelling.

Safety Equipment

VHF

There are now few cruising boats not fitted with some kind of VHF radio. VHF has an obvious value in an emergency, but it also helps with decision-making in all kinds of more marginal situations. The ability to receive up-to-date local weather reports and fore casts is a significant aid to passage-making and can considerably reduce the risk of becoming caught out by bad weather. But the facility for communicating with port officials or coastguards can be another important safety factor. Imagine a boat which is making a passage along a rather inhospitable lee shore, keeping a prudent five miles off. The skipper can see that the weather is freshening and he knows that there is a harbour within reach under his lee, but he is not sure whether the depth of water and the conditions over the bar would actually allow him to get in. The alternative is to press on for another 30 miles for the next secure port-of-call.

He could approach the first harbour to see what the entrance looked like, although this would be putting himself in a vulnerable position close to the coast if it became obvious that he couldn't reach shelter safely. With VHF, however, the skipper could probably contact the harbourmaster, pilot or coastguard at this first harbour and obtain local advice about entering. If there appeared to be no problem about getting in, the skipper would have avoided the unnecessary risk involved in continuing along the lee shore in deteriorating weather.

Bilge pumps

All boats intending to venture offshore should have two reliable large-capacity hand bilge-pumps, regardless of any other more fancy pumps that her owner may like to install. Electric pumps are convenient when they are working, but a real flooding emergency is quite likely to put all electrical equipment out of action at a stroke. One advantage of electric pumps is for when a boat is being left at her moorings for any length of time, when a pump connected to an automatic level switch can save the day in case of any unexpected leak.

The best type of hand bilge-pump is the diaphragm type, which can cope with minor obstructions and has an efficient rate of discharge. Make sure that at least one of your pumps is 'much too large', to the extent of causing comment when other skippers look over your boat. There is nothing quite like peace of

Choosing a VHF may seem a bewildering task, but most modern sets offer a similar range of facilities.

mind at sea, and if you ever need a pump in anger, you will need one which can shift water at a rapid rate. Strum boxes should always be fitted at the bilge end, to avoid pumps becoming clogged by debris.

Lifebuoys and danbuoys

Horse-shoe lifebuoys are normally the most convenient type to have aboard a yacht, because they are comparatively easy both to mount and use. Careful thought should be given to the stowage, because lifebuoys need to be ready for throwing at a moment's notice, and yet not liable to become dislodged accidentally.

Motor yachts with a flying bridge should have at least three lifebuoys, two mounted in the cockpit and one up on the bridge within easy reach of the helm. One of the lower lifebuoys should be fitted with a flashing light for night emergencies. Danbuoys, which are floating markers with a long flag-pole, are often carried aboard sailing yachts, but you don't see them so often aboard motor yachts. Admittedly it is usually more difficult to find a convenient stowage aboard a motor yacht, but a danbuoy is a highly practical aid for locating a man overboard and well worth carrying at sea if you can find space.

51

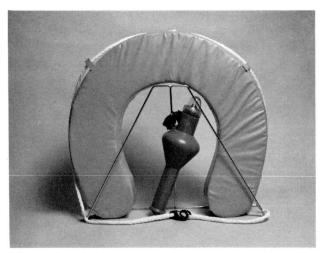

Horse-shoe lifebuoys are the most convenient. The light should be stowed upside down because the activating switch operates in the upright floating position.

Liferafts

For some reason, the subject of liferafts is apt to arouse strong arguments in clubroom bar discussions. Newcomers to boating tend to feel more secure if they know that there is a liferaft on board, while some older hands regard them as rather flimsy and dubious pieces of equipment. Stories may be told about liferafts which have failed to open, which become perished in a few seasons, or which break up quickly in heavy seas. You really have to try and envisage the kinds of situation in which a liferaft might be used in anger, and it is worth remembering that heavy weather probably comes a good way down the list for a well-found cruising boat. There are three more likely reasons for having to abandon ship as a last resort: (1) Sinking caused by collision with another vessel; (2) Sinking caused by collision with floating debris at speed; (3) Fire on board.

Any of these three emergencies could occur in absolutely calm conditions, when the seaworthiness objections to liferafts would mostly be academic. Of the three incidents, a collision with floating debris seems particularly likely these days, judging by the quantity of flotsam and jetsam that you come across

in open water. Such a collision also becomes increasingly dangerous as boats travel at faster cruising speeds.

Taking to a liferaft in heavy weather is a different matter altogether. Experience has shown time and again that, however chaotic, unpleasant or tenuous life appears to be aboard a gale-battered yacht, the chances of her actually foundering because of weather alone are usually slight. By contrast, it is extremely difficult to transfer a crew safely into a tiny bobbing liferaft and the chances of the raft subsequently capsizing in steep or breaking seas can be quite significant. It is therefore important to appreciate what a liferaft can and cannot be expected to achieve. Although there is everything to be said in favour of carrying a regularly maintained liferaft if you can afford it, you should only consider abandoning ship for this frail craft as a last resort. In the case of certain boats I have come across, the money spent on buying and maintaining a liferaft would have been much better spent on making the parent ship safer and more seaworthy.

Lifejackets and harnesses

The best type of lifejacket is the fully inflatable type which you can blow up either with the mouth-pipe or by using a CO_2 bottle. You would normally wear this type of jacket deflated or only partially inflated as you move about the boat, in which state it is not at all cumbersome. All cruising boats should carry at least as many lifejackets as there are likely to be crew members, and they should be stored in a dry airy locker to guard against mildew.

Who should wear lifejackets and when is largely a matter of personal judgment, although small children should wear them all the time they are afloat, especially in a dinghy. Newcomers to boating or non-swimmers may prefer to wear a lifejacket as a matter of course, whatever the weather. Anyone going out on deck in choppy conditions should put on a lifejacket first, and some skippers will insist that everyone wears them in heavy weather. It is prudent to issue lifejackets if you should run into thick fog in the vicinity of shipping lanes, because there is then a real risk of collision with another vessel at very short notice.

Safety harnesses are standard equipment aboard sailing boats, but they also have their uses aboard motor yachts. Some helmsmen wear them on a tight rein while they are up on a flying bridge, while anyone going out on deck at sea is arguably more secure using a harness than he is by simply wearing a lifejacket.

However, you should only use harnesses on a *very short line* aboard high speed motor boats, because it would be much safer for a crew member to fall into the water unattached than to fall in at the end of a longish line and be pulled along at 20 knots until someone noticed what had happened!

Flares

These vital items of safety equipment often work their way to the bottom of a wheelhouse locker, only to lie forgotten until they have gone out of date and turned rather mouldy. It is very important, however, to store your flares carefully and easily to hand, to renew them regularly, and to carry considerably more than the minimum recommended number. There are several different types of flare and every cruising boat should be equipped with several of each type:

—Red parachute flares, which are the most effective form of visual distress signal by day or night.
—Red hand-held flares, which are effective at night but have nothing like the visual range of parachute flares.
—White hand-held flares, which are not distress signals but can be used at any time to indicate your position to other vessels.
—Orange smoke flares, which are the traditional way of indicating distress during daylight, but are usually less effective for this purpose than parachute flares.

Fire extinguishers

Most people dread the possibility of fire on a boat more than any other emergency, with very good reason. It is absolutely essential to carry sufficient extinguishers of the correct type, of as large a capacity as you can reasonably accommodate. Anyone who has ever seen fire extinguishers demonstrated will know how quickly they fizzle out, so it is prudent to regard any coastguard recommendations as a basic, minimum provision.

The engine-room extinguishers need careful consideration. The best system to install is an inert gas extinguisher, preferably one which is activated manually from the wheelhouse rather than automatically. By all means fit a heat alarm in the engine room to indicate when a fire has started or is about to start, but it is usually more effective to trigger an extinguisher manually rather than have it go off either by accident or when the engines are still running at full tilt. The gas will have a much greater chance of smothering a fire when the engines have been stopped and, if possible, the fuel has been turned off. For this reason there is also much to be said for having fuel taps that are remotely controlled from the wheelhouse.

To fight fires elsewhere on board you need a number of carefully placed hand extinguishers, some of which are accessible from outside the accommodation. The more you can fit the better, in my view. A useful size of extinguisher is $2\frac{1}{2}$ kilograms, which is large enough to have an effective capacity but compact enough to handle at sea. Most marine extinguishers use either dry powder or BCF. An asbestos fire blanket is a must for the galley area, but make sure that it is mounted so that it can be reached easily if the stove should catch alight.

Tools and spare parts

These are not usually classed as safety equipment, but that is exactly what they are. Once you have put to sea you are thrown onto your own resources and any mechanical problem has to be dealt with using the skills, equipment and materials on board. The better equipped your tool and spares locker, the more seaworthy your boat. It is sensible to carry a selection of different sized screwdrivers and the right spanners for every nut on board, but it is amazing how even the owners of highly expensive motor yachts can be extremely parsimonious when it comes to buying tools. You should have a solid vice on board, even if it lives in a locker and has a temporary mounting somewhere. Engine spares may include fan belts, water pump impellers, injectors, high pressure fuel pipes, fuel and oil filters. It is wise to carry a comprehensive selection of nuts, bolts and screws, and a good hacksaw with plenty of spare blades.

Behind-the-Scenes Equipment

Charging facilities

Some larger motor yachts run to a separate generator, which may provide 12 or 24 volts DC for charging the batteries, or it may be able to supply 112 or 240 volts AC to a domestic ring-main. If the generator is permanently installed in the engineroom it will probably run on diesel, assuming that the main engines are diesels. However, some boats carry a portable petrol generator for emergency use or perhaps for driving power tools. These generators are usually very reliable, but they should always be stowed upright in a dry, well-ventilated locker, and the petrol should be carefully stored in a metal can. Most production motor yachts now have a shore power system, basically a built-in rectifier which converts shore supply AC to low voltage DC for charging. The input supply comes from a heavy-duty cable which plugs into a marina socket and into a suitable weatherproof socket somewhere convenient on board.

It is now feasible to use solar panels in order to provide top-up charging, a useful facility if your boat is left unattended for longish periods of time. Solar technology has become much more efficient and considerably less expensive in recent years. The robust plastic panels suitable for yachts are usually mounted on a horizontal surface such as a cabin roof, and you can walk on them quite safely.

Tankage

Fuel and water tanks are important items of equipment aboard a boat, but they are not always given the careful consideration they deserve. The ideal material for fuel tanks is stainless steel, although ordinary steel is perfectly serviceable if the tanks are well painted before being installed. A well-made fuel tank is fitted with baffles inside, to reduce the movement of the fuel when you are at sea; half a tank of diesel weighs a considerable amount and can put a lot of strain on the tank mountings if it is allowed to swill about freely. A good tank also has a sump at its lowest part, with a tap to allow any water and sediment to be drawn off. Boats with twin engines should have two completely separate tanks and fuel supply systems, although there is something to be said for an arrangement of cocks which allows you to supply either engine from either tank. This can have advantages in heavy weather if, for example, there is something wrong with one engine, you are low on fuel, and need to draw upon both tanks of fuel to get you into port safely.

Chapter 4

Handling your Boat

Manoeuvring in a restricted space is a complex art which most cruising folk acquire very gradually, over many years' experience and after exposure to a wide range of circumstances and conditions. Whenever I am running a course for comparative beginners, I am faced with the difficulty of putting over the unfortunate fact that polished manoeuvring is not a skill which can be taught quickly, or dealt with *en passant* as just another item in a syllabus. There is a certain amount of 'theory' you can draw upon, but practice is another matter. However, it is possible to teach some basic general principles, to try and analyse the various forces acting on a boat under power, to explain something of how different types of hull ought to behave, and to consider specific examples of mooring situations.

By way of 'drill', you can get beginners to practise circuits and bumps by coming alongside a stretch of quay or a moored pontoon, or picking up a buoy dozens of times. You can take them carefully through the intricacies of berthing in a crowded marina. Yet despite all this, it can sometimes be difficult, when faced with a novel mooring problem, to articulate all the factors which may be running through your mind as you perhaps shift the wheel just a fraction, edge up to windward a shade or open the throttle slightly to stem the tide.

Some people seem to have a natural feel for boat handling, while others will probably never get the hang of the finer points, however many courses they attend and however much they practise. Having said this, most would-be mariners can learn a basic competence in manoeuvring, given some sound initial instruction, a willingness to analyse and learn from mistakes, and two or three seasons' experience.

I have divided this chapter into two distinct sections. The first looks at some basic principles of power boat handling, while the second considers specific manoeuvres and their associated problems and techniques. For those interested in reading further, there are various books which give a detailed treatment of the whole subject of boat-handling. One that I particularly like and recommend is called *This is Boat Handling at Close Quarters* by Dick Everitt and Rodger Witt, published by Nautical Books.

Some Basic Principles

Subtleties of steering

When manoeuvring at close quarters, it is important to remember that a single-engined boat which has a conventional propeller and a rudder close astern of it will tend to slide and swing when turning ahead under power. If port helm is applied, the rudder will move to port, the boat will turn to port, but the stern will swing out to starboard and describe a larger radius than the bow.

At the same time, the boat will slide bodily in the direction of her original course for a short way, until the rudder begins to bite properly and the new turning circle is established. These two factors are vital when, for example, you are making a right-angle turn into the narrow space between two lines of marina pontoons. If you leave the turn too late, you'll find yourself too close to the far row of boats, with your stern swinging even closer as you try to correct the situation and steer towards the middle of the fairway (see Fig 4.1).

Twin-screw boats exhibit a similar swinging effect if they are being steered with the rudders. Of course a twin-screw boat is often turned by going ahead on one engine and astern on the other, but a different kind of 'creeping' effect can also catch you unawares. You will not necessarily pivot 'on the spot' by running slow ahead on the port engine and slow astern on the starboard, because the drive from a prop turning ahead is more efficient than that from a prop turning astern at similar revs. Therefore, the boat in Fig 4.2 may describe a small turning circle to starboard as shown. To achieve a pure pivot turn, so that the boat is not actually moving anywhere, you usually need to run the astern engine at slightly higher revs than the ahead one, to keep the push and pull effects more or less equivalent. It is worth experimenting with your own boat to discover this differential, so that you can easily execute a pivot on the spot if you need to.

Tight turns are also possible with a single-screw boat, so long as you appreciate how the transverse thrust of the prop, often known as the 'paddle-wheel

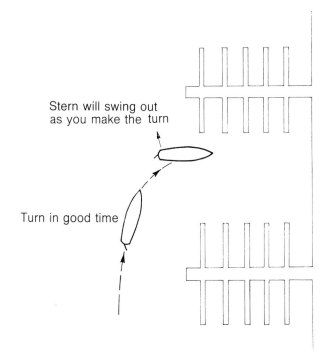

Stern will swing out
as you make the turn

Turn in good time

Fig 4.1 *Don't leave it too late to make the turn between two lines of marina pontoons.*

Fig 4.2 *By running slow ahead on one engine and slow astern on the other the boat may describe a small turning circle.*

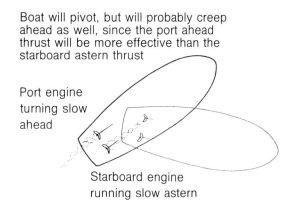

Boat will pivot, but will probably creep ahead as well, since the port ahead thrust will be more effective than the starboard astern thrust

Port engine turning slow ahead

Starboard engine running slow astern

Fig 4.3 *A right-handed propeller, viewed from aft, rotates clockwise when driving ahead.*

effect', can be used to your advantage. Propellers do not simply produce thrust forwards or backwards: there is usually a significant sideways component which can either help or hinder in confined spaces. Fig 4.3 shows a right-handed propeller, i.e. one which rotates clockwise, viewed from aft, when driving ahead, and therefore anti-clockwise when driving astern.

Forgetting, for a moment, the main forward or astern driving force of the propeller, try to envisage it as a paddle-wheel acting *across* the boat. Now you might think that such a paddle could only be effective if the top half was out of the water, Mississippi-style. With the prop fully immersed, surely any sideways drive produced by the bottom blades would be cancelled out by sideways drive in the opposite direction produced by the top blades? Not so. In fact any sideways thrust from the bottom blades is more effective than that from the top blades, since the lower half of the prop is acting in slightly deeper water, and is also less prone to the turbulence which occurs nearer the surface. Therefore, the bottom blades of the prop usually win the battle of the sideways thrust. So a right-handed prop will tend to swing the stern to starboard when driving ahead, and to port when driving astern.

When you start moving ahead from rest, you normally only notice transverse thrust for a moment. Once the boat gathers way you automatically correct any side-swing with the helm. But when the prop is driving astern transverse thrust becomes much more significant, especially if the boat is barely moving through the water and the rudder is therefore largely

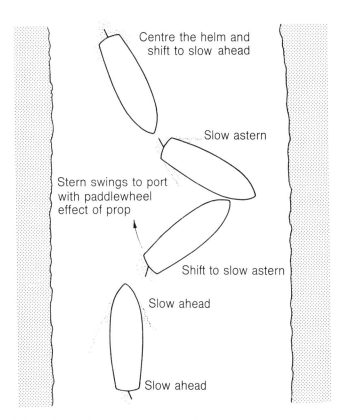

Centre the helm and shift to slow ahead

Slow astern

Stern swings to port with paddlewheel effect of prop

Shift to slow astern

Slow ahead

Slow ahead

Fig 4.4 *A single-screw turn in a narrow channel. The prop is right-handed, so the stern will swing to port in reverse.*

ineffective. Note that paddle-wheel effect is most pronounced with larger props, since there is then a greater difference in drive between the top and bottom blades. Craft with large, slow-turning props have an appreciable transverse thrust, while the effect is much less in a faster boat having a small, high-revving propeller.

When you are trying to turn a single-screw boat in a confined space, it follows that it is much easier to turn to starboard if you have a right-handed prop, or to turn to port with a left-handed one. Fig 4.4 shows a straightforward single-screw turn in a narrow channel. The prop is right-handed, so the boat's stern will swing to *port* when the engine is put astern. Imagine that the wind is blowing from dead ahead before the manoeuvre is started. The copy-book procedure is first to make a swing to port, to give yourself as much room as possible. You then apply increasing starboard helm to start the turn, soon afterwards shifting the engine astern. Reverse drive will put the brakes on, to prevent you hitting the bank, but it will also increase your stern swing to port as the transverse thrust comes into play.

For most boats in this situation, the wind will help rather than hinder, since it will tend to affect the bow to a greater extent than the stern. This is because the forward part of the hull usually has the shallowest draught and is therefore least able to resist sideways movement. So once the wind is blowing from one side or the other, the bow will generally fall away from it and the boat will tend to pivot about her stern.

What is often rather difficult to judge is at which point to change your helm direction as the boat is slowing down, coming to a stop, and then starting to move backwards. While you are moving significantly ahead, it is clearly best to maintain starboard helm, so that the flow of water past the rudder continues to assist the turn. You will also facilitate the transverse thrust stern-swing to port, since the rudder will be partly 'feathering' when moving in that direction. If you apply port helm too soon, three undesirable effects can occur:

—The boat will begin to steer to port if she is still moving ahead, thereby counteracting your intended turn.

—Until your stern has sufficient port momentum, the rudder blade's paddle effect as you move it across will hinder the swing.

—Once in the port-helm position, the rudder may form a kind of scoop which will also inhibit the swing of the stern to port.

In some cases, where you are trying to turn without gathering much sternway, it may be effective to keep the same helm angle almost throughout the whole manoeuvre: starboard helm during a starboard turn with a right-handed prop, and port helm during a port turn with a left-handed prop. When the engine is driving ahead, the stream deflected off the rudder will kick the stern in the required direction; when the engine is driving astern, the trans-

verse thrust of the prop will reinforce the swing and the then feathering rudder will help this swing continue unimpeded.

Of course once the boat starts moving steadily astern, you have to turn the rudder in the opposite direction. You will then need a delicate yet nifty touch on the helm at the point where you shift ahead once again. For a backing-and-filling turn to starboard, you will have port helm applied on the backing leg. But if the helm is *still* to port when the prop next starts driving ahead, your stern will start swinging back to starboard and some of the advantage of reversing will be lost. On the other hand, if you apply starboard helm too soon before shifting ahead, the rudder will steer the stern to starboard as you reverse, so you also lose some ground. Every boat seems to react differently, but it is usually best to shift gear first. As the prop bites and starts driving ahead, you often feel the helm go dead as the forward and reverse flows oppose each other; this is generally the best time to swing the wheel for the next forward leg.

If you are forced to make a backing-and-filling turn in the 'wrong' direction, i.e. to port with a right-handed prop or to starboard with a left-handed prop, you should take some positive steps to try and ensure that the manoeuvre actually comes off and you don't get stuck halfway round. The wind is often the most important factor here; ideally, you want it more or less on your bow just as you start to make the turn.

The first main swing assumes much greater importance on a wrong-handed turn. It should be made as boldly as possible because (a) you really want to get the boat as far round as you can while she is still travelling ahead under full control, and (b) you need to impart a good sideways momentum to the stern, because the transverse thrust will work against your swing as soon as the engine is shifted into reverse.

When backing-and-filling wrong-handed, it is usually best to apply plenty of throttle after the change-over from astern to ahead, immediately the helm is full over in its new position. This positive ahead thrust with full helm will help kick the stern round, but don't let the boat gather too much headway unless you have room to complete the turn. Otherwise you will have to apply plenty of astern power to 'back up' again and the transverse thrust will lose you a lot of ground.

The seasoned single-screw helmsman will go to great lengths to avoid making a wrong-handed turn, even if it means reversing into a marina berth or coming alongside a different stretch of quay from the one he would prefer. There is nothing more embarrassing than starting a backing-and-filling manoeuvre and getting stuck halfway round. It is amazing how quickly a dockside crowd begins to gather as soon as you look like becoming embayed up a blind alley.

Boats with outboards or outdrives have their own turning and steering techniques and are, in some ways, the most difficult types of craft to handle. For one thing, they are usually very shallow-draughted and therefore prone to being blown sideways in the slightest breeze. They also have no rudders, since steering is achieved by actually turning the drive units to direct thrust in the required direction, which means that steering is typically very positive with power engaged in forward or reverse but is largely non-existent in neutral. So coming alongside can be quite tricky with an outdrive boat, because you don't have much scope to lose way simply by slipping into neutral and ghosting. When manoeuvring, you should always take note of your helm position *before* engaging gear, because the prop thrust has an immediate effect on your direction. This is particularly important when you are just about to shift astern in order to bring yourself to a neat halt alongside.

Fig 4.5 shows an outdrive boat approaching a quay. At position C the helmsman will shift into astern gear to slow down and stop. But just before he does this, and while the drive is in neutral, he should put on a certain amount of starboard helm, as if steering the boat further in towards the quay. The boat will slow down when the reverse thrust bites, but her stern will also swing slightly to starboard so that she ends up lying parallel with the quay. Don't overdo either the degree of helm or the burst of reverse power, or the stern will swing in rather faster than you intended and give the quay a nasty clout.

With this example in mind, you can appreciate that the backing-and-filling technique for an outboard or outdrive boat is similar to that for a car. You don't experience the same changeover problem that you do with a conventional prop and rudder arrangement, because wherever an outdrive is pointing it will have a positive steering effect so long as power is applied, ahead or astern.

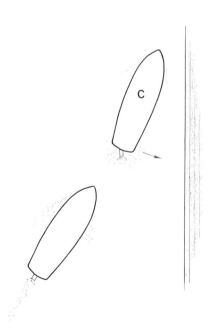

Fig 4.5 *An outdrive boat approaching a quay. At position C, shift into astern so as to slow down and swing parallel to the quay.*

Using stream and wind

One of the real arts of boat handling is that of exploiting any stream or wind. Beginners often take a while to realize that a strong stream can actually make manoeuvring simpler, so long as you are able to turn more or less into the stream and use it both to control your speed over the ground and to help you steer.

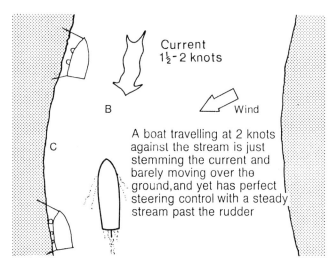

Current
1½–2 knots

Wind

A boat travelling at 2 knots against the stream is just stemming the current and barely moving over the ground, and yet has perfect steering control with a steady stream past the rudder

Fig 4.6 *Manoeuvring is often simpler when you are stemming a powerful river current.*

In Fig. 4.6 a traditional single-screw boat is stemming a powerful river current with her engine ticking over at slow ahead. Her speed through the water is exactly equal to the speed of the current, so she remains stationary relative to the quay off which she is hovering. A light breeze is blowing towards the quay. Now here is an ideal situation for manoeuvring alongside, because the balance of forces gives you a fine control over the position of your boat. Open the throttle a shade and you will edge forward very slowly. Reduce the engine revs and you'll begin to drop astern. But even while you are stationary, you can gently cant the boat sideways, either towards or away from the quay, by applying a little starboard or port helm.

Under these conditions, it should be a fairly simple matter to land against any selected stretch of quay. If C looks like a good spot, you can edge forwards to position B, pretty much abreast of where you hope to end up. Even though there is little spare space between the two boats already there, you can sheer gently sideways into this slot by putting on a spoke or two of port helm. The onshore breeze will help you in. When you are almost alongside, you can centre the helm again in order to straighten up and stop your sideways movement. Small adjustments to the throttle will allow you to creep ahead or drop astern, and you should keep in mind that the current may be less powerful once you are tucked between the two moored boats.

In some circumstances it can be useful to edge stern-first into a quayside berth. You might have passed a likely looking spot with the tide behind you, and then find it difficult to turn round in order to stem the stream in the normal way. Fig 4.7 illustrates this kind of manoeuvre, similar in principle to the previous one and equally dependent upon a strongish current for its success. The paddle-wheel effect of the prop will be relatively insignificant compared with the power of the rudder inclined against a reasonable stream. It should therefore be easy to come straight astern, so long as you don't try to reverse too quickly and provided that you only use small helm movements. The boat will effectively be 'hanging' in the tide by her propeller and her natural tendency will be to align herself with the flow.

The wind can complicate matters, since most boats tend to 'weathercock' when going astern (Fig. 4.8). In Fig 4.7, a fresh breeze is blowing from ahead while the boat is making sternway, so any appreciable deviation from a straight course could be greatly accentuated if the wind were to catch one or other side of the bow and try to swing the boat round. This would be most likely, and inconvenient, once you had drawn abreast your mooring space and were starting to sheer sideways towards the quay. Softly softly is the trick, as it often is with boat handling. Try to make only a gradual slant across the tide, so that you don't give the wind a chance to catch the bow squarely.

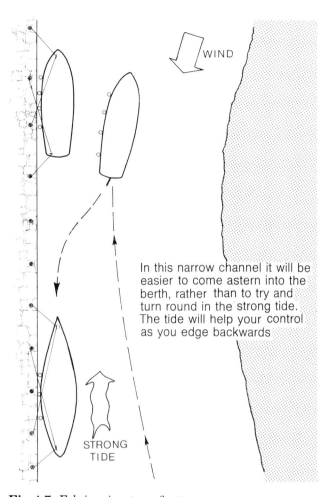

In this narrow channel it will be easier to come astern into the berth, rather than to try and turn round in the strong tide. The tide will help your control as you edge backwards

Fig 4.7 *Edging in stern first.*

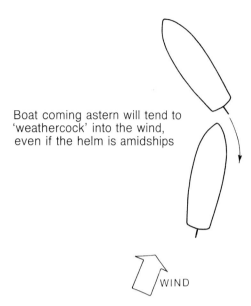

Boat coming astern will tend to 'weathercock' into the wind, even if the helm is amidships

Fig 4.8 *The effect of a wind from aft of the beam, when going astern.*

One of the hallmarks of an experienced helmsman is his continual awareness, when manoeuvring, of how the wind may be affecting, or could possibly affect, the position of his boat. Most yachtsmen soon get to grips with tides and currents, probably because these forces have a comparatively tangible, steady quality. You can often see the direction of flow past a quay or a mooring buoy, but you will have to pick up rather more elusive clues in order to gauge wind direction from inside a wheelhouse.

In a crowded marina keep an eye on masthead indicators, but remember that they don't always pick up those stray gusts and eddies which can confound a close-quarters manoeuvre at the critical moment. In a more open harbour, watch for the tell-tale cats-paws of wind as they ruffle the surface, and take note of how nearby dinghies are lying to their painters. It should be almost instinctive to look for these signs whenever you enter confined waters, and to try and assess the implications for any manoeuvre that you have in mind.

You should know exactly how the wind will act on your boat if she is left to her own devices. With most boats you find that the bows tend to fall away from the wind, because the forward part of the hull is usually the shallowest and has limited resistance to sideways movement. This is useful if you are making a turn away from the wind, but a hindrance if you are trying to turn into it.

Motor Cruising

You will no doubt be familiar with this effect if you've ever had to reverse out of a marina berth with a fresh wind blowing from astern. In Fig 4.9 the two lines of pontoons leave only a narrow fairway to play with, and yet you have to come out as far as possible in order to give yourself room to turn before the wind takes control. The manoeuvre is considerably more difficult with a single-screw boat than with twin screws. The situation in this example is helped if the prop is right-handed, because the transverse thrust will swing the stern to port as you reverse clear of your 'finger'. Unfortunately, the more the bow swings out to starboard, the more the wind will try to push it back.

The secret of success with this manoeuvre is to have your lines ready to let go at a moment's notice, to wait for a brief lull in the wind, and then to come out quickly and boldly, using plenty of throttle. The helm should be slightly to port to start with, but you should put on increasing port helm as you reverse clear of your slot. You need to come back as far as you dare, to give the bow plenty of swinging momentum and to allow yourself as much room for wind drift as possible. The nifty moment comes when you have to shift from astern to ahead gear and then starboard the helm, almost simultaneously. I would shift into ahead while I still had the helm to port, but then switch quickly to starboard helm as I opened the throttle. The prop thrust would thus help to swing the rudder back through amidships as quickly as possible.

The situation is not quite so critical with a twin-screw boat. You would probably come out of your berth with a little port helm applied, first with both engines at slow astern and then with the starboard engine slow astern and the port engine in neutral. Again, you'd want to come back as far as possible, but you would make the turn by shifting the port engine ahead while the starboard engine was still running slow astern. As the boat straightened up, you would shift the starboard engine to slow ahead to meet the port engine.

With twin engines the actual turning process is greatly simplified, because the push-pull pivot effect should overcome even a strong wind. Yet you are

62

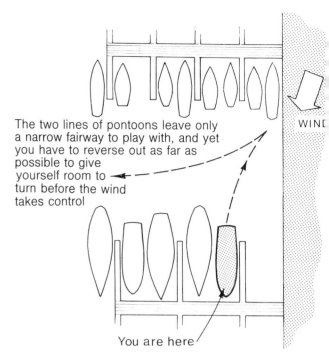

The two lines of pontoons leave only a narrow fairway to play with, and yet you have to reverse out as far as possible to give yourself room to turn before the wind takes control

You are here

Fig 4.9 *Wind can be a critical factor when leaving a tight marina berth.*

still not immune from being set sideways onto the line of pontoons you have just left, so it is still advisable to reverse out as far as you can and to complete the turn as soon as possible. If the wind catches your exposed beam before you have forward steerage way, you are in trouble. At the same time though, whenever you are manoeuvring with twin engines it is important to keep mental track of which gear each engine is in and to use only as much power as is necessary. You often see quite straightforward operations getting completely out of control because the helmsman has been too heavy-handed with four or five hundred combined horsepower. Violent bursts of throttle should be saved for those rare occasions when they are really needed.

Romara using her 14hp Atlantic Richfield bow-thruster to manoeuvre in a restricted space. A bow-thruster can be a great help in today's crowded harbours, but it is important to install a unit which is powerful enough to be effective 'in anger'.

Some Specific Manoeuvres

As I mentioned earlier, it is not my intention that this chapter should attempt to tackle the whole complex subject of power boat handling, right from the basics up. In fact I have assumed, throughout this book, that the reader has a fairly solid grounding in general seamanship and I have therefore tried to

focus attention upon some of the issues that become increasingly relevant as you cruise further from home. In considering a number of specific manoeuvres in this section, I am taking it for granted that the reader is more or less competent to handle his boat. I have chosen to concentrate on various strategic factors that an experienced yachtsman will try to keep in mind when planning his manoeuvres.

Marina berthing—plan your retreat

Manoeuvring in crowded marinas these days can undoubtedly be a nerve-racking business. Quite apart from the physical risks of collision, the damage to your ego can be considerable if you make a hash of things in front of a large audience. Most of our modern nautical parking lots are laid out with a view to maximizing capacity, and this economic constraint is apt to take priority over ease of entry and exit. It also means, of course, that there are likely to be plenty of observers around when anything goes dramatically wrong.

Permanent berth-holders become used to their own niches and the local vagaries of wind and tide, but strangers arrive fresh to each intricate layout. A visiting skipper has to size up the geography quickly, at the same time avoiding residents who know where they are going. While hovering about, he will probably receive 'helpful' and conflicting suggestions from several quarters. He will finally settle on a likely spot and dive in hopefully, perhaps not quite sure what size berth he will find or even whether there is room to turn into it.

It is worth underlining one important aspect of this problem of searching for a parking space. More a state of mind than a skill, it is linked to that sound boating premise which says that if something can go wrong then it probably will. On this basis, it must surely be sound practice to adopt that well established military maxim 'always plan your retreat'. I remember a classic case in point while we were moored in that attractive yet rather compact marina at Lézardrieux, on the North Brittany coast. The sun was over the yardarm and we were relaxing in the cockpit, watching the comings and goings. A Birchwood 33 was edging along the fairway between the pontoons, as someone had apparently told her skipper that there was an empty berth right inside to port. He began to line up for the vacant slot, but then discovered that the space was too narrow and that there was nowhere else to go.

While the boat was moving steadily forwards she was under full control and her skipper was able to compensate for the cross-tide that filters insidiously through this marina. But he had come in expecting success and had kept to the downstream side of the fairway, ready to swing to port into his intended berth. Once he realized he couldn't get in, there was a problem. While the Birchwood was lining up to reverse into open water, the tide set her onto the starboard pontoons and much fending-off ensued.

A more pessimistic approach would have been better, with the skipper working out a retreat plan before committing himself to the narrow fairway. There was clearly no turning room, so he would have to come out astern. With the tide setting persistently to starboard, he'd need to allow for a brief period of drift in which to straighten up and get going in reverse. Preferable, therefore, to skirt the *up-tide* pontoons on the approach, keeping well to port even though the target berth was on the port-hand (see Fig 4.10). If the space was seen to be clear, it would be easy enough to back off a shade, allow the stream to take the boat towards the middle of the fairway, and then pivot to port using both engines. But if the berth was a no-go, the boat would be positioned safely up-tide and the skipper could get going astern without the risk of being carried onto the starboard-hand pontoons. In the tight marina at Lézardrieux, this strategy would make all the difference between a foul-up and getting out safely.

Fig 4.11 represents a similar situation, but now suppose that we are talking about a single-screw boat with a right-handed propeller. Assume there is negligible wind or tide, and that the lines of pontoons are sufficiently widely spaced to allow for a three-point turn. Once again, the skipper is aiming for a finger berth some way in to port, but he's not sure whether it is actually vacant. This time there are two possible strategies for retreat—to come out astern or to turn round and come out ahead. Each requires a different approach.

If the skipper would prefer to come out forwards then the approach would best be made on the port side of the fairway. The plan would probably be to reverse into the berth if it were vacant, or to turn round to starboard if not. In either case, there would be room to make a swing ahead to starboard and

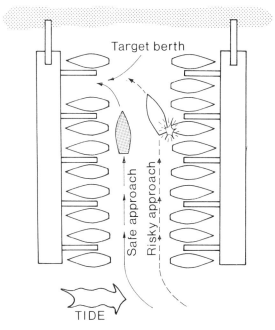

Fig 4.10 *Skirt the up-tide pontoons on the approach.*

then go astern to bring the transverse thrust of the prop into play.

If the skipper would rather make his escape backwards, it would be advisable to make the approach along the starboard side of the fairway. Given a clear slot, he could then swing in forwards. But if a retreat proved necessary, there would be room to cant the boat to port before going astern. The transverse thrust would bring her back straight, by which time there should be sufficient sternway to steer normally in reverse.

Of course wind and tide will usually provide a further complication, and every boat has her own quirks of handling which need to be taken into account. However, the important principle is to cultivate the habit of always considering your retreat. When faced with a tricky berthing problem it is natural to ask 'How best can I get in?', but you should also be wondering 'How can I get out again if I need to?'

Mooring abreast

Many harbours have a designated stretch of quay or set of pontoons for visiting yachts. These 'town' berths are often very agreeable places to lie and the overnight rates are generally less expensive than commercial marina charges. However, they can become rather crowded in high season, and you may find yourself lying abreast several other boats of various shapes and sizes. There are a few points to bear in mind before you get too embroiled in one of these gregarious rafts.

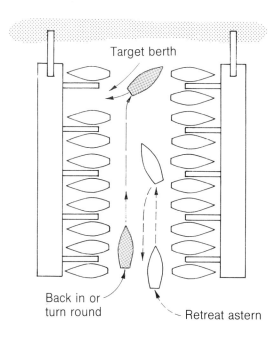

Fig 4.11 *Plan a retreat carefully in case you cannot find a vacant berth.*

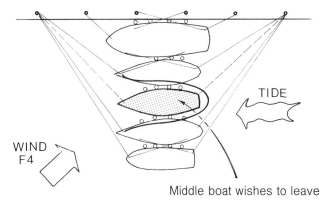

TIDE

WIND
F4

Middle boat wishes to leave

Fig 4.12 *When rafting alongside, each boat should lead head and stern warps ashore. Here the middle boat wishes to leave.*

When choosing a spot, remember that it is preferable to moor alongside a boat of similar length or longer, with a freeboard at least as high as your own. The raft will lie more easily with the larger boats on the inside and the smallest outside. Breast ropes and springs should be used between boats, and everyone should lead head and stern warps ashore to take a share of the raft's weight as it tries to pivot in the wind or tide (Fig 4.12).

Before you decide to berth alongside someone else, especially if there is any likelihood of new arrivals mooring outside *you*, it is important to check your echo-sounder and make sure that you will remain afloat at all states of tide during the period you intend staying. This is part of the 'plan your retreat' principle, because there is nothing more embarrassing than discovering that you are just about to go aground, but there are four other boats outside you—mostly without crews aboard—and you therefore have precious little chance of escaping in time!

If another boat secures outside you, and then someone else outside him, try to work out exactly how you would extricate yourself if you needed to leave in a hurry. If the raft is lying in a tideway, this strategy would hinge around how the stream was flowing at the time, but would also depend on the strength and direction of the wind. Fig 4.12 show a raft of five in which the middle boat wishes to leave by going forwards. Everyone is facing the same way and there is a moderate tide running from astern The wind is about force 4, blowing from half-ahead towards the quay. Now the inside boat is not directly affected by the intended manoeuvre, but the skipper or crew of number two should be present to help take warps, adjust fenders, or fend off where necessary. The boat intending to leave should remove her head and stern warps, as well as the lazy spring secured to number two—probably the aft spring in this case if the tide is stronger than the wind.

There are now various options for letting the middle boat out. One possibility is for the two outside boats to cast off their head lines *at the boat end* passing them across, still attached to the quay, to number two. Number four can then detach herself from the middle boat, who in turn casts off her forward breast rope, aft breast rope and forward spring in that order. The middle boat can then slip gently forwards with the tide behind her, and the two outer boats, still moored together, should swing in toward number two. Two and four can make fast together and then the two outer boats can re-secure their bow lines at their leisure.

If there seems any risk of the two outer boats being blown astern against the tide, number five should have her engine running so that she can nudge them both back alongside if necessary. This would be particularly wise precaution if the wind was blowing offshore instead of onshore; in this case, it would also be prudent to pass a head line from number four boat, around the stern of three to the bows of two. As soon as number three has slipped clear, four can then pull herself and five alongside two, and there is no chance of the wind catching the two outer boats and holding them off. However, when using a slack head line like this, be careful that (a) it is kept well away from the leaving boat's propeller, and (b) doesn't snag anywhere on her hull as she moves ahead.

Another possibility for letting number three out is for the two outer boats to cast off in turn, as they were themselves planning to leave, and then make a circuit under power and come alongside again afresh. This tactic might be preferable and ultimately less complicated if, for example, there were other rafts of boats either side of your own raft, and there was barely enough room for the leaving boat to escape.

The situation in Fig 4.13 is not uncommon at busy town quays or in some marinas. The leaving boat may be planning to cast off as per Fig 4.13 and then to manhandle herself round the bows of the two outer boats. Although this can work in quiet conditions when the stream is fairly slack, it can lead to chaos in a strong tide or wind. With the tide running as shown, the main potential hazard is for the leaving boat to become pinned against the raft of boats immediately ahead of her. She could avoid this problem by coming out astern instead of ahead, but then the two outer boats of the middle raft would themselves be in danger of being set forward, since they'd have to detach their stern lines in order for number three to slip out. In these particular circumstances, it would be safer for the two outer boats to peel off astern, stand a little way off the quay until number three is clear and then return to their spaces. When manoeuvring alongside number two again, they could either turn round and come in head-to-tide, or reverse in as per Fig 4.7.

Before getting involved with a sampan-style raft alongside, it is worth considering the potential damage which could be caused by other boats coming and going, or perhaps sustained when you yourself have to leave. It can be somewhat disconcerting to know that a boat in your line may decide to 'slip out' at some inconvenient time for you, or that similar operations ahead or astern of you could easily result in a chipped topside, or maybe a bent stanchion or davit. If you are looking forward to a quiet dinner either ashore or on board, you might find it more agreeable to anchor off somewhere in uncomplicated solitude.

While on the subject of gregarious berths, it is worth mentioning some of the conventions of good manners appropriate when boats are rafted alongside each other at a quay or pontoon. The primary rule is that you should always ask permission before

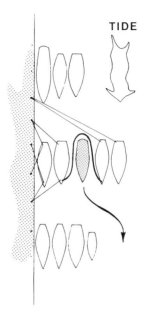

Fig 4.13 *This situation is not uncommon at busy town quays or in some marinas: the leaving boat may plan to manhandle herself round the bows of the two outer boats.*

you first walk across another boat to get ashore, and you should then cross via the foredeck, *not* through the cockpit or over the aft deck. This is a straightforward matter of respecting other people's privacy. You should also try to walk very quietly whenever you are crossing someone else's boat, especially if you are returning aboard late at night and your neighbours have turned in. It is amazing how loud a well-dined crew member on deck can sound from below, even when he imagines himself to be creeping silently; a nocturnal reveller who manages to trip over an anchor or stumble across a spring will not be at all popular.

Try to give your neighbours plenty of notice of your own intention to leave, and do your best to stick to your estimated time of departure. There is nothing more irritating than to have someone knocking on your deck and wanting to move off just as you are starting lunch. It is equally irritating to have been

Mooring abreast can be a sociable method of berthing. Motor cruisers are rafted up here in the small harbo[r] at Wangerooge, easternmost of the German Friesian Islands.

given a departure time for a boat next door, to have therefore made an effort to have a couple of crew members aboard and ready at that time, and then to be kept hanging around for half an hour while the would-be passage-makers return from the pub!

If you are leaving early in the morning, it is courteous to conduct your manoeuvres in a quiet and orderly fashion, without voices being raised or any undue revving of engines. You should make all your preparations before starting up, rather than have your exhausts burbling away and disturbing other people's sleep while you potter about with warps and

springs. If you need to detach someone else's line[s] make sure that they are carefully made up agai[n] even if this means leaving a crew member ashore [to] do so, and then picking him up afterwards when [all] is secure.

A nudge on the engines will sometimes help wh[en] you are man-handling yourself out of a tricky corn[er] but use just a touch ahead or a touch astern as ne[c]essary. An uncontrolled burst of throttle can cau[se] a considerable amount of damage if you are ma[n]oeuvring at close quarters and make contact wi[th] another boat.

Mooring fore-and-aft between buoys

In some harbours and estuaries you may come across visitors' moorings laid out in continuous trots, with floating fenders between them (Fig 4.14). The principle is that two boats can secure fore-and-aft to each pair of buoys, although the system is not always so simple in practice. A problem occurs when you have a strong tide setting across the trots, making one side difficult to leave and the other difficult to arrive at. A cross-wind can cause similar complications. Of course, if you can pick a completely vacant pair of buoys, you will usually have a choice of directions for approaching or casting off; with a boat there already, the possibilities are somewhat constrained.

In Fig 4.14 a visiting yacht has been allocated a mooring which is already half occupied. A strong river ebb is running aslant the trot and there is a moderate breeze from a similar direction. Careful preparation and crew briefing provide the key to this manoeuvre. You will be approaching from near position A, making for the upstream buoy first, passing a slip line through the ring, and then holding yourself alongside the floating fenders until you can secure to the downstream buoy. You'll need a longish warp ready at the bow, secured some way along its length rather than right at the end. The *tension-bearing end* should be ready to lead through the ring and back to a separate deck cleat.

A shorter warp should be ready on the port quarter, secured at one end. While the forward crew member is making fast, another crew (or the helmsman if there are only two people aboard) should be using a long boathook to pull the boat and the floating fenders together before the cross-wind can take charge. Slip the free end of the aft warp round either the fender rope or the wooden fender bar, hauling up tight and making fast. This leaves you temporarily but safely secured in position B.

There are now two options for securing to the downstream buoy. You can either launch the dinghy take out the stern warp, or you can work your boat slowly aft by gradually letting out the head rope and holding yourself close to the fenders. The first

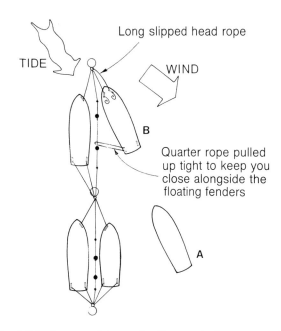

Fig 4.14 *Approaching a half-occupied trot mooring, with a moderate breeze and a strong river ebb running aslant the trot.*

method will be preferable if your boat is heavy and the tide powerful because, by dropping astern on a long head rope, your bow would almost certainly be carried right out to starboard by the stream. The strain on the warp would be considerable and you'd have a hard job to haul back towards the forward buoy once you were secured aft.

One way to prevent this sheering is to rig a slipped breast rope forward, which would be used to hold your bow close to the fenders as you worked your way downstream towards the aft buoy. Once the stern rope is secured, centralize your boat between the buoys and neatly alongside your neighbour.

For an overnight stop, you may need a few of your own fenders and perhaps even springs or breast ropes. You should also use two separate warps forward and aft, rather than just rely on the slip ropes with which you first made fast. A warp doubled round a buoy ring has a persistent sawing action which can chafe surprisingly quickly. One of the most secure knots for mooring to a ring is the round turn and bowline, although this should never be used on a single warp in a tideway, since it is impossible to cast off under strain. With a slipped warp rigged as well, however, you can take the tension off a bowline before trying to untie it.

Fig 4.15 shows a tricky situation for boat Y when she wishes to leave a trot, with both tide and wind holding her tightly against the floating fenders and making it difficult to escape. Your tactics in such circumstances will depend on the handling characteristics of your boat, whether she has a single or twin screws, and how strong the wind is compared with the tide.

A twin-screw boat has a natural advantage in her ability to pivot. So long as the wind is not too fresh, she can cast her stern warp off straightaway, leaving only a single slipped head rope ready to run clear at a moment's notice. The trick is to wait for a brief lull, go ahead on the starboard engine and astern on the port, and hope to pivot sufficiently to port so as to give yourself room to reverse quickly away from the trot.

For this manoeuvre to be successful, the helmsman and foredeck crew need to be well co-ordinated. The helmsman won't want to cast off forward *before* he knows that he can reverse safely clear, otherwise he loses the 'abort' option of swinging back on the head line and either attempting the same operation again, or else trying something different.

On the other hand, once the helmsman has decided to go, he ought to go quickly, before the wind and tide have a chance of setting the boat alongside again. At this point, there must be no hiatus on the foredeck; the head line should be slipped quickly and efficiently, but not so frantically that there is any risk of the loose end flicking about and getting jammed under itself. To be unwillingly pinned by

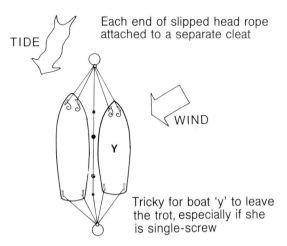

Each end of slipped head rope attached to a separate cleat

TIDE

WIND

Y

Tricky for boat 'y' to leave the trot, especially if she is single-screw

Fig 4.15 *A tricky situation for boat Y, with both wind and tide holding her tightly against the trot.*

Fig 4.16 *A single-screw boat poised to leave a trot mooring in moderate conditions.*

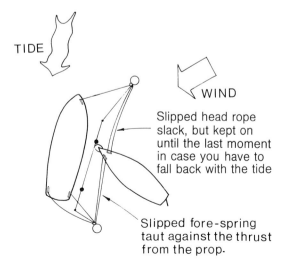

TIDE

WIND

Slipped head rope slack, but kept on until the last moment in case you have to fall back with the tide

Slipped fore-spring taut against the thrust from the prop.

e bow at this late stage could have some dramatic
nsequences.

The head line must therefore be ready to slip in
l respects. It is best if each end is secured to a
parate cleat on the foredeck, so that it's always
ite clear to the crew which he or she will be re-
asing. Once one end is free, the other should be
lled in smoothly and steadily. Avoid quick jerky
lls, which are more likely to cause the loose end
double over itself and form a perverse impromptu
tch. This is worth remembering during any de-
rture which involves a slip warp being cast off at
critical moment.

In a gentle tide and a light wind, a single-screw
at may be able to use a slipped forespring to the
wnstream buoy, going ahead with full helm to kick
r stern out before reversing clear. You'd want to
ep a slipped head line secured until you were sure
 swinging out far enough for the manoeuvre to
ork.

The problem with this tactic is that, by driving
ead on the engine, you put an unfair strain on the
ating fenders, the boat next door and on the trot
elf. You have to consider the speed of the tide, how
ur neighbour is lying, the strength of his warps
d the size of the lines used to moor the floating
ders. You may also need to rig one of your own
ders low down across the bow. This type of man-
uvre is not feasible in fresh winds and powerful
eams, since there is a real risk of doing some dam-
e with the potentially large forces involved.

However, Fig 4.16 shows a single-screw boat poised
leave in moderate conditions. It is decision time
r the helmsman, with the forespring under tension,
e head line slack and the trot pushed sideways by
e combined weight of prop thrust, wind and tide.
 fast if you decide to go; head line slipped, engine
fted astern with the helm swung amidships and
ring cast off as soon as tension comes off it. Once
ur bow is clear of the trot and both warps are safely
 you can port or starboard your helm depending
 which way you prefer to pay off and turn round.

In a strong tide, the alternative is to rig a slipped
 spring to the upstream buoy, using the stream
d perhaps a touch of engine to swing your bow

clear of the trot, prior to driving off ahead. There are
three possible hitches in this manoeuvre. The first
is that your sterngear could foul either the trot itself,
the floating fenders or any loose ropes streaming
between the buoys. Softly softly is the secret. Only
come astern with the engine if you have to, and even
then very cautiously. The second point is that, in
springing off, you have to be sure that you bring the
tide well onto your inner bow before trying to leave;
otherwise there is a danger of being forced back towards the trot and becoming entangled with the upstream buoy as you draw away. Finally, once you
have swung out far enough to be able to start edging
clear, the aft spring needs to be slipped smartly,
without the risk of any snarls.

In Fig 4.17, with wind and tide as they are, you
can cast off everything except a slipped head rope
and aft spring. Rig your own fenders on the port
quarter, where you will nudge close to the floating
fenders and the boat next door. If you have plenty
of crew, station someone forward to handle the head

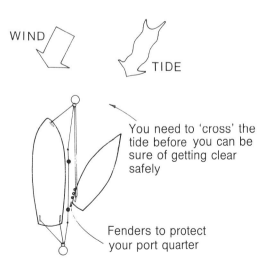

WIND

TIDE

You need to 'cross' the
tide before you can be
sure of getting clear
safely

Fenders to protect
your port quarter

Fig 4.17 *Cast off everything except a slipped head
rope and aft spring. In a lull in the wind, slip the
head line and wait to see if the bow swings out.*

line and someone aft to slip the spring and watch your stern. When you feel a lull in the wind, slip the head li..e and then wait to see if the tide is strong enough to swing your bow out.

Much depends on the angle at which the stream is running across the trot. If you can 'cross' the tide without recourse to the engine, all well and good. But if nothing much happens when you sit back on the spring, shift the engine slow astern and keep an eye on your port quarter as it tucks in towards your neighbour. Make sure that your prop and rudder are clear of any trailing ropes, gradually increasing the revs to swing yourself out until the tide is on your port bow. Your swing will accelerate once you reach this critical position and you can then start drawing away from the trot. Now is the time to cast off the aft spring, but try to give your crew as much time as possible to accomplish this by alternating between neutral and slow ahead until the warp is gathered in.

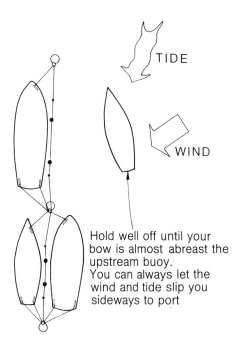

TIDE

WIND

Hold well off until your bow is almost abreast the upstream buoy. You can always let the wind and tide slip you sideways to port

Fig 4.18 *Use the minimum of power when approaching a trot with the wind and tide working in your favour.*

It is comparatively simple to *approach* a trot wi wind and tide setting you onto it, but there is sor skill involved in stopping with your bow near t upstream buoy and the boat more or less paral with the floating fenders. You should use a minimu of power, creeping forward and sideways against t tide and shifting between slow ahead and neutr: The trick is to hold off until your bow is almc abreast the upstream buoy, especially with a sing screw boat. If you let the bow fall in too soon, the is a risk of becoming tangled with the floating fe ders, or even driving across them (Fig 4.18).

Mooring fore-and-aft between piles

Pile moorings can be easier to deal with than pa of buoys, simply because they are higher and ther fore easier to reach. On the other hand, a timber p is a pretty solid obstacle to collide with if things do quite go according to plan.

The various techniques for coping with trots a equally relevant to pile moorings. A brisk wind a the close proximity of other boats are apt to provi the main hazards, but it is also worth rememberii the following tips:

—Because it is usually more straightforward to fet up alongside a pile than to manoeuvre next to buoy, it may sometimes be feasible to secure the *aft* pile first, and then to carry on towards t forward pile, paying out the stern line as you g

—When making fast to a pile, use the mooring b rather than passing your line right round the tir ber. The warp will then ride up and down easi with the rise and fall of the tide.

—If you make fast with a bowline, it's useful to t a very long bowline which can be cast off witho having to come right up to the pile again.

—Unlike trot moorings, piles have no 'give' and warps are more likely to snatch in a strong wii or chop. During a spell of heavy weather it can I a good idea to run out your anchor chain as t bow warp: the catenary will absorb some of tl

Local motor boats moored to piles on one of the Danish islands. There is negligible tide in the Baltic, which makes life a bit easier when it comes to berthing.

snatch and reduce the strain on cleats and fair-leads. Another solution is to tie a heavy weight near the middle of both the bow and stern lines.

Anchoring

Today's motor yachts are generally better adapted to cruising between out-of-the-way anchorages than were their counterparts of twenty years ago. Conveniences such as fridges and showers reduce the need to call frequently at towns. Large battery capacities and efficient charging systems supply plenty of power on board, not only for lights but also for more decadent comforts such as cabin and water heating, shavers, hair-driers, music centres and the

like. Anchoring was never so straightforward as with the help of modern winches. Lightweight tenders can be stowed in easy-to-handle davits, ready to launch at a moment's notice.

Natural anchorages offer practical advantages as well as seclusion. Entering and leaving is usually simple compared with the backing and filling required to negotiate many marinas. There can be a certain amount of stress involved in trying to reverse into a narrow slot at the end of a long line of pontoons, with a mischievous cross-wind waiting to foul things up and a large audience watching from the comfort of their cockpits. The intricacies of quayside rafts and mooring trots can be just as daunting, so why is it that so few yachtsmen take up the option of passing a quiet and economical night in an attractive and sheltered anchorage? And how much more agreeable to be able to come in at your own pace, make a circuit or two, and have a good look round before deciding where to fetch up.

Of course it is important to study the large-scale chart well before your arrival, and to note the position of any potential hazards such as drying rocks, shoal areas, submerged jetties and so on. The chart will also give you an idea of how sheltered the anchorage ought to be in different weather conditions. You should consider the likely state of the bottom and try to work out in advance where the best holding ground might be found. Look carefully for possible obstructions to anchoring such as weedy or rocky patches, ground chains, power or telephone cables, or those deeper wrecks which are not directly dangerous to your boat but are almost impossible to escape from if your ground tackle should become entangled with them.

You will need to look up the times of local high and low water and calculate the expected range of tide and how much further the present level should fall before low water. What will be the depth at high water? With this basic information at your fingertips, you can interpret the soundings as you feel your way in. But remember that you are not simply interested in the range of depths at the point at which you drop anchor. You will need to anticipate where your boat might actually be lying at various states of tide and to assess whether the whole swinging area will be safe.

In the example shown in Fig 4.19, Crab Cove is a small bay sheltered from between north through west to about southwest. Kipp Point obviously requires a good berth on the way in, with its pair of above-water rocks and the off-lying tail of drying ledges known as The Saints. At high water you will see only the two islets, although most of The Saints should be visible near low water. At half-tide it may be tricky to decide which rock is which and how far out the dangers extend. It would be safest to approach the bay on its west side, using the jetty as a reference point.

Suppose that the forecast was for northwesterly force 4, backing west or southwest overnight. This

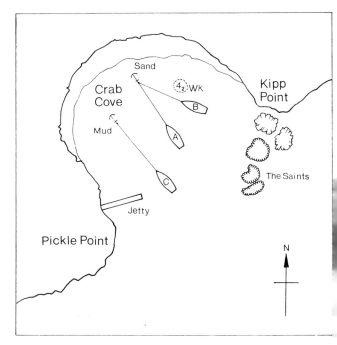

Fig 4.19 *Crab Cove would make an ideal anchorage in offshore winds, but where would you fetch up?*

wind shift would have to be taken into account when you were deciding exactly where to anchor. Position A is quite feasible so long as the wind stays offshore, but backing conditions will bring two potential problems: (a) your swinging room is greatly reduced as the northeast side of the bay becomes a lee shore, and (b) there is a risk of your cable snagging the underwater wreck as you turn through position B. Better to anchor at C, towards the west side of the bay. This allows you space to swing as the wind backs, and also makes the most of the shelter afforded by Pickle Point. Your chain should stay clear of obstructions, and the mud bottom at C offers more secure holding than the sand at A. Even if you end up lying over the wreck, there is at least 4.2m of water at LW.

If your selected anchorage is shallow, don't get caught out by allowing your anchor to become stranded by a falling tide. Suppose, for example, you were to enter Crab Cove at half-ebb, intending to stay for a couple of hours over lunch. The wind is offshore and you might decide to edge in close to the beach. You drop the hook, fall back with the breeze into deeper water, and then read the echo-sounder before settling down. You might check the depth occasionally, but don't forget that, when you come to leave, you will have to haul yourself shorewards to recover the anchor. Although there may be enough water under the keel where you are actually lying, the anchor itself could now be lurking where you can barely float.

The use of two anchors is sound seamanship under any of the following circumstances.

—If you are expecting the wind to freshen, especially overnight.

—If you are not too sure of the quality of the holding ground and simply want to double up with 'belt and braces'.

—If you are planning to leave your boat unattended at anchor for a few hours, perhaps while you go ashore for a meal.

—In order to reduce your swinging circle in a crowded anchorage.

When you moor to two anchors in a tideway, such as a river estuary, it is usually best to lay the two in line with the stream so the boat lies to one anchor on the ebb and the other on the flood. I generally find that the most reliable method is to settle down to your main anchor first and then use the dinghy to carry out the kedge. You can thus position the second anchor accurately and ensure that it has plenty of scope. A second anchor laid in response to a dodgy forecast would normally be taken out in the direction from which the freshening wind is expected—and it should be your heavy anchor.

In a tideway or a river, as alternatives to using the dinghy you can carry out either a 'standing' or a 'running' moor. With a *standing moor*, settle back to your main anchor first and then veer at least twice as much cable as you actually need for safe holding. When you are lying back nicely on this, lower your second anchor over the bow in the normal way, hauling the main cable back in when the kedge is on the bottom. By paying out the kedge warp as you go (make sure that you keep it slack), you can pull yourself up-stream again to a point midway between the two anchors and then take in the slack kedge warp. In order to keep the 'lazy' cable clear of the props and rudders, you can attach the kedge warp to the main cable with a rolling hitch and then veer more of both until the hitch is lying somewhere below the keel.

With a *running moor* you lower your second anchor *first*, as you are going against the tide to reach your main anchoring position. It is usually easiest and safest to do this from the cockpit, making sure that the slack warp stays well clear of the props. Continue upstream until you have paid out at least twice as much kedge warp as you need for safe holding. Then lower your main anchor as normal, settling back to the moored position midway between the two anchors and taking in the slack of the kedge warp as you fall downstream. To complete the moor, lead the kedge warp up to the bow.

Those relatively new to cruising are inclined to regard anchoring as a complicated business, and yet it is a piece of cake compared with marina berthing. It is also considerably more prudent than securing to a poorly maintained mooring, the actual condition of which you may be blithely oblivious. By casting your eye over the large-scale chart you can usually find an anchorage to suit the requirements of your crew, as well as the prevailing and expected weather conditions. You can opt for perfect seclusion or a degree of company, and even our own coasts still have plenty of delightful retreats which are outside the jurisdiction of men with invoice pads.

Berthing stern-to

Lying stern-to a quay with an anchor out ahead is much favoured in Mediterranean harbours, but can be rather tricky until you get the hang of it. The knack is to know where to lower the anchor among your neighbours' and at the right distance from the quay; then to reverse into a narrow slot between two expensive yachts with maybe a fresh cross-wind doing its best to foul things up.

Fig 4.20 shows the finished job, with boat Q lying neatly with her anchor laid out at just the right angle to counteract the prevailing wind and plenty of scope of cable to allow for freshening conditions. An important point to remember about berthing stern-to is that you don't have the option of veering more cable later if the weather blows up: you need to be sure of good holding first off. Of course if you anchor *too* far out, you may run out of cable *before* you reach the quay. It is irksome to have gauged your angle of lay to perfection and to have come astern nicely under full control, only to be brought to a grinding halt before your stern lines can reach the quay. Another trap is to cross your cable over someone else's, so that your anchor becomes a cat's cradle of chains and warps when they come to leave.

Fig 4.20 shows a single-screw boat berthing stern-to in circumstances which make the manoeuvre much easier to draw than to execute. A brisk wind is blowing across the line of the moorings, so that backing in towards the quay will be rather unpredictable. You ought to lay the anchor a little up-wind of perpendicular, and there will be a tendency for your boat to swing to her anchor unless the cable is kept completely slack as it is paid out. Your propeller is right-handed, which means that your stern will throw to port in reverse gear.

This is one of those occasions when it will almost certainly pay to lower the anchor while you are *stern-to* the wind. If you tried to approach from downwind, following line X, there would be a better-than-even chance of swinging back towards Y1 once the anchor was down. Although, in theory, the bow ought to fall off the wind more readily than the stern, the transverse thrust of the prop will give the stern a good

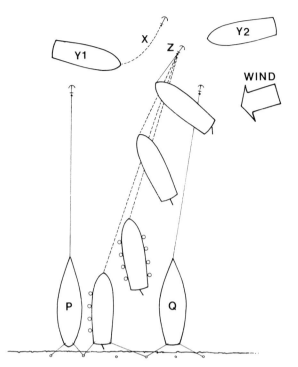

Fig 4.20 *Berthing stern-to. Hold well up to wind-ward whilst going astern, until close to the vacant berth.*

initial shove in the wrong direction; it would also be a skilled crew indeed who could keep the cable running out steadily without it pulling your bow up to starboard. Better to make the approach from apparently the 'wrong' direction, from position Z. It is relatively simple to hold a single-screw boat with her stern into the wind, nudging astern if necessary to check forward drift, and veering to port or starboard in order to edge closer to or further from the quay.

Once you have dropped anchor near Z, the trick is to let the combined forces of the wind, the transverse thrust of the prop, and the drag of the cable help swing you neatly towards your selected slot. It's a good idea to agree two basic hand signals with your crew—'pay out' or 'stop'. Go astern with a little port helm first while the crew keeps the cable slack as it runs out. Ideally, you want to hold well up to windward until you get close to the vacant berth. Depending on the handling characteristics of your boat, you will probably put on starboard helm once you start coming astern, in order to try and maintain station upwind.

Have plenty of fenders on both sides. If the manoeuvre goes as planned you will be cutting Q's bow fairly close, so be prepared to fend off from your starboard quarter at first. But as you drop astern into your slot the wind will be trying to push you alongside boat P, so that's where you are likely to end up until you get the stern lines ashore and can haul yourself neatly central. In some harbours you will come across a line of mooring buoys opposite the quay. This makes life a bit easier in a way, although your crew still has to be sensitive about controlling the tension on the bow line as you reverse. You need to make fast to the buoy as soon as possible, for which a 'grabbit' boathook is worth its weight in gold. It is normally easier to control the tension on a *single* rather than a slipped bow line.

Manoeuvring in Locks

Traditionally, there is something of a divide between those who do most of their cruising inland and the salt-water types who suffer from claustrophobia once any kind of lock gate closes behind them. Personally, I've always enjoyed both. There is nothing quite like chugging gently along a canal or river—and lunching off a horizontal table—if you know that depressions, cold fronts and gale warnings are on the menu offshore. But I also know well that excitement which comes from sniffing sea air again after a spell in narrow waterways among green fields.

Sea locks, where the two worlds meet, are often viewed with suspicion by those who approach with spray on their decks. Indeed I have come across yachtsmen who try to steer clear of all gates and sluices on principle, because they believe them to be complicated, restricting, time-consuming and sometimes downright dangerous. Yet it is surprising how frequently you need to negotiate locks when coasting, especially since many marina basins are now

entered in this way. Lockmanship really ought to be in the repertoire of anyone who goes cruising. All that's required is sound boat handling, competent warp and fender work, a quiet understanding between helmsman and crew and some idea of how lock-keepers like things done.

If you are likely to be faced with a set of gates at the end of a passage, try to find out in advance about opening times and tidal constraints, perhaps from an almanac or pilot book. Most sea locks are geared to the tides, some operating for a set period either side of high water and some for longer before high water than after. Others may work only during daylight, or between certain times when the tide serves. Large commercial locks generally prefer to let yachts through when shipping is also expected.

Signal lights or shapes near the lock entrance are often used to direct traffic and to indicate what's happening inside. Although many harbours are now beginning to adopt the International Port Traffic Signals (refer to your current almanac for the latest details), there is still no universal system of signalling and you will need to find out what the local arrangement is. Lock-keepers may use a loud-hailer as well as or instead of lights or shapes, but their more or less distorted messages are not always easy to understand, particularly in a foreign language. Some locks have VHF and working channels vary.

It is usually best to approach a lock slowly, a little earlier than the scheduled opening time. This gives you a chance to size things up and also allows the keeper to register your presence. The art of hovering is useful; it is better to creep towards a lock under full control than to roar up to the gates, find they are closed, and have to retreat from a tight corner. If there is a special 'waiting' berth you should use it unless you expect the lock to open imminently. Sound your horn once if nothing seems to be happening, but don't overdo this or you will risk irritating the man who matters.

When a lock is emptying, the water drains out through sluices in the gates or culverts built into the lock itself. In either case turbulence is created *in front of* the gates, which can linger for some time after they've opened. Watch out for this as you are coming into an ascending lock and be prepared to be swung off course. Similarly, when approaching a *descending* lock, beware of cross-currents caused by the canal draining over a sill or through a side sluice; this kind of eddy can be difficult to spot until you suddenly find yourself being set sideways out of control! Always let traffic come out of a lock before you start to enter. It is normal practice for ships to be called in before yachts, to reduce the risk of the smaller boats being damaged. However, some lock-keepers like to pack yachts right at the far end of their lock before ships come in, which at least keeps the smaller craft clear of powerful prop washes.

I like to have plenty of fenders out both sides, with a bow and stern warp also ready either side (Fig 4.21). Lock-keepers can sometimes seem contrary by asking you to moor starboard-to when everything is rigged to port! Warps should be long enough to reach up over the lock wall and along to a possibly distant bollard. Once you have been called into the lock, try to enter at a steady pace, not so slowly as to make the lock-keeper impatient but not so fast that you cannot stop where you want to. Having safely negotiated any eddies at the entrance, watch out for current setting straight through the lock, especially if you are descending and the stream is behind you: in this case get tucked alongside in good time and put your stern line ashore first.

Entering an ascending lock, you sometimes meet a slight drift coming out. This can help slow you down as you come alongside, but you have to get your head line secured first, to prevent the bow swinging out. When ascending, I usually make for a ladder near the outer end of the lock, just inside the gates and nicely away from any turmoil caused by the sluices. With a single screw boat try to moor port side to if your propeller is right-handed, or vice versa. The lock-keeper or his assistant *may* take your warps, perhaps on a long boathook, but otherwise be prepared to send two crew members up the ladder. You can then either stay in the quieter outer position, or edge forwards to wherever the lock-keeper indicates. Flexibility is the key.

If you are short-handed, only one crew may be available to take both warps up the ladder. He or

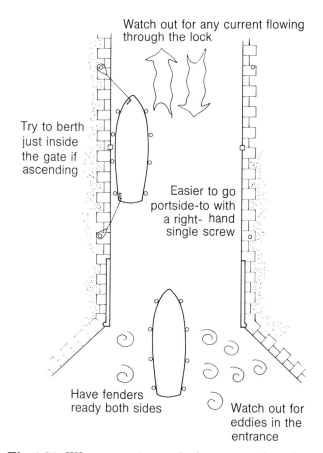

Watch out for any current flowing through the lock

Try to berth just inside the gate if ascending

Easier to go portside-to with a right- hand single screw

Have fenders ready both sides

Watch out for eddies in the entrance

Fig 4.21 *When entering a lock you need to have plenty of fenders out on both sides, with bow and stern warps ready either side.*

she should try not to heave too much on either warp before they are made fast. The helmsman will probably have to leave the wheel at some stage and chase up and down between foredeck and stern cleats. When tending warps aboard, always take in the slack *from the free end* and not from the standing part under tension. Whenever you secure a warp to a deck cleat it is important to make sure that you can easily cast it off under strain. This is vital when you are descending a lock, when you need to let out line steadily as the water level falls, without the risk of getting hung up. If you are rising, take up the slack in both warps as you go.

Locks are a way of life on the European waterways. In the Netherlands, most locks are automated and yachts simply follow instructions and traffic lights. Keep out of the way of barges though, and remember that they are working while you are there for pleasure.

Sometimes, it can be handy to lie alongside a barge or a fishing boat in a lock, avoiding having to adjust warps as the level changes. But not all commercial skippers appreciate how frail yachts are compared with working ships. If, as occasionally happens, they allow their bow or stern to swing across the lock chamber, you may find your boat acting as an impromptu fender. Amidst such comings and goings, be prepared for an official to be demanding attention, maybe asking for lock dues, canal dues or dues for lying in a wet basin. Even if there is nothing to pay, you often have to fill in a form when passing through a lock. It's a good idea to have a pen in your pocket, your registration documents ready and some money to hand.

Leaving a lock can be something of a free-for-all once the gates open. Don't be rushed into casting off before you are ready, but don't hang about if yachts are let out before ships. If the ships go first, it is wise to stay safely secured until their propeller wash has subsided; it can cause instant chaos if your crew have untied your warps and are just standing on the quay holding on. The salt-water sceptics are right about one point: if things do go wrong in a lock, it is quite possible to sustain more damage than you would ever risk by going to sea.

The Art of Towing

There can be few of us who have never given or accepted a tow at some time. The circumstances can range from helping a becalmed sailing dinghy home on a summer afternoon to a full-scale lifeboat rescue in gale conditions. Having to be towed in because of engine failure is less common than it used to be, partly because modern marine engines are mostly highly reliable, and partly because many motor boats now have twin installations which greatly reduce the risk of their becoming incapacitated. Yet there are still plenty of incidents each season in which a passing skipper's ability to undertake a tow can help someone out of a fix. A timely pull to safety may prevent a minor mishap, such as a stray rope round a prop, from developing into something more serious.

Towing and being towed are skills of seamanship with which all cruising yachtsmen ought to be reasonably well acquainted. As an example, imagine that you are approaching a familiar coast at the end of an uneventful passage. You know your position, about five miles seaward of your destination. The weather is deteriorating, with the wind freshening from offshore. Your 33ft twin-engined boat is cruising at 14 knots, but her motion is becoming lively as the sea starts to build. The blue skies of the early afternoon are giving way to thickening cloud. There is an open boat ahead and one of her crew seems to be waving something orange. Since there is nobody else about, you throttle back and edge over to see what's wrong. She is about 20ft overall, of heavy clinker construction, and has a fishing party aboard. It appears that her engine has overheated and seized. The boat is based at your destination, so you offer to tow her in.

Now I don't want to get embroiled here with the question of salvage, a complicated enough subject in its own right. I have towed various boats home where there was no immediate danger to vessel or life, and have accepted tows myself, without the issue ever being raised. Most yachtsmen and fishermen are pleased to help when they can and I've never felt that remuneration ought to change hands, except perhaps in a tumbler at the end of the day.

One of the first practical questions is what sort of towrope to use. A long nylon warp is usually best, especially if there is any sea running. Nylon is comparatively elastic and a decent scope will absorb much of the inevitable surging that you get when the two boats are moving about on different waves. You sometimes hear of anchor chain being recommended for towing in heavy weather, but chain can be tricky to pass between boats. It is difficult to lay down rules for the length of a tow, except to say that, at sea, you will probably need to let out more rope than you first think! A short towrope not only has minimal elasticity but, in a following sea, it can encourage the towed boat to slide down the front of a wave into her rescuer's stern.

It's a good idea to try and visualise a tow in terms of boat-lengths. Three lengths of the towed boat is a working minimum in *quiet* conditions, but snatching will soon occur if the sea starts to build up and if the towed boat is as heavy as or heavier than her tug. Use five lengths in a moderate sea and increase the scope if things become more boisterous. The thickness of the towrope is an important consideration. There's a compromise to reach here between strength, elasticity and ease of handling. Modern nylon can take a surprisingly large load, but the sharp jerks that arise when towing can generate tensions many times greater than a steady resistance.

For example, good quality three-strand nylon has a breaking strain of something like 3000kg, or nearly 3 tons. Taking the safe working load (SWL) to be about half the breaking strain, this cuts you down to $1\frac{1}{2}$ tons. Yet a floating deadweight of only $\frac{1}{2}$ ton can easily generate $1\frac{1}{2}$ tons tension in a rope when the load is jerked on. A workmanlike size of cable is 16mm diameter nylon, thick enough to be easy on the hands, yet elastic and not too heavy for throwing short distances. With a SWL of over $2\frac{1}{2}$ tons, a long coil of 16mm can double as a towrope or an extra anchor warp.

A towrope should be prepared carefully for running out and this is normally best done by flaking it down loosely, either in the cockpit if you have one, or otherwise on the aft deck. Try and carry out this operation before getting too near your tow. It is worth holding off for a while in order to get things ready, rather than making a hasty approach, a tangled throw, and ending up with your own towrope round your prop. In moderate conditions you should be able to manoeuvre within close range and throw the rope across directly. Throw downwind if possible, but take care to avoid being blown onto your tow (see Fig 4.22). In heavy weather you won't be able to approach so closely and you will probably be trying to pass over thicker warp. Under these circumstances you may have to use a heaving line, or perhaps float a light messenger line down towards your tow using a fender or other float (Fig 4.23).

The next problem is to find strong securing points on both the towed and towing boats, since modern cleats tend to be rather inadequate when subject to real seagoing forces. The fishing boat in this example

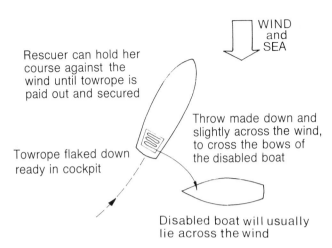

Fig 4.22 *Aim to throw your towrope downwind if possible, but take care to avoid being blown onto your tow.*

Fig 4.23 *It is sometimes possible to float a rope downwind tied to a fender.*

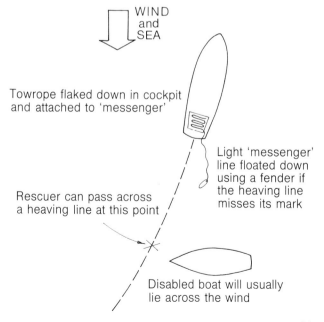

may well have a solid, old-fashioned samson post which will do the trick. However, the towing boat also needs a strong securing point which, under load, will not hamper her ability to manoeuvre. If a heavy tow is secured right aft, the drag on the stern can make steering difficult. Commercial tugs always have their towing hooks well forward, near the centre of the ship, because it's easy to pivot about this point and alter course at will, as shown in Fig 4.24.

You can ease this problem by securing the tow to *both* quarter cleats. The towrope is made fast to one cleat, on the starboard side say, and another warp of similar or slightly smaller diameter is fastened to the towrope with a rolling hitch. The tow is then let out for not quite another boat's length, with the second warp being made fast to the port quarter cleat. You end up with a kind of bridle, as in Fig 4.25, which has two advantages. The weight of the tow is now shared between two cleats, and whenever you find yourself pinned by the stern, you can slacken off one of the warps and allow the boat to pivot about the other. If you are having difficulty turning to starboard, slacken off the port towing warp, and vice versa. Once you are on course again, centre the bridle by easing out the pivot warp.

If you are doubtful about the strength of your aft cleats, they can always be backed up by taking the falls of both towropes forward, heaving tight and then making fast a second time to the sidedeck or foredeck cleats, or even to the anchor winch (Fig 4.25). This 'belt-and-braces' strategy is advisable at an early stage if conditions look like becoming heavy later.

Once you've successfully passed your own nylon rope across and the end has been made fast aboard the tow, some close co-operation is now required between helmsman and crew as you start edging forwards in the direction you want to make good. Your crew should pay out the towrope steadily as the distance between the boats increases. If it goes out too quickly, you run the risk of a stray bight getting caught round a prop or rudder; if it is paid out too slowly, the strain will come on prematurely.

You, the helmsman, will need to keep looking back

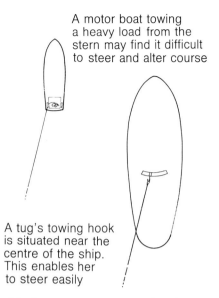

A motor boat towing a heavy load from the stern may find it difficult to steer and alter course

A tug's towing hook is situated near the centre of the ship. This enables her to steer easily

Fig 4.24 *If a heavy tow is secured right aft, the drag on the stern can make steering difficult.*

Fig 4.25 *Towing with a bridle allows you to manoeuvre and steer more easily.*

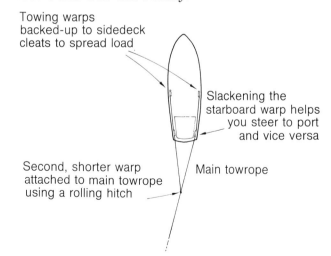

Towing warps backed-up to sidedeck cleats to spread load

Slackening the starboard warp helps you steer to port and vice versa

Second, shorter warp attached to main towrope using a rolling hitch

Main towrope

to see how things are going. When the required length of towrope has been let out, slow right down and come into neutral to allow the rope and anti-chafe protection to be secured. Now ease forward gently until the strain comes on and the towed boat straightens up. Speed should be increased very gradually. Once under way, you can assess how your own boat is handling and decide whether or not to use the bridle shown in Fig 4.25.

Your final speed will depend on the sea state and on the type and size of your tow. In this example, it is unlikely that you'll be able to make more than about six knots: you are pulling quite a heavy boat with four people aboard, there is now a significant head sea, and you don't want to generate excessive surging tension in the towrope. Remember that even if you have enough power, pulling a smaller boat, especially a sailing boat, *too* fast can make her break up, or at least put a heavy strain on her fittings and hull. Stay below *her* hull speed. In deciding on a safe speed, you have to strike a balance between caution and trying to cover ground. If you lose the tow because the rope parts or a cleat carries away, you'll have all the trouble of getting things rigged again, often in worsening conditions. On the other hand, you don't want to linger unnecessarily: the sooner you can obtain some lee from the land the less vulnerable you will be to the deteriorating weather.

The tow's crew can assist in various ways. Careful steering will keep her nicely in line with the tug. Her trim can also be critical; she will be more likely to sheer about and take green water over the bow if down by the head, so her crew can help by keeping aft. If the securing point is well aft—a samson post, or the base of a sturdy mast—the towrope should also be lashed down near the stemhead so that the effective lead is from right forward. This will help keep the tow on a straight course. The towrope should be protected from chafe wherever it might rub any part of the boat, e.g. in a fairlead or over a chain roller. Rag, canvas or heavy plastic tube can be parcelled around the rope for this purpose.

In a following sea the tow may tend to 'surf' down the wave fronts, over-running her rope so that it falls slack periodically. When the load comes on again it can do so savagely, putting a heavy strain on both towrope and fittings. An improvised drogue can sometimes help keep the tow steady: a bight of heavy warp streamed astern, or even a strong bucket on a long line (Fig 4.26). Towing alongside is not a technique to be used at sea and should be reserved for the quiet waters of a harbour. Even apparently quite small waves can grind two boats together with alarming force.

Near harbour the towrope should be shortened to less than two boat-lengths, in preparation for manoeuvring. Approach a quay or mooring very slowly and against any tidal stream, because your tow has no active means of slowing down. Finally, as your rope is cast off and you carry on about your own business, it's always worth remembering that, next time out, it could just as easily be you in need of a friendly tow home!

Fig 4.26 *An improvised drogue can sometimes help keep the tow steady.*

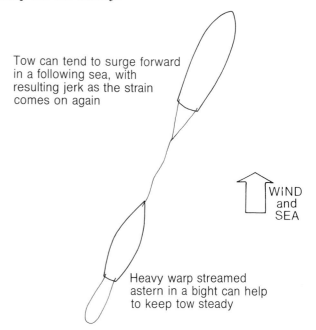

Tow can tend to surge forward in a following sea, with resulting jerk as the strain comes on again

WIND and SEA

Heavy warp streamed astern in a bight can help to keep tow steady

Handling with One Engine

Twin-engined boats can lose the use of one engine at the most inconvenient moments. It may happen at any time, as a result of dirty fuel, a fractured pipe or simply a piece of thick plastic or a rope's end round a propeller. If you are out in open water, getting home on the remaining engine may be relatively straightforward, but what about the problem of man-oeuvring in today's crowded harbours with the remaining, unaccustomed offset screw? It is a wise precaution to practise handling your boat occasionally with one engine only, but few of us ever get around to doing it.

So, bending the mind to some of the theory and forces involved may pay dividends. Consider first what happens to a twin-engined hull if you start from rest with only one screw. You will begin to move forwards, of course, but there will also be a swivelling force—turning the boat to starboard if the port engine is used and vice versa. The significance of this force will depend on a number of factors, such as the separation of the props, their direction of rotation, the underwater profile of the hull and so on. But for a modern, fairly beamy, planing hull this initial turning effect will be considerable (see Fig 4.27).

On an outdrive-powered boat you will have steerage the moment the engine is put into gear, so the effect can be countered, as it were, before it occurs. With inboards, however, there will be a short delay between the prop beginning to bite and the boat gathering sufficient way for the rudders to become effective. During this period the hull will start to pivot and you must therefore allow room for this swing to take place. Once she has gathered momentum and steerage, you will be pointing in the required direction but actually moving at an angle to your heading (see Fig 4.28). I will call this the 'angle of yaw', and because of this you have to travel slightly crab-wise in order to progress in a given direction (see Fig 4.29). The extent of the crabbing depends largely on the boat's resistance to sideways motion. A displacement hull will tend to need less helm than a planing one, and there is a wide range

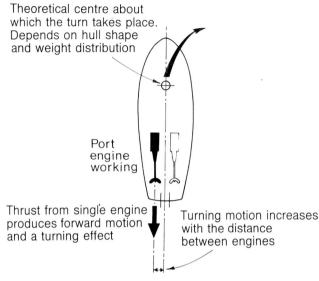

Fig 4.27 *When a twin-engined boat starts from rest with only one screw, the initial turning effect can be considerable.*

Fig 4.28 *Once the boat has gathered momentum, you will actually be travelling at a slight angle to your heading.*

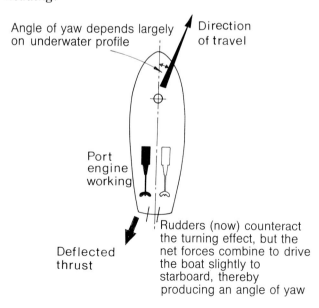

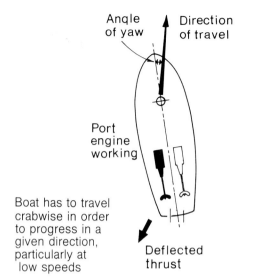

Angle of yaw

Direction of travel

Port engine working

Boat has to travel crabwise in order to progress in a given direction, particularly at low speeds

Deflected thrust

Fig 4.29 *Because of the angle of yaw, you have to travel slightly crabwise in order to progress in a given direction.*

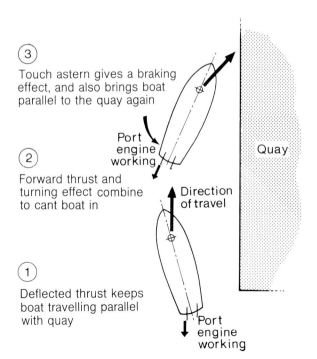

③ Touch astern gives a braking effect, and also brings boat parallel to the quay again

Port engine working

② Forward thrust and turning effect combine to cant boat in

Quay

Direction of travel

① Deflected thrust keeps boat travelling parallel with quay

Port engine working

Fig 4.30 *Hold the bow well off until you are nearly up to your chosen spot and then centre the helm, allowing the bow to fall towards the quay.*

of handling characteristics in between. You can see, therefore, how it is usually easier to come alongside a pontoon or quay starboard-side-to if using only the port engine, or port-side-to on the starboard engine. The sideways drift can actually help you into a restricted space and this is worth bearing in mind even when both engines are fully operational.

Hold your bow well off the quay until you are nearly up to your chosen spot and then centre the helm, thus letting the bow fall in towards the quay for the 'landing'. Bring her up with a touch astern: as well as braking, this will have a reverse turning effect that should leave you lined up with the quay (Fig 4.30). Most twin-screw boats have outward-turning propellers, in which case the paddlewheel effect will help counteract stern-swing even more. All very nice in theory! The effects of wind and tide have to be considered on top of all this, and it is also important to maintain an even approach speed that will just allow the rudders to work. Gentle use of the throttle is a must, unless you suddenly need the pivoting effect to get you out of trouble.

Approaching port-side-to using the port engine (or vice versa) is tricky, often requiring more flamboyance if the manoeuvre is to come off successfully. The bow should be canted in much harder much sooner, to ensure that the boat has a reasonable quay-wards momentum. You will be coming in at a steady speed with some port counteracting helm to stay on course. When the pulpit is almost there, a rapid switch to starboard helm should send the stern swinging in nicely and bring the boat straight. The final touch astern stops this swing as well as the forward motion, leaving you parallel with the quay. The catch is that if you switch the helm over too soon you can end up neatly parallel to the quay but several feet away, although this obviously isn't a problem if the wind is blowing you on.

Setting off. What sort of passage will we have? Where will we end up?

Chapter 5

Basic Navigation

At its simplest, navigation is just a form of map-reading. Suppose, for example, that you plan to cross a wide bay, in order to reach a harbour whose entrance is marked by an offshore buoy. The buoy is out of sight some distance away, but your chart shows its exact position in relation to everything else. You can therefore find out how far and in what direction to steer to reach the buoy and enter the harbour. This is essentially the same process as, having looked at a road-map, deciding to 'carry on north up the A38 for a couple of miles and then take the first left after the roundabout.'

Navigational charts differ from road-maps in two important ways. First, the depth of water indicated on a chart usually has a vital significance for the navigator, whereas height on a road-map is, more often than not, only of passing interest; second, whereas many maps are crammed with physical features, charts tend to be filled with wide tracts of watery open space. It is when you come to cross this nothingness that the map-reading analogy breaks down. You can no longer point to the chart and say, 'Ah yes, we are just coming up to this headland, so we must be here.' Away from the land, one area of sea looks much like another. You then begin to use the chart not only as a source of information but also as a plotting sheet on which to record your progress, accurately and to scale. Tidal streams and currents complicate matters, keeping the sea on which you are floating continuously on the move. However, before you graduate to this stage in navigation, you need to be fully conversant with how a chart is set out, and particularly how it represents the various hazards that sea-goers have to avoid.

Reading a Chart

One of the knacks of chart reading is 'seeing the wood for the trees'. It is important to take notice of those features which are relevant to your passage, but not to worry about those that are not. In this respect, modern charts, with their clear symbols and use of colour, make life much easier than did the old black-and-white charts. Keep in mind that official or Admiralty charts are produced for the use of *all* mariners, and the navigator of a motor yacht drawing no more than, say, $1\frac{1}{2}$ metres, can often ignore marked 'shoals' which may nevertheless concern the master of a large ship. Sometimes though, even quite deep shoals can cause troublesome overfalls on the surface, especially when there is a strong tide running.

Soundings The depths of water, or soundings, marked on a chart are all pessimistic depths: what you would encounter at an exceptionally low spring tide. This baseline is called *datum*. On British Admiralty charts it is the Lowest Astronomical Tide (LAT), and represents the lowest tide that can be predicted from the known orbits of the heavenly bodies. (Chart datum may be different according to chart publishers, but will be identified on the chart itself and should be noted.) So at an average low spring, you've got a bit more depth of water than the chart indicates. But remember that tide tables are only predictions, so never cut your depth calculations too fine. Tide levels are also affected by imponderables such as atmospheric pressure and recent weather.

Chart symbols for dangers The complete list of symbols, abbreviations and conventions used on Admiralty charts is contained in the excellent publication *NP5011*, but it is useful to look here at some of the more common danger symbols, those indicating rocks and shoals.

Fig 5.1a shows a rock which never covers; its height (above Mean High Water Springs) is often shown in brackets alongside. It can sometimes be difficult to pick out small above-water rocks among a mass of other dangers on a chart, but they can make useful seamarks if you are navigating close inshore and very certain of identifying them.

Fig 5.1b shows an area of rock or foreshore that is exposed at LAT, one of the most common danger symbols and coloured green on metric charts. The *drying height*, which is simply a negative depth, is shown as a sounding with a line under it. For example, 2 on a metric chart means that the tip of the danger stands 2m *above* the water at LAT.

Fig 5.1c shows a rock that is just awash at LAT, an innocuous looking symbol which can easily slip the eye if you glance quickly over the chart. Fig 5.1d on a metric chart shows an underwater rock with 1.3m over it at LAT.

Fig 5.1e represents an underwater rock or rocks over which the depth of water is not so certain— 2m or less at LAT. This symbol can also denote an

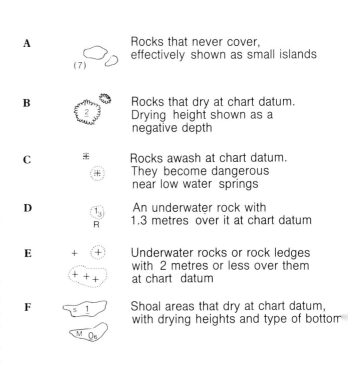

A — Rocks that never cover, effectively shown as small islands

B — Rocks that dry at chart datum. Drying height shown as a negative depth

C — Rocks awash at chart datum. They become dangerous near low water springs

D — An underwater rock with 1.3 metres over it at chart datum

E — Underwater rocks or rock ledges with 2 metres or less over them at chart datum

F — Shoal areas that dry at chart datum, with drying heights and type of bottom

Fig 5.1 *Some symbols for navigational dangers on metric charts.*

underwater rock over which the exact depth is unknown but which is nonetheless considered to be a danger to surface navigation.

Fig 5.1f shows two banks which dry at LAT, the S denoting sand and the M mud. Drying banks are shown as enclosed green areas on metric charts, similar to drying rocks but with a smooth enclosing line instead of a jagged one.

Navigation buoys and beacons

These mark navigational dangers of all kinds, thereby directing shipping into safe water. Buoys float and are anchored to the bottom, while beacons are solid structures built on rocks, banks or the foreshore. Although you can glean a limited amount of information from either mark just by observation, the full value of a seamark is only obtained when you can identify it, unambiguously, on an up-to-date chart of the area in which you are cruising.

The buoyage systems used by different countries are gradually converging towards a universally accepted standard. IALA Maritime Buoyage System 'A' has been widely implemented within Europe at least, and most local variations are fairly readily understood. Within this system, navigational buoys and beacons really fall into three classes—lateral, cardinal and others.

Lateral marks are used for well-defined channels. As you approach a harbour, river mouth or other fairway *from seaward*, red buoys or beacons are left to port and greens to starboard (Fig 5.2a). You sometimes come across lateral marks some distance offshore, where the direction of buoyage cannot be deduced by reference to any specific entrance. In such cases, the direction of buoyage may be shown on the chart by a broad arrow (Fig 5.2b).

Port-hand (red) buoys are generally cylindrical or can-shaped, and they have similarly shaped topmarks. If lit at night, they exhibit red lights. Starboard-hand buoys and their topmarks are usually conical. If lit at night, they exhibit green lights. The same conventions apply to lateral beacons, although their shapes are less predictable.

The IALA Maritime Buoyage System 'B' adopts an opposite 'green to port, red to starboard' convention for its lateral marks and is used in North, South and Central America, Japan, South Korea and the Philippines. It may seem odd that these completely opposite conventions are still in force in different parts of the world, but I suppose it is a bit like driving on the left or right hand side of the road: those countries which have grown up with either system would find it difficult and expensive to change.

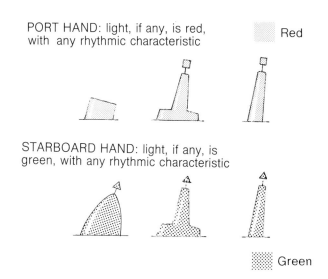

PORT HAND: light, if any, is red, with any rhythmic characteristic ░ Red

STARBOARD HAND: light, if any, is green, with any rhythmic characteristic

▓ Green

Fig 5.2a *Lateral marks of Region A, used in Europe, Africa, India, Australia and most of Asia. Note that America is part of Region B, where the lateral convention is reversed and green marks are left to port, red marks to starboard.*

Fig 5.2b

This symbol is used on Admiralty charts to indicate the direction of buoyage, wherever this seems ambiguous

The Local Direction of Buoyage is that taken when approaching a harbour, river estuary or other waterway from seaward

The General Direction of Buoyage is determined by the buoyage authorities, but follows broadly clockwise around continental land masses, i.e. from SE to NW off NW Europe

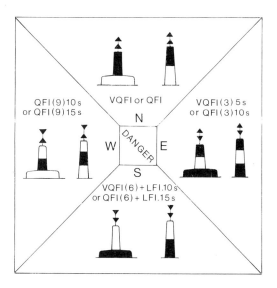

Fig 5.2c *The cardinal system of buoyage, showing the direction in which clear water lies.*

Fig 5.3 *Other common marks.*

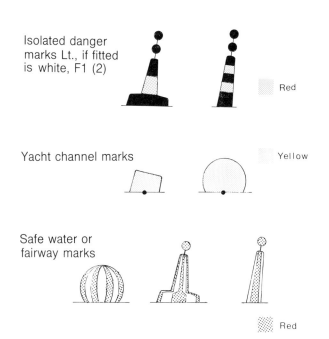

Cardinal marks are common to both System 'A' and System 'B'. As their name suggests, they use the quadrants of the compass to indicate where clear water may be found. Fig 5.2c shows the four types of cardinal mark. Each type can be identified by its colours, the shape of the topmarks and by its light characteristics. A north-cardinal mark is situated to the north of a navigational danger and the clear water therefore lies to the north of the mark, and so on.

Cardinal colour bands on the buoys usually show up well at a distance, although you must be careful not to jump to conclusions too soon. An east-cardinal buoy tilted over in a strong stream sometimes looks as though it has north-cardinal colours. On the other hand, a north-cardinal beacon at low water may appear to be coloured black-yellow-black, the lower 'black band' actually being the seaweed-covered rocks on which the beacon is standing. The cardinal topmarks are easy to remember as pairs of opposites; north cones pointing upwards and south pointing down; the west-cardinal's two cones' points together look like a **W** on its side, and the east cones are the other way round.

The 'odds and ends' include those buoys and beacons shown in Fig 5.3. **Isolated danger marks** are black with one or more red bands and the topmark usually consists of two black balls. They indicate dangers of limited extent which are steep-to with navigable water all round. If lit at night, isolated danger marks exhibit a white light, usually group flash 2.

Safe water or 'fairway' marks have red and white vertical stripes, or sometimes red and white horizontal bands. Often moored some way off a harbour or river entrance, a fairway buoy is the first point to make for before the channel is picked up. If lit at night, fairway marks exhibit a white light, usually either isophase, occulting, long flash every 10s or Morse **A**.

Yellow buoys and beacons are **special marks** which have a number of possible local applications. They are sometimes used to indicate the seaward end of underwater sewer outfalls, in which case it would be unwise to anchor anywhere between a yellow buoy and the shore. Yellow buoys labelled **DZ** cordon off 'Danger Zones', the most common type of which is a military target practice area.

In Europe, yellow buoys sometimes indicate a comparatively shallow channel into a harbour or river (or between deeper channels) which is normally navigable by yachts and other shallow draught boats but not by larger ships. In this case the yellow buoys are left close on either side. If lit at night, yellow buoys usually exhibit yellow lights.

Distance on a chart

A nautical mile is a fundamental measure defined as that distance subtended by a minute of latitude at the earth's surface. This means that nautical miles can be read off directly, using a pair of dividers, from the latitude scale at the side of a chart. When doing this though, four points should be borne in mind:

—Don't inadvertently use the longitude scale at the bottom of the chart. Minutes of longitude are not the same thing at all, and vary greatly in length depending upon your latitude.

—Make sure that you get the scale units right. It is possible, for example, to confuse 5 minute blocks for single minutes when you are tired or in a hurry.

—Always read off minutes from that part of the latitude scale on the side directly opposite where the divider distance was taken. A slight 'distortion' occurs when the earth's curved surface is projected onto a flat sheet of paper: for example, on a chart of the English Channel, a minute opposite Weymouth is not quite the same length on paper as one opposite St Malo.

—It is best to use large, brass dividers of the one-handed type.

Direction

An official chart usually has two or three compass roses, each with a magnetic scale inside the true scale. The two scales exist because the earth's magnetic pole, towards which all compass needles point, is not exactly at the 'top' of the earth. This difference between magnetic and true north is called *magnetic variation*. It changes as you move about the globe and is expressed, for a given area, as so many degrees 'west' or 'east'. To convert a true course to magnetic, you add westerly variation and subtract easterly, and vice versa from magnetic to true. Variation also changes slowly over time, so on the compass rose an approximate rate of change will be given, e.g., '7°15'W (1987) decreasing about 5' annually', usually now shown as (5'E).

In practice, it doesn't much matter whether you work directly from the magnetic scale or work in true and convert to or from magnetic as necessary, so long as you always know which you are doing. The true scale on a compass rose is larger and easier to read than the magnetic, but there is always the chance of applying variation the wrong way. However, when using French charts you *have* to work in true and convert: they don't have compass roses printed on them and you can only extract and lay off true courses, using a protractor.

There are now numerous types of navigation protractors and rulers to choose from. I was weaned on parallel rules, but they can easily slip when used in a bumpy sea. The Breton Plotter is quite good, with its swinging arm and rotating scale, provided that neither swings or rotates when it is not supposed to. Some navigators swear by the Douglas Protractor, which has no moving parts, although I have never quite found the knack of using it quickly without doubting the result. The best thing is to try them all, find out which you get on with and then stick to it. When organizing your navigation area, though, remember that when motor cruising most of your detailed plotting will be done before you set out. Whereas the relatively slow speeds and damped motion of a sailing boat make it quite feasible for the navigator to work at a chart table on passage, the higher speeds and harder motion of a motor boat make this much more difficult.

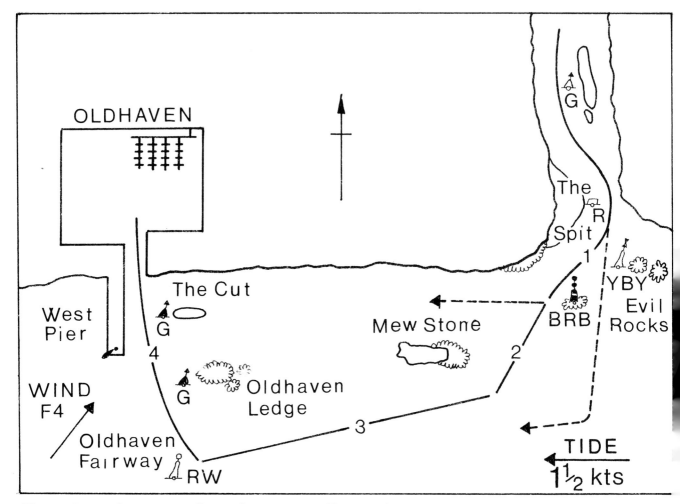

Fig 5.4 *Route planning usually results in a series of legs, as shown in this short passage to Oldhaven harbour.*

'Round the Coast' Navigation

The first stage of even a short coastal passage is to work out the safest route to your intended destination. For a motor yacht this generally means the route which, while being no longer than necessary, nevertheless keeps you in deep enough water, uses land for shelter wherever possible, stays well clear of any rocks or shoals and is far enough off headlands to allow a reasonable margin of safety in case of engine or steering failure. For this exercise you need a large-scale chart of the harbour you are leaving,

a large-scale chart of your destination, and a smaller scale chart or charts covering the whole area in between.

Route planning usually results in a series of legs, as Fig 5.4 shows. In this example of a short passage from a navigable river to the nearby harbour of Oldhaven, the legs work out as follows.

1 Leaving the river safely: remember that you are travelling out *against* the direction of buoyage, so avoid the shallow bank in midstream by leaving the green conical buoy to *port*, standing on for a short distance to be sure of clearing the tail of the

A south-cardinal beacon on the rocky coast of Brittany. Note the disturbed water on the 'wrong' side of the beacon.

shoal. Now turn to port to avoid the sandspit which extends from the west shore, leaving the red can buoy to *starboard*.

In the estuary, keep west of the cardinal buoy marking Evil Rocks. Which side should you then leave the isolated danger beacon? There is clear water on either side, but it's probably best to leave it to port because (a) you are bound westward along the coast anyway, and (b) other things being equal, it is preferable to pass down-tide of a danger, so that in the event of machinery failure or something nasty round a prop, the stream will carry you clear instead of setting you on.

With a stronger wind and a heavy sea, there would be a case for passing east of the isolated danger beacon, keeping the sea more comfortably on your starboard bow rather than having it dead on the nose. Once offshore a little way, turning west along the coast would bring the sea nicely on your port bow.

2 Having passed west of the isolated danger, on which side do you now leave the Mew Stone? There is an inside passage and you could reach Oldhaven by hugging the coast, but it would be more prudent to keep a good offing given the moderate onshore wind. Therefore pass outside the Mew Stone, giving it a wide berth because (a) the tide is setting onto it, and (b) there is an underwater ledge extending east from the main rock.

3 Having cleared the Mew Stone, the next leg leads out to Oldhaven fairway buoy. You can pass just inside this buoy, but head towards it first to be sure of giving a good offing to Oldhaven Ledge, a drying rocky shoal only marked on its west side. The onshore wind makes it all the more important not to cut this danger too finely.

4 Approach Oldhaven harbour from near the fairway buoy by leaving Oldhaven Ledge green conical buoy to *starboard* (you are now travelling in the direction of buoyage) and The Cut green conical to *starboard*. Oldhaven entrance looks narrow, so take it slowly and watch out for any traffic coming out.

This coastal hop involves chart-reading rather than any detailed navigation, although there are clearly some tactical decisions to be made en route. In good visibility you'd probably only need to work out a compass course for the leg from Mew Stone to Oldhaven fairway: the buoy might not be visible at a distance and it is important to clear Oldhaven Ledge. Provided you can make at least 6 knots the tide is not too significant on this passage, except when you are deciding which side and how far off to leave dangers. Since the stream is flowing against the wind, you could expect more chop than if it was flowing east. Oldhaven is accessible at any state of tide, but this is not true of all harbours; you often need to time your arrival near HW, or at least above half-tide.

Basic Navigation Equipment

Compasses

A reliable main compass is vital for stress-free navigation. I was once told that the only way to choose a compass is to work out how much you can afford to pay and then buy one at twice the price! This isn't always true, though. You get what you pay for to some extent, but there are now some very good compasses available at quite modest prices. Most are accurate in the sense of having virtually no error when standing still, clear of magnetic objects. However, when buying a compass you are looking for sustained accuracy in use, as much as absolute accuracy. You should therefore ask yourself the following questions before deciding:

—Is it well built? Motor boats can suffer quite violent motion, so a steering compass must be able to withstand this as well as the constant vibration from the engine(s).

—Is it easy to read from the steering position? This seems an obvious point, but many compasses aren't. Look for a bold, clearly marked card with not too many sub-divisions, and a good magnification of the card by the compass bowl. Make sure that the ship's head line is clearly visible against the card from the angles at which you would normally be viewing it.

—Is it well damped? That is, does the card settle down quickly having been swung off course? This is particularly important in high-speed boats. However, there is a compromise to be made here, because a compass which is too heavily damped will make accurate steering difficult.

—Can it be easily corrected for deviation? Most reputable compasses have adjusting screws or compensating magnets, which are used to correct the worst of any deviation (see right).

—Is there a suitable light for night use? The card should be easy to read, but not so bright that night vision is impaired.

Deviation Sometimes confused with variation, magnetic deviation is simply compass error caused by various ferrous metals on board. There are many possible sources of deviation, of which the engines are usually the most significant. Electrical equipment can also play its part. Whereas variation depends upon your location, deviation changes as your boat's heading changes. This is because the total effect of all sources of on-board magnetism is a local magnetic field which competes against the earth's field for the compass card's attention. As the boat changes heading, the two fields combine differently, and if you plot deviation against heading the resulting curve usually looks something like Fig 5.5a.

There are two ways of coping with deviation. You can try to adjust the compass, using either its own adjusting screws or some external compensating magnets, hopefully reducing the error to an acceptable level. You can also calibrate or 'swing' the compass by comparing, on various headings, what the instrument actually reads with what it should read. Swinging a compass is tricky, and although you *can* do the job yourself, it is best left to a professional compass adjuster. The result of this operation is a deviation card (Fig 5.5b) which can be used to convert between magnetic courses and compass courses.

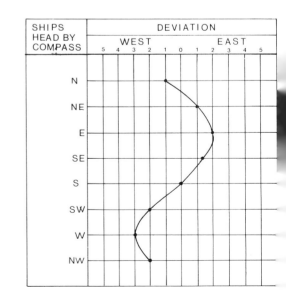

A reliable main compass is essential for stress-free navigation. When installing a compass, make sure that the ship's head line is clearly visible against the card from the angles at which you would normally be viewing it. (Photo: Ron Dummer)

Fig 5.5a *A typical deviation curve.*

Fig 5.5b *A typical deviation card.*

DEVIATION CARD	
SHIP'S HEAD BY COMPASS	DEVIATION
N	1°W
NE	1°E
E	2°E
SE	1°E
S	0
SW	2°W
W	3°W
NW	2°W

The hand-bearing compass is a small hand-held compass with a prism sight, used for taking bearings of navigational marks. Hand-bearing compasses need to be especially well damped and the better designs are normally reasonably free of deviation provided that you use them as far away as possible from any sources of magnetism, i.e. out on deck if possible and standing as high up as you can manage. There are many makes of hand-bearer on the market, but I prefer those which are encased in a kind of miniature rubber 'tyre'. Light to handle, it can be hung safely round your neck as you move about.

The British company Nautech Ltd. now manufacture a rather neat electronic hand-bearing compass. This has no moving parts, gives instant readings and has a roll-over memory capable of storing nine bearings. The only disadvantage of this instrument is that it must be held on a horizontal plane for accurate results.

The Autohelm personal hand-bearing compass is easy to use, and accurate so long as you keep it horizontal when taking readings.

Speed and distance log

This essential item of equipment, at its simplest, clocks distance run through the water, enabling you to plot your progress on the chart with a fair degree of accuracy. Most electronic logs display speed as well as distance, and digital logs often have a host of extra features. Some instruments are driven by through-the-hull impellers, some use small paddle-wheels, some use flush-mounted 'doppler' transducers and some use a propeller at the end of a trailed line or wire. You pay your money and take your choice, but you need not spend a fortune: the most expensive logs do not necessarily give the best results. You must, however, follow the installation instructions to the letter.

Echo-sounder

This is not strictly indispensable, because not long ago cruising folk managed perfectly well without them. But echo-sounders are so convenient, and now so reliable and inexpensive, that it makes sense to have one aboard. I would personally avoid the type with sophisticated alarm systems: they are always a menace to set, you are never quite sure that you've got it right, and the alarms can get on your nerves by going off as you pass over a shoal of fish or patch of seaweed. 'Keep it simple' is an excellent rule with any kind of cruising equipment, and especially so with electronics.

Coastal Navigation

Let us now examine what can be involved in making those short coastal passages which nevertheless require a little more preparation than a careful perusal of the chart. In thus taking your navigation a stage further, there are three important new aspects to think about:
—working out an accurate 'course to steer', to allow for the displacing effect of tidal streams
—calculating tidal heights
—making and using a passage plan.

Working out a course to steer

Unless you are lucky enough to do most of your cruising in the Mediterranean, passage-making will usually be complicated by the inconvenient fact that the sea doesn't stand still while you career about on it. Tides or currents generally keep things on the move, providing a tricky source of uncertainty in small-boat navigation. The practical significance of a tidal stream or current really depends upon two factors: its rate in relation to your own speed; and whether it is flowing against, behind or across your course.

If, for example, you can cruise at 20 knots, the effect of a knot of foul or fair tide is about 5 minutes lost or gained over a 30 mile passage. If this stream was flowing at right angles to your heading, your boat would be set sideways by $1\frac{1}{2}$ miles on the same trip, equivalent to about 3° difference in the course made good. If, at the same cruising speed, you encountered a tidal stream averaging $2\frac{1}{2}$ knots over the same distance, the difference between having this against or behind you would be something over 20 minutes. If this faster stream was at right angles to your course, your boat would be set sideways by $3\frac{3}{4}$ miles in 30 miles, equivalent to just over 7° shift in the course made good.

Tidal streams clearly become more significant at lower boat speeds. Cruising at 9 knots, a 1 knot cross-tide means a sideways drift of nearly $3\frac{1}{2}$ miles over a 30 mile passage, or just over 6° on the course made good. If this stream was running at $2\frac{1}{2}$ knots, the drift over the same distance would be nearly $8\frac{1}{2}$ miles, or about *15°* on the course made good. Cruising at 5 or 6 knots, the displacement would be even more marked. Now motor boat owners differ widely on the question of how to treat tide in practice. Some high-speed navigators ignore it altogether, but this can be a dangerous habit except in the most straight-forward coastal hop. There tends to be enough uncertainty in navigation without deliberately adding to it, so whenever you work out a course to steer, you ought to make allowance for any tidal or current set.

There is no black magic involved in this process; you really only need to be able to draw simple scale

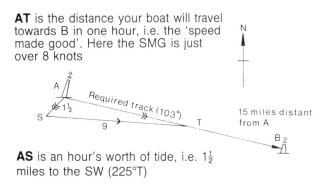

AT is the distance your boat will travel towards B in one hour, i.e. the 'speed made good'. Here the SMG is just over 8 knots

AS is an hour's worth of tide, i.e. $1\frac{1}{2}$ miles to the SW (225°T)

ST is an hour's worth of boat speed, i.e. 9 miles at 9 knots cruising speed

A course equivalent to the direction *ST* (095°T) will take you from A to B so long as the tide continues SW-going at $1\frac{1}{2}$ kts, and so long as your predicted cruising speed is maintained

Fig 5.6 *Calculating a course to steer to counteract a given tidal stream.*

triangles. Fig 5.6 shows the basic calculation. Suppose that part of your passage involves travelling between buoys A and B, a distance of 15 nautical miles. Your cruising speed is 9 knots and the tide will be setting SW at $1\frac{1}{2}$ knots. The first step is to draw a straight line on the chart between A and B: this is the required *track*, along which, ideally, you would like your boat to proceed.

Now ask the question; in one hour, if you just sat and drifted with the tide, where would your boat end up? Clearly she'd be set SW from A for $1\frac{1}{2}$ miles, and so you draw this vector to scale on the chart. The term *vector* simply means a combination of direction and distance. Lay off the tide's direction using either the compass rose and parallel rules, or a navigation protractor, and mark off an hour's drift by opening the dividers to a distance equivalent to $1\frac{1}{2}$ minutes of latitude.

Given that the tide, if left to its own devices, would have set you to S in one hour, how do you 'get back' to the required track over the same period? Well, all you know about your boat's likely progress is that she can cruise at 9 knots. So with dividers open to 9 miles, that is 9 minutes of latitude, locate one point at S and strike across to where this radius cuts the track at T.

Now the direction ST, transferred to the compass rose, is the course you will need to steer, *at 9 knots*, to counteract the tide and reach B. The length AT represents the speed you will make good along the track—less than your cruising speed in this case because the tide is partly foul. Although the tidal triangle appears as a sequence of vectors, the components obviously act simultaneously. Your boat will travel through the water at the same time as the surrounding sea moves bodily sideways. So long as your estimates of the rate and direction of tide are correct, and provided you average the planned cruising speed, you will, in effect, be continuously side-slipping along the track AB.

You can, of course, work out tidal triangles other than by drawing them on the chart. A scientific calculator can be handy, if you are fairly fluent in trigonometry, and there are various special navigation calculators on the market. A low-tech solution is to use a patent course corrector, although these simple devices have rather gone out of fashion in this microchip age. Looking like a kind of slide rule, with a swinging arm to represent tidal set, they are quick to use once you know how.

Having calculated the true course to steer, you apply variation and deviation to arrive at the *compass course*. When cruising with a wind on the beam, you may also need to allow for some leeway. This factor is never easy to quantify, but can easily represent 5° drift for a planing boat in a force 5–6.

Calculating tidal heights

We saw earlier that soundings on a chart are referred to a base datum, usually Lowest Astronomical Tide or LAT. It is important to appreciate how the tide's rise and fall relates to that datum, so that you can estimate the depth of water at a given position at any point in the tidal cycle. There are two high and two low tides every 24 hours, but successive highs or lows are something over 12 hours apart, so that tide times advance each day.

Spring tides occur twice each lunar month, when the sun and moon are in opposition (near full moon) or in conjunction (near new moon); springs bring the highest high water and lowest low water levels, and consequently the fastest tidal streams. Neap tides occur between periods of springs, bringing lower high water and higher low water levels, as well as more moderate streams. Fig 5.7 shows how the various levels compare with each other and with chart datum. The heights above datum of each high and low water can be found from tide tables, along with their times.

Fig 5.8 shows a river entrance with a bar whose least shoal part dries 1.5m at LAT. The nearest port for which tide tables are published is Sedmouth, not far upstream. Suppose that, on a particular day when you are planning to enter the river, low water at Sedmouth is at 1435 and high water at 2022, with heights of 0.8m and 4.4m respectively. Referring back to Fig 5.7 you can see that, at low water, the deepest part of the bar uncovers by 0.7m, i.e. the difference between the sounding and the low water height. For the purpose of entering the river, you might be interested to know when, after low water, you would find a depth over the bar of, say, 2m.

Now tides don't rise or fall at a constant speed. Both flood and ebb begin slowly, build to a maximum rate of change around half-tide and then finish slowly. Most tidal curves are roughly sinusoidal, and you can see examples in the Admiralty tables and in almanacs such as *Reed's* or *MacMillan's*. But in practice, you rarely need to get involved with using these curves. A useful approximation, known as the Rule of Twelfths, serves for almost all circumstances that yachtsmen are likely to meet. This rule says that in the 1st hour of ebb or flood the tide falls or rises by 1/12 of its range; in the 2nd hour by 2/12; in the 3rd hour by 3/12; in the 4th hour by 3/12 again; in the 5th hour by 2/12; and in the last hour by 1/12.

Now at Sedmouth, the tidal range on the afternoon concerned is 3.6m: the total predicted rise, calculated from the difference between the low and high water heights. According to the Twelfths Rule, in the 1st hour of flood the tide should rise by 1/12 of its range

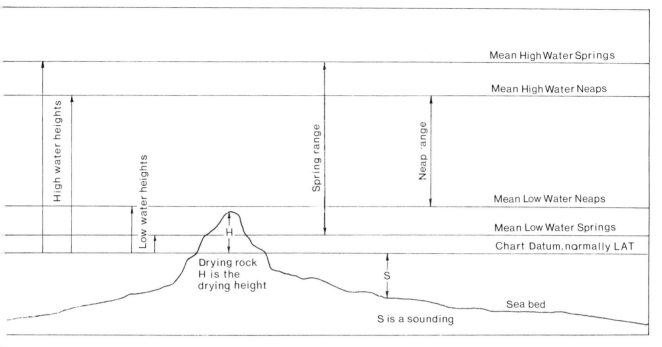

Fig 5.7 *Different tide levels referred to chart datum.*

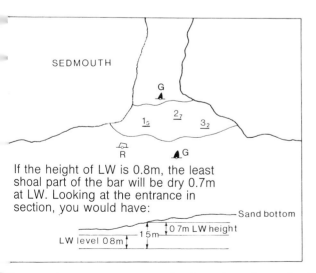

SEDMOUTH

If the height of LW is 0.8m, the least shoal part of the bar will be dry 0.7m at LW. Looking at the entrance in section, you would have:

Fig 5.8 *A river entrance with a bar whose least shoal part dries 1.5m at LAT.*

i.e. 0.3m. So at 1535 there should be 1.1m above chart datum and the bar will still be dry by 0.4m. In the 2nd hour of flood the tide should rise by 2/12 of 3.6m, i.e. a further 0.6m, so by 1635 there ought to be 0.2m of water *over* the bar. In the 3rd hour the tide should rise by a further 0.9m, giving 1.1m over the bar by 1735. In the 4th hour you can expect another 0.9m rise, giving 2m over the bar by 1835.

Once you have worked out this earliest entry time, it is important not to cut things too fine when you arrive on the scene. Tide tables, although generally accurate in themselves, are only theoretical predictions. Bear in mind that a high barometer or sustained winds from a given direction can easily depress tide levels by significant amounts. You also have to allow for any sea that may be running; even in apparently calm conditions, ½m of swell at a river mouth is not uncommon. In brisk onshore weather, shallow bars tend to break and may only then be passable near high water, if at all.

Passage planning

Constraints on arrival time There are various reasons why you might wish to reach a destination before, at, or after a certain time: so as to enter harbour during daylight perhaps, or to get ashore to your favourite restaurant. However, it is the tide which often provides the least flexible constraints upon your arrival time.

Some marinas have a retaining sill which can only be crossed when the tide has risen to a certain level. You may plan to lock into a basin, but sea-locks usually only work for a set period either side of high water, and sometimes to a timetable. As in the last example, a river mouth may be complicated by sandbanks or a bar where a minimum rise of tide may be required before you can enter safely. If the river itself is shallow, it may be prudent only to venture upstream on the flood, in case you go aground.

Constraints 'on passage' It is generally preferable to make any passage when the tide is fair, but the slower your cruising speed the more this is true. The fastest streams are usually encountered off headlands, which may therefore represent key points or 'gates' in your plan. Some headlands have off-lying patches of locally rough seas or 'overfalls' which are apt to be least boisterous at slack water. Even high-speed boats should take notice of tide to this extent, avoiding the worst periods of overfalls by careful timing. Strong winds can influence your passage planning, and it is sometimes prudent to take a less direct route in order to stay as much as possible under shelter of the coast, or to give a wide berth to a potentially dangerous lee shore. A contingent strategy can be valuable, so that you follow a route which allows the option of making for a port of refuge if the weather should deteriorate. In poor visibility, you may prefer to arrange your passage to stay within sight of land.

Constraints on departure time The various constraints mentioned earlier in relation to arrival time

can also set limits on your departure. For example, the tide may dictate when you can leave a particular marina, or you might need to catch the last lock out of a commercial harbour, or carry the first of the ebb down a river. There are also other 'administrative' considerations to bear in mind. Before you set off on a day trip you will need to listen to the morning weather forecast or perhaps phone the local met office. An unhurried breakfast is a good idea before a passage, and if you are going to be at sea for more than a couple of hours you should build time into your pre-departure schedule for preparing sandwiches and filling Thermos flasks with hot drinks or soup. You may need to top up with fuel, do some last minute shopping or settle harbour dues. All these jobs take time and should be allowed for realistically.

ETD and ETA Suppose that you have got as far as working out a safe-water route for your passage and have measured the total distance; you have considered the constraints on arrival time and worked backwards, considered the constraints on departure time and worked forwards, and made some allowance for diversions in case of bad weather. Balancing all these factors will enable you to estimate times of departure and arrival, which can then be used to begin the process of drawing up a more detailed passage plan.

Leg planning A typical coastal passage usually divides into several legs between convenient 'way points'. These can be tangible seamarks such as buoys, beacons or lightships, or more arbitrary, such as a position 2 miles off a particular headland. The example in Fig 5.9 shows a passage of about 40 miles in which three navigated legs of 15, 5 and 12 miles form the main haul. There are short, 4 mile stretches of pilotage at the start and finish of the trip.

Imagine planning to make this passage at the beginning of a fortnight's summer holiday. You have heard the forecast the previous evening—fresh to strong northwesterlies overnight, force 5–7, gradually easing to force 3–4 tomorrow as a weak ridge moves in behind a depression which is just passing through. The next local forecast is at 0745 on the

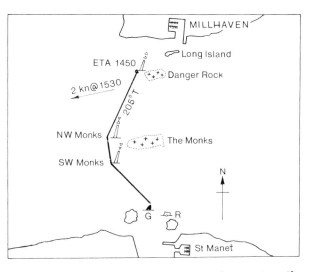

Fig 5.9 *A typical day passage of about 40 miles, which has 3 distinct legs.*

have moderated by then, and you'll be able to keep an eye on the barometer during the morning and hear the next local weather forecast. Assuming the weather looks OK, you can cast off at 1410 say, and be clear of the harbour approaches by about 1430.

It is 20 minutes along the coast before you reach the first waypoint, Danger Rock N-cardinal buoy, at about 1450. You'll be sheltered by the land until then, but if conditions still look boisterous offshore you can always come back to the outer harbour and try again next day. Here you have the basis of a passage plan. Because you can now put likely start and finish times against each leg, it is possible to start extracting some more specific information from the tidal stream atlas.

Tidal stream atlases It is important to distinguish between a tidal stream atlas and a set of tide tables. The latter are published in all-purpose almanacs, where the full tables for principal ports show, for each day of the year, times of high and low water and their heights above chart datum. Tidal 'differences' are given for secondary ports. Tide tables, like calendars, go out-of-date as each day passes.

Tidal stream atlases contain information about directions and rates of tidal streams for a given sea area. Although tide times and heights are always changing, the pattern of tidal streams, relative to tide times, remains constant. The directions of flow are shown by arrows on chartlets of the sea area concerned, there being a separate chartlet for each hour of the tidal cycle. Times normally refer to a Standard port (1hr after, 2hrs after, etc) and sometimes to a local standard port. Because rates obviously vary between a maximum at springs and a minimum at neaps, both these values are given alongside the appropriate arrow, and you have to interpolate between them depending on whether you are closest to springs or neaps. Some atlases help you carry out this interpolation by including a table of differences which refer to the actual height of tide on a given day.

morning of your proposed passage. You are moored in a marina accessible for 3½ hours either side of high water, which will be at 1105. Your well-found 32ft boat has a semi-displacement hull and you normally cruise at about 12 knots. The trip should take 4 hours or so, 'door-to-door'. You are bound for a marina which is inaccessible for about an hour either side of low water: that will be at 1720, so you won't be able to enter between 1620 and 1820. The tidal stream atlas indicates that the streams will be mostly across your route, so they don't materially affect your decision about when to leave.

The weather looks like the main constraint at the moment. The depression *seems* to be moving away, but the wind is probably going to be brisk for the first part of tomorrow. It will almost certainly be best to delay your departure until later in the day, and to keep a careful watch on conditions in the meantime. You don't want to kick off your holiday with a trying passage in a rough sea. The latest exit time from the marina is 1435, so why not aim to get under way soon after 1400? The wind and sea should

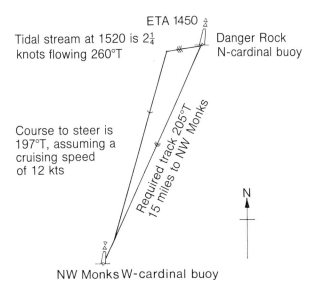

ETA 1450

Tidal stream at 1520 is 2¼ knots flowing 260°T

Danger Rock N-cardinal buoy

Course to steer is 197°T, assuming a cruising speed of 12 kts

Required track 205°T
15 miles to NW Monks

N

NW Monks W-cardinal buoy

Fig 5.10 *Working out the course to steer.*

Working out the 'course to steer' for each leg Fig 5.10 shows the first navigated leg of the example passage, the 15 miles from Danger Rock buoy to the NW Monks buoy. Your ETA at Danger Rock is 1450 and it is just over an hour's run from there to the NW Monks. From the tidal stream atlas, you now have to estimate the average stream rate running in that particular area during that period. In practice, this probably means extracting the direction and rate which applies at around 1530.

Suppose that the atlas indicates a stream flowing at 260°T at 2¼ knots. The required track between the buoys is 205°T and the tidal triangle is constructed in the same way as for the first example in Fig 5.6. The course to steer comes out at 197°T and the speed made good at 13.1 kts. At this rate of progress you would cover the 15 miles of the 1st leg in 1hr 09min. If you pass Danger Rock buoy dead on 1450, you should therefore come up with the NW Monks buoy at 1559 (say 1600).

Note that the angular difference between the track and the course to steer is 8°. If you didn't make this compensation for the tidal stream, you would end up 2½ miles W of the NW Monks buoy. On a hazy sum-

mer day this displacement could easily lead to you missing the buoy altogether.

Having worked out an ETA for the NW Monks you therefore have a starting time for the second leg. Calculate the next course to steer in exactly the same way as before, extracting the appropriate rate and direction of stream from the tidal atlas. Remember that you are now in a slightly different position and that time has moved on. This second leg, between the NW and SW Monks buoys, should take less than half an hour, so look for the stream which applies at around 1610.

Setting out the plan Once you have calculated courses to steer for each leg of a passage and ETA for each waypoint, it is important to set out your plan clearly and concisely. Fig 5.11 shows a useful pro-forma for this purpose which, once completed, can be kept handy in the wheelhouse for easy reference. This particular form was designed by Cameron Meikle of Jersey, but you could easily devise something similar to suit your own way of working.

At the head of each sheet are entered the height and time of high water at the reference port for tidal stream information. Then comes the departure time which I normally take as the expected time at the first waypoint; you can either express this in the 24h clock, or as a difference before or after high water. There are also spaces for local magnetic variation, likely cruising speed and the initial log reading.

The main part of the form is for details of each leg of the passage. The waypoint identifier columns are used in conjunction with Decca, Loran or satellite navigation systems, which I will look at later in the chapter. Otherwise, the various sections are filled in as follows.

Track: the direct course between waypoints, in degrees True.

Tidal stream: an estimated average rate (in knots) and direction of flow (in degrees True) over the expected duration of the leg.

Course: the course to compensate for the tide, i.e. what we have been referring to as the 'course to steer', in degrees True.

PASSAGE PLANNING CHART

DATE: *15th July* FROM: *MILLHAVEN* TO: *ST. MANET*

HEIGHT OF TIDE: *5.9 M* TIME HIGH WATER: *1105 BST* DEPART: HW *+3 hrs.*

LOCAL MAG VARIATION: *7°W* CRUISING SPEED: *12 kts.* LOG READINGS: FINISH: ___ START: *114.6*

FROM	WP	TO	WP	TRACK True	TIDAL STREAM Knots	True	COURSE True	COURSE Mag	DEV	STEER Mag	DIST NM	SMG Knots	TIME	ETA	ATA
MARINA		*DANGER ROCK BOUY*		*PILOTAGE – N of LONG ISLAND*										*1450*	
DANGER ROCK BOUY		*NW MONKS*		*205*	*2¼*	*260*	*197*	*204*	*2°E*	*202*	*15*	*13.1*	*1.09*	*1559*	
NW MONKS		*SW MONKS*													
SW MONKS		*ILE MANET GREEN CONN.*													
ILE MANET GREEN CONN.		*MARINA*		*PILOTAGE – Via GRAND CHENAL*											
				Can't enter marina before										*1820*	

ig 5.11 *A useful passage planning sheet.*

ourse (mag): the previous column expressed in egrees Magnetic, i.e. after applying variation.

eviation: the magnetic deviation for that particular heading, obtained from the ship's deviation rd.

teer: the final course, corrected for ship's deviation, e. the course that you actually steer by compass.

istance: the leg distance, measured directly between waypoints in nautical miles.

peed made good: the effective speed 'over the ound' between waypoints, obtained from the ngth of the track side of the tidal triangle.

ime: the calculated time to cover the leg.

TA: the estimated time of arrival at the next wayint.

TA: the actual time of arrival at that waypoint, th the log reading at that time alongside it.

With this basic information carefully worked out d entered, your passage navigation, at least on latively short coastal trips, should become a fairly utine matter of following the plan, identifying the rious seamarks which have been chosen as way-points, recording times and log readings, and making minor course or speed adjustments as necessary. The faster your cruising speed, the more important this kind of preparation becomes. The motion at sea in a motor boat is rarely conducive to lengthy deliberations over a chart, but if you've done your homework properly, only quick references should be required. Possible 'bolt-hole' routes should be tabulated on a separate planning sheet, in case of deteriorating weather.

Offshore Passage-making

Passage legs offshore are usually longer than coastal legs, and any errors in either calculations or steering become more significant the further you travel. Being well away from the coast also reduces the opportunities for verifying position from buoys or landmarks. These two facts heighten the importance of careful chartwork as you venture offshore. The use of electronic aids will be covered later in this chapter, but I will first consider the more traditional methods of navigation, as they are best applied in a cruising motor yacht.

Because they lead out into open water, offshore passages invariably involve more strategic planning than coastal trips. You are more vulnerable to changes of weather, so you must have a feel for how far ahead you can rely on settled conditions. How long will your proposed passage take at normal cruising speed? Do you have a good idea of fuel consumption at various speeds, and what is the boat's safe and maximum range? You should check on possible ports of refuge in case of bad weather, but (a) can you be sure of being able to reach them if you needed to, and (b) could you actually enter having got there? You will probably need to prepare food for the passage, and for longer trips devise a simple watch-keeping system which will allow all the crew to get some sleep. How much of your proposed passage will be at night? if you are delayed and arrive at your destination in the dark, will you be able to enter harbour safely?

Passage planning

Having taken these factors into account, the basic navigational preparation is similar to that for coastal passage-making, with one or two provisos. You will need to weigh up the various constraints on arrival and departure time, but because of the increased length of the legs there is bound to be more uncertainty about the duration of the passage. Your ETA should allow for a good margin of error if you need to arrive at your destination at a certain time. Working out the course to steer is slightly more complicated because you will generally be covering more than one hour of the tidal cycle. In Fig 5.12, imagine that you are bound from Draymouth to Selly Island, just over 60 miles. Normal cruising speed is something like 15 knots, so the passage should take about four hours if all goes well. Because the direction and rate of the stream will vary over that period, you need to draw four separate tidal vectors.

Once you have decided on your likely departure time, plot the required track (AZ) on the largest scale

104

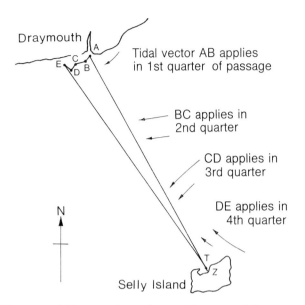

Fig 5.12 *Allowing for tide on a longer offshore passage.*

chart which shows both Draymouth and Selly Island. Now turn to the tidal stream atlas for this area and mark each chartlet of the tide cycle with the relevant time for the day concerned. Sometimes it also helps to pencil the track lightly into the atlas, dividing the line into the estimated number of hours of travel. Supposing you plan to leave Draymouth at 0900 subject to a reasonable weather forecast. Your first hour of passage-making will be from 0900–1000, so you need to estimate an average direction and rate of stream for that period over the first quarter of the trip. The nearest chartlet to 0930 would be the best bet if the tide time happened to fall conveniently close, but you often have to calculate a mean between successive hours in the atlas.

Plot this first tidal vector (AB) on the chart and then turn to the tidal chartlet for the second hour of the passage. From this you need to extract an average direction and rate of stream to cover the second quarter of your required track. Plot this vector (BC) onto the end of AB, and repeat the process for all four hours of the trip. Thus, from your proposed starting point, you will have mapped out the total effect of the tide.

You now have to account for your own travel. With dividers open to 60 miles, i.e. four hours of boat speed, strike the radius ET from the end of your composite tidal vector back to the required track. This line, transferred to the compass rose, gives you the course to steer for Selly Island *assuming* (a) that you leave Draymouth at 0900, (b) you experience the tide as predicted, and (c) you keep up an average of 15 knots. The length of AT is equivalent to the total distance you will make good in the four hours.

You should now write down the details of your proposed passage, preferably on a planning sheet such as that described earlier. We saw that, for a short coastal hop, this sheet would be your principal navigational reference and you would simply enter the actual time of arrival against each waypoint as it came up. For longer offshore passages, though, it is advisable to plot your position on the chart at regular intervals.

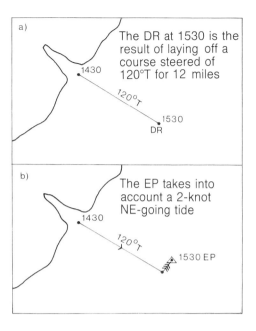

a) The DR at 1530 is the result of laying off a course steered of 120°T for 12 miles

1430
120°T
1530
DR

b) The EP takes into account a 2-knot NE-going tide

1430
120°T
1530 EP

Fig 5.13 *Dead Reckoning (D.R.) and Estimated Position (E.P.)*

DR and EP

The term 'dead reckoning' or 'DR' tends to be used rather loosely in practical navigation. Many yachtsmen, including myself, often talk about 'marking up the DR' when they mean the whole process of plotting their latest position on the chart. But dead reckoning started life more specifically, referring to the position obtained simply by laying off the course steered by compass and distance run by log. Strictly speaking, DR takes no account of the effect of the tide (see Fig 5.13a).

Adding a tidal vector to your DR gives you an 'estimated position' or 'EP' (see Fig 5.13b). Clearly, the difference between DR and EP becomes more significant with faster tides and slower cruising speeds. Ideally, if conditions permit, the prudent way to keep your navigation up to date when making an offshore passage is to mark your EP regularly on the chart. Every hour after departure, for example, the navigator would read the log and calculate the distance run during the previous hour. He should also ask the helmsman for an estimate of the mean course steered over that period. These two pieces of infor-

mation enable the navigator to plot the latest DR, as per Fig 5.13a. He would then turn to the tidal atlas and try to assess the average effect of the stream over the last hour. Adding this vector to the DR would give the latest EP, which becomes the best estimate of the boat's position at that time.

It is important to remember that, when you are working out a course to steer as per Fig 5.12, you are effectively doing your navigation backwards. You are trying, by using simple geometry, to calculate a course which will counteract the tide you expect to meet and thereby fetch you up at a planned destination. However, once you have set off, the first purpose of navigation is to keep track of what is *actually* happening to your boat, even if this differs from the plan. You can only do this by regularly plotting the *course steered* (as opposed to the course the helmsman was asked to steer) and the *distance run* each hour (as opposed to the hourly runs that you thought you'd make).

Again, plotting an EP is comparatively easy on a slow-moving yacht so long as you have a reasonable chart table to work on. But things become pretty difficult in a high-speed motor boat offshore, where the lively motion and vibration tend to work against any sort of precision with pencil and parallel ruler. Yet offshore passages, including many open sea crossings, require something more than simply working out a course to steer, filling in a planning sheet and hanging onto the wheel until you sight land. Good seamanship involves keeping a running estimate of your position in case of emergency, or in case you are forced to change your destination en route because of engine trouble or deteriorating weather.

High-speed motor boats really need some kind of rough and ready EP which is both accurate enough for practical purposes and easy to plot at sea. It would be useful if, for example, having worked out passage legs and courses to steer, you could assume your boat would travel more or less along the required track throughout the trip. Is this a fair approximation? If the tidal vectors were all equal in Fig 5.12, the calculated course to steer would certainly have had the boat crabbing continuously along the track. But because each of the four vectors is slightly different, a boat steering the course ET will not remain exactly on the line AZ. If things work out as planned, she will *end up* on track, at position T, only after the four hours have elapsed.

Now if you had two hours of tide setting in one direction and then two hours in the opposite direction, the boat would be more positively displaced (see Fig 5.13c). The course to steer would be almost identical to the required track, but you'd be set, say, eastward for the first half of the passage and then westward for the second half. The maximum drift might be only a mile or two in moderate neap tides of the western English Channel, but could be up to five miles if stream rates increase. You clearly need to bear in mind your particular spread of tidal vectors. However, for high-speed boats and moderate tides, it is often quite reasonable to calculate a course to steer, stick to it as far as possible, and assume that you'll stay close to the drawn track.

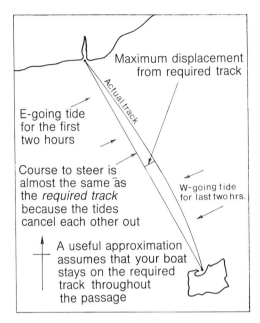

Fig 5.13c *The effect of a turning tide.*

EP navigation would thus boil down to estimating how far along the track you were at any given time. With moderate tidal streams and high cruising speeds, you can simply use your log readings for this purpose, marking off distance run each hour along the track. With slower cruising speeds and faster tides, it is usually more accurate to take appropriate proportions of the speed made good. Referring again to Fig 5.12, remember that AT is the total distance your boat should make good in four hours, if all goes according to plan. Dividing AT by four gives the predicted speed made good which, if the proposed cruising speed is maintained, you can mark off every hour as progress along the track. All you need for this is a pair of dividers.

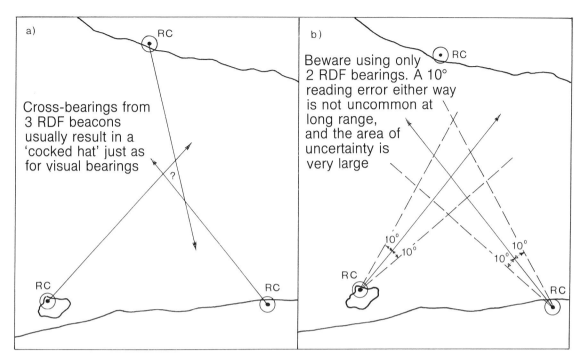

Fig 5.14a & b *Taking bearings using a radio direction finder.*

Radio-direction finding (RDF)

Although RDF is an electronic aid, it really belongs to an earlier generation of technology and can thus be said to fit under the heading of 'traditional' methods of navigation. Although of limited accuracy aboard a bucking motor yacht, RDF can nevertheless be used to back up an uncertain EP plot which has been running for some distance. It can also provide valuable moral support in poor visibility. Often it is best to take an RDF fix with your engine(s) stopped, both to ease the motion and to cut out any stray interference from poorly suppressed alternators. Remember that hand-held sets should be used as far away as possible from any likely sources of compass deviation. The principle of RDF is simple. Each coastal radio beacon transmits a repeated Morse code identification signal, so that you know which station

you are receiving; this is usually followed by a continuous tone used for taking the bearing. Your receiver has a directional aerial and, most commonly, a built-in compass. When the set is pointing straight at the beacon to which it is tuned, the received signal will be at its quietest, i.e. at a *null* point. Read the bearing of this null and then plot it on the chart as a position line with the time written against it, just as you would any other compass bearing.

If you repeat this operation with other beacons, you will end up with a set of cross-bearings whose intersect, in theory, is somewhere near your actual position (see Fig 5.14a). There is, however, considerable scope for error when using RDF, although results and speed definitely improve with practice. The first potential problem, if you are taking bearings on the move, is the likely time lag between position lines. Having tuned to a particular beacon, you may have to wait a while before you pick up the required call-sign: many beacons are grouped in cycles on the same frequency, and you often just miss the one-minute transmission of the particular station in which you are interested. This is no great problem on the first bearing but, if you are travelling quickly, you ought to take any subsequent bearings as soon as possible after the first.

In the open sea, near the maximum range of RDF transmitters, the apparent signal null can occupy a surprisingly large angle. As you swing your receiver to find the null, you will hear the tone disappear at some point and you may have to continue swinging through 20° or 30° before you pick it up again. The trick is to note the bearings at which the signal disappears and reappears, and then to assume that the null lies midway between the two. But a lot of practice is required before you can obtain reliable results. As you swing the RDF set its compass card will also be swinging, partly in lag and partly because of the motion of the boat. There is considerable skill involved in trying to compensate visually for this swing and also to gauge equal volumes of tone on either side of the null. You can expect large areas of intersection in your first few sets of bearings.

There are certain propagation errors associated with RDF signals, such as land and night effects. Also, when you are using Mercator charts (which most are), there is a small difference, known as half-convergency, between the line along which a radio bearing is received and the line along which it is plotted. However, these 'system' errors are apt to be nowhere near as significant as those due to the difficulty of judging the null. Fig 5.14b shows how large the area of uncertainty can become when there are reading errors in each of two RDF bearings.

Navigation at night

This is really no more difficult than navigation by day. In some ways it is simpler, particularly when you are a safe distance offshore but are still able to see and identify lights. The following points should be borne in mind, though.

If you have just started cruising, you'll probabl find it easier to leave or enter harbours in daylight Once you have the experience of a few landfalls, tr to graduate to dusk approaches, when you can se both land and lights. The knack of night pilotag lies in visualizing the layout of an unknown por from its lights, identifying navigation lights agains the confusion of the shore, and judging distances.

It is best to avoid busy shipping lanes and fishin boats at night. Although you might be able to se and identify ships clearly, they can't usually see yo so well. At night it is also more difficult to estimat a ship's speed and distance off.

There is more risk of colliding with flotsam a night. It is surprising how many large baulks of tim ber and other floating objects there are offshore; a least during daylight you stand some chance o avoiding them. Crab-pot markers are another haz ard, particularly off certain headlands.

There is often much to be said for making a land fall an hour or so before dawn. The coastal ligh houses should still be operating and they will hel you to fix your position with more certainty than b day. It is usually easier to identify a lighthouse fron its light characteristic than from an ethereal profi seen through a morning haze. At the same tim you will soon have daylight coming on for enterin harbour. However, if you are contemplating a nigh passage, remember that most people are not at the best around 4am! The metabolism takes a bit adjusting to the wee small hours and this can sho up if problems occur or there are any trick navigational decisions to be made.

When you sight a lighthouse, lightship or lit buo it is important to be thorough about timing its cha acteristic and checking this against the latest a manac or *List of Lights*. The light you are expectin to see first doesn't always turn up first, and man otherwise successful passages run into trouble b cause the navigator jumps to the wrong conclusio about which light is which. A common source of co fusion is attempting to identify characteristics fro too far off. A light seen at the limit of its range ma appear to be flashing when, in fact, it is disappearin behind wave-tops periodically. Sometimes you ca pick up the glow or 'loom' of a light from beyond its nominal range, but even then it is easy to misread the characteristic.

Navigation in fog

Contrary to popular belief, navigation offshore in fog is generally no more difficult than navigation in gin-clear visibility, so long as you are well out in deep water. The main difference is that you are forced to travel more slowly, in order to comply with Rule 19 of the Collision Regulations. Passage times are therefore longer and tidal streams will have a more significant effect on your track. Because of this, you should avoid approximations and maintain as accurate an EP as possible. This means plotting your position every hour, taking individual account of each hour of tide.

The two principal dangers in fog are (a) risk of collision with other vessels, and (b) closing with an unknown coast. However, if you are not far from land when fog comes down, the safest strategy is often to try and make for an uncomplicated stretch of coastline which has a gently shelving seabed. It should then be possible to sound your way inshore and anchor in a moderate depth of water until visibility improves (see the later section on the use of the echo-sounder).

Making a safe landfall

The transition between the open sea and the coast is critical and sometimes rather traumatic. At sea, given reasonable weather and a well-found boat, you are relatively safe—even if you're not sure exactly where you are. It is when you close the shore that potential dangers start to raise their heads. Stronger tides, steeper seas, rocks, shoals and sandbanks are usually features of landfalls, not of passage-making. For this reason it is a mistake to heave a sigh of relief when you sight the coast. Your problems, far from being over, are usually just beginning.

Even after a modest offshore passage of between 60 and 100 miles, there will be a degree of uncertainty surrounding your position. If you've been keeping a regular EP on the chart, you should have a fair idea of when you might expect to spot the coast, but fickle cross-tides can put a question mark over the actual point of landfall. If you are blessed with reasonable visibility and have picked up land or lights from some distance off, your job as navigator becomes tinged with a curious mixture of opportunism and caution. You will need to gather as much information as possible and try to draw logical conclusions about where you are and what you are seeing. At the same time, it is prudent to keep an open mind about your position until this is verified by hard evidence.

One thing you mustn't do is to disregard your passage navigation unless you have good grounds. A carefully maintained EP provides the best idea of your position *until* you have some reliable observations or bearings which indicate that you are somewhere else. Don't throw all your previous work out of the window and alter course precipitately just because you happen to spot a distant blob that might possibly be a fairway buoy, or because some hazy stretch of coast looks vaguely like a harbour entrance.

Taking and plotting bearings

The ability to use a hand-bearing compass quickly and accurately is a valuable skill when making a landfall. Towards the end of a longish passage, with some doubt surrounding your EP, a good fix from three clearly identifiable shore marks will provide a sound navigational base from which to approach the coast. Not that life is ever that straightforward, because you won't always be able to make out more than one or two unambiguous features, and sometimes not even that. The practical art of taking bearings often lies in using what you can see and then squeezing as much information as possible from the resulting position lines. If the coast has off-lying dangers and it is particularly important that you obtain

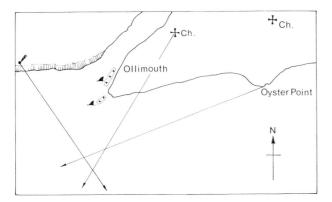

Fig 5.15 *The importance of identifying shore marks correctly.*

a fix before getting too close, it can be a good idea to stop your engine(s) and drift for a little while, to enable you to take and plot your bearings carefully.

Fig 5.15 illustrates the basic principle of plotting position lines. Imagine you are approaching a strange shore and you think you can identify two landmarks: a church spire some way inland to starboard and a lighthouse on the cliffs to port. You are making for a particular river which joins the sea at an angle, and you will need to fetch up with the outer starboard-hand buoy before turning into the entrance. Further off to starboard is something that could be a short headland, although it is rather difficult to make out.

If you can be sure that the lighthouse *is* a lighthouse, it will probably provide your most reliable position line, but you should carefully scan the large-scale chart of your landfall coast to see how much scope there is for confusion. Read the entry in the relevant pilot book, which will briefly describe the coastline and its various marks and features. Yacht pilot books may contain useful photographs taken from some distance offshore, although these are not always as easy as you might think to match with reality. When you come to take bearings, brace yourself firmly somewhere outside and try and let the compass settle down before you decide on the reading.

Even the best hand-bearing compasses are not completely dead-beat, so you will need to learn the trick of judging the mean point of the compass card's swing. Once you have taken the first bearing, don't try and keep it in your head while you take the others: it is better to jot each figure down or call it out to someone else. If possible, have one of your crew take the same set of bearings as a double check. Always note the time of each fix and mark this on the chart when you plot bearings. Remember that compass readings are in degrees *magnetic*.

Landmarks such as church spires and water towers can be problematic for the navigator, simply because they are often difficult to identify with certainty. Fig 5.15 shows two spires; Ollimouth should be the most prominent, but there is another further inland along the coast. If you were to take a bearing of the latter believing it to be Ollimouth spire, the intersect with the lighthouse bearing would put you further inshore than you actually were. This mistake would work on the safe side, but confusing the spires the other way round could be more dangerous. This is why you should try and use at least three bearings for obtaining a fix. A large disparity between them indicates that something is amiss, but bear in mind that reading errors become more significant when position lines cut at a fine angle (Fig 5.16).

In practice, even if you take three very careful bearings of correctly identified marks the lines are unlikely to intersect exactly. You'll generally end up with a small (and sometimes a large) triangle or 'cocked hat'. It is usually fair to assume that your actual position is somewhere inside this triangle with the best estimate being its geometric centre. In Fig 5.15, a useful third bearing would be the end of Oyster Point, but you can see from the geography that it might be difficult to distinguish this headland from some way offshore.

When you are approaching the coast from a position obtained from a large cocked hat, keep in mind that, although your most likely fix position was somewhere near the centre of the triangle, you *could* have been setting off from one of the edges of your cocked hat, or even from outside it, depending on where the error(s) lay. A useful way to take account

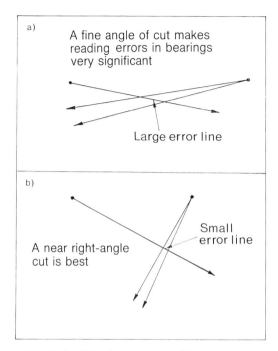

a) A fine angle of cut makes reading errors in bearings very significant

Large error line

b) A near right-angle cut is best

Small error line

Fig 5.16a & b *Obtaining a good intersect.*

of this is not simply to plot a single track from your fix position to your next waypoint, but also to draw in a set of 'tram-lines' either side of your most likely track, which will then represent the outer extremities of a corridor down which you might be travelling. You will want to be sure that there are no dangers anywhere in this corridor, particularly as you draw close inshore. Having this band actually marked on the chart will help to maintain an open mind about your position as you scan the coast for landmarks.

Taking bearings at night

Using a well designed hand-bearing compass at night is not difficult; most are now lit by the almost perpetual glow of a 'beta' light, a source which needs no batteries and provides just the right amount of illumination for a small compass card. The important point about taking night bearings is that you must be sure which lights you are looking at and where they are located on the chart. It is best to time flashing, occulting or isophase lights with a stop-watch; and you should always check and re-check the observed characteristics against one of the almanacs and/or a current *List of Lights*.

Transits, clearing lines and danger lines

On the final approach to a strange coast, there is often insufficient time for continually taking bearings and plotting fixes. Yet it isn't always necessary to know precisely where you are so long as you are obviously proceeding along a safe track. Local transits (marks in line) can be a great help in close-quarters pilotage, since they are quick to use and involve minimal work at the chart table. Suppose that you can see two prominent landmarks ashore *and*, most important, identify them with certainty on the chart. If these marks come into line, one behind the other, you are said to lie on their *transit*. In other words, if you join the two marks with an extended line on the chart, you'll be somewhere on that line when you see them come into transit.

Leading lines are a special kind of transit, specifically located to indicate a safe passage. While some leading lines use daymarks only, others are lit at night. However, any pair of marks or lights can serve as an impromptu lead, provided you can identify them on the chart. In Fig 5.17, if you are entering Midhaven Bay from westward, the transit of the conspicuous white house and the Mewstone leads safely west of The Devils, a ledge of unmarked drying rocks. Once into the bay, the transit of Midhaven church and the end of the breakwater leads safely inside The Devils as far as the harbour. Approaching Midhaven Bay from eastward, you can stay safely between The Devils and South Rock by keeping the white house just open to the west of Gull Rock.

Safe-water transits are known as *clearing lines*, because they lead you clear of danger. But transits can also act as *danger lines*, by warning that you are on course for something nasty. If you were approach-

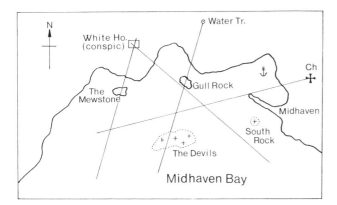

Fig 5.17 *Using transits and dangerlines.*

ing Midhaven Bay and saw the water tower on the hill in transit with Gull Rock, you'd know you were sharing a position line with The Devils! A great advantage of transits is that they can be improvised for your own purpose as coastal features begin to take shape. They can often be handy when you are simply 'map-reading', without putting pencil to chart. One common use in pilotage is for identifying a turning point in a channel; you might, for example, decide to stay on a set course until a particular rock was in line with a given headland.

Of course you can plot a transit, together with one or more compass bearings of other marks, in order to obtain a fix. Because it is not subject to any reading error, a transit is a completely accurate form of position line, so long as you have identified the marks correctly and noted the time at which they came into line. If there is any doubt about what you are looking at, take a bearing of the transit and compare this with what the chart says it should be.

Identifying buoys

When you make a landfall on a strange coast and sight a buoy that you've been expecting to pick up, it is generally a good idea to motor close up alongside it. Not only can you then check that what you've

seen *is* a buoy, but you can also identify its colour and topmarks, read its name and thus verify your position beyond doubt. There are many cases of boats making a landfall after a long passage, spotting a buoy in the distance and assuming, wrongly, that it was the mark they expected to see. It usually costs little time to stand in close to a buoy, but it can save a good deal of uncertainty later on. It also gives a check on whether the tide is running the way you expected.

Using the echo-sounder

The assistance that your echo-sounder can give when you are making a landfall depends largely upon the profile of the seabed. Where the bottom shelves gently but steadily towards the shore, soundings will provide a fairly reliable indication of your distance off, which is valuable information in poor visibility. Sometimes it is possible to register off-lying shoal patches and use them as rough underwater marks. However, some coasts have a more or less level seabed, where the depth doesn't vary much even quite close in.

Fig 5.18 shows an example of how an accurate

Fig 5.18 *Navigating by echo sounder.*

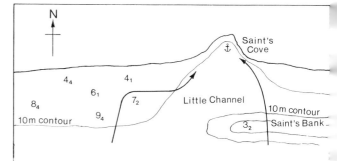

If water continues to shoal beyond the 10m contour, you will have made a landfall to the west of the Little Channel

If water shoals and then gets deeper, you will have been crossing the Saint's Bank

echo-sounder can earn its salt. Suppose you are approaching a low coast on a murky day, bound for the anchorage at Saint's Cove. You believe that your landfall ought to be somewhere along this stretch, but that is about all you can say. By watching the echo-sounder, though, you'll be able to tell when you reach the 10m contour. Standing on for a while after that, you will either discover that the bottom is steadily shelving, which it does to the west of the Little Channel, or it will shoal quickly and deepen again, which it does over Saint's Bank east of the Little Channel. Of course you could be unlucky and hit the entrance to the Little Channel dead on. In this case, you might strike the 10m contour too far inshore for comfort—the depth would shoal quickly, as if you were crossing Saint's Bank, but then it would continue to shoal.

In very poor visibility, it would be prudent to aim to make your landfall positively to the west of the Little Channel, *to be certain of missing it*! Having found the 10m contour, you could then follow this depth east and then NE into Saint's Cove. A landfall coastline will not always provide this sort of interesting scope for using the echo-sounder, but you should always be on the lookout for ways of 'feeling your way in' if necessary.

None of the navigation described hitherto, apart from RDF, need rely upon electronics for its successful application. A simple, mechanical trailing log can be used to measure distance run, and there's always the lead-line if the echo-sounder packs up. It is important for anyone new to cruising to appreciate that extensive cruises are quite feasible without having to install huge banks of high-tech plant. Even if our boats are bristling with antennae, we still ought to remain competent in the basic principles of navigation.

However, there is no denying that today's electronic aids, intelligently used, can make passage-making safer, quicker and generally more enjoyable. It is also true that most people buying new boats above a certain size expect them to be fitted with the latest navigation equipment. So I will now consider some of the pros and cons of using Decca, Loran, satellite navigators and radar.

Electronic Navigation Aids

The term 'navigation aid' is becoming something of a misnomer, because many new boat-owners are now obtaining their first experiences of navigation by using either a Decca, Loran or a satellite system. Cruising folk of an older school often look on in horror as these high-tech mariners start their passage planning, not by drawing tidal vectors on the chart, but by entering waypoints into a computer memory and setting up a sailplan program.

The range of marine electronics exhibited at the boat shows grows wider and more sophisticated each year; prices tend to be competitive and, nowadays, lower in real terms. The better quality gear is robust, easy to operate and offers carefully designed facilities which are of practical value. However, be on your guard against equipment which is not adequately protected against the elements, is complicated to use, and which performs tricks which may seem impressive in the safe surroundings of a boat show but are of precious little use at sea. I will concentrate here on three types of equipment; Decca navigators (Radio Position Finders), satellite navigators and radar. The first two are position-fixing systems; radar fulfils a different function by providing a penetrating extra eye which can be especially reassuring in poor visibility. It can earn its keep aboard any motor boat which regularly ventures offshore for more than a mile or two.

Decca and Loran-C navigators

Decca was pioneered during the last war and tested in anger at the D-Day landings. The Decca Navigator Company established its first chain of transmitting stations in the late 1940s and the system soon became widely used for both civil and military applications, and by fishing vessels. It is only comparatively recently that small yachts have been using Decca, since the manufacture of light, moderately priced sets which could be purchased outright. Prior to this, the receivers were bulky affairs which could only be leased from the Decca Navigator Company.

Main coverage is concentrated in the busy waters of NW Europe, from the Bay of Biscay across to the Baltic. Most of the Mediterranean cannot receive Decca, although the extreme western end can pick up the South Spanish chain. There are several other Decca chains throughout the world where shipping provides a particular demand. The Americans operate a similar system called Loran-C, not so accurate as Decca but covering much of the northern hemisphere. Loran can be picked up in most of the Mediterranean.

Basic principle The essentials of the Radio Position Fixing systems are simple. A low frequency (medium wave) radio transmitter is sited where its signals can easily cover a given sea area and a similar transmitter is located, say, a couple of hundred miles away in a similarly commanding position. These two stations transmit continuous wave signals of identical frequency which are locked in phase. Now if you, at sea, are equipped with a radio which can receive and analyse these signals, your set will detect a *phase difference* between the two as you travel about in the area between the transmitters. At some points the signals will be received in phase, but as you move closer to one transmitter and further from the other, you will receive the 'peaks' of the former signal sooner and those of the latter correspondingly later.

Locations which experience a constant phase difference between the signals lie on position lines which are hyperbolic in shape and printed on Decca or Loran lattice charts. Now if the first (master) station transmits a second signal on a different frequency, synchronised in phase with an identical signal from a third transmitter, you generate a second set of position lines which, if crossed with the first, can provide a fix. In practice, Decca chains use a master transmitter and three 'slaves', a configuration which produces three pairs of synchronized signals and three possible sets of position lines.

Yacht receivers Most of the larger marine electronics companies now market either Decca or Loran-C receivers. The latest designs are extremely compact and incorporate sophisticated passage-making software which is becoming increasingly simple to use. Latitude and longitude are displayed directly, so that lattice charts are not required. The sets are generally splash-proof and take only a modest current from the batteries. Installation is straightforward: you just need a fused 12V or 24V supply and a suitable location for the aerial. Because incoming signals are of a relatively low frequency, aerial height is not too critical; somewhere above the wheelhouse is the most common mounting for motor yachts. Some manufacturers supply a sealed repeater which can be fitted on a cockpit bulkhead or up on a flying bridge.

From the navigator's point of view there are really two distinct stages to the receiver's capabilities. The first is the valuable fact of the yacht's position being continually updated and displayed. I know many owners who only use this basic facility, preferring not to get too involved with the various navigation programs which provide the second stage of information. With these, the operator is able to enter and store a number of key positions or waypoints in the receiver's memory. Because the present position is always available, the software can monitor the boat's progress in relation to the waypoints and calculate up-to-date distances and bearings to each. It can also measure how far you are drifting away from a given track between two waypoints, and knowing this cross-track error allows you to make course adjustments to counteract the actual tidal set and drift.

Some of the latest receivers incorporate a graphical display which allows you to set up, on the screen, a simple scale chart of a given coastal area. This might include key marks such as buoys, lighthouses or headlands, and your own progress is indicated by a flashing marker moving across this pictorial chart. A latitude and longitude display is also provided, so that you can also plot position on a real chart in the usual way. Improvements to receivers will doubtless continue, so that the passage-making and waypoint functions will be even cleverer and easier to use.

Loran is the American equivalent of the Decca system but, unlike Decca, it can be used across a large part of the northern hemisphere.

Loran-C

The first version of Loran was developed in the USA in the early 1940s. Loran-A was in place rather earlier than the Decca system and a good many stations were operating around the world by the end of the Second World War. Loran-C came into use in 1957 and incorporated a number of improvements and sophistications. Most of the present Loran chains are now operated and maintained by the United States Coast Guard.

Basic principle Loran-C radio navigators work on a similar principle to Decca, in that they define hyperbolic position lines by measuring specific differences in the received signals from several transmitters. But whereas a Decca navigator detects phase differences in medium wave transmissions, Loran-C calculates time differences (TDs) in synchronised pulse transmissions. As with Decca, there

is a network of different chains, each comprising a master station and between two and four secondary stations. Loran-C stations all transmit on the same frequency and each chain is identified by its own characteristic or *group* of pulses.

Although Loran does not have quite such a fine resolution as Decca, it offers a much wider coverage and can be used accurately across a large part of the northern hemisphere. European boat owners will find Loran of particular value in the Mediterranean and up in the Baltic, where Decca coverage is very weak.

Yacht receivers The receivers look almost identical to Decca or Sat-nav receivers and usually have an equivalent range of waypoint navigation facilities. As with Decca, your position is up-dated continuously and displayed in latitude and longitude. Loran receivers consume about the same amount of power as Decca sets.

Using radio position fixers

Yachtsmen use these systems in different ways. At one extreme, the more conservative tend to navigate much as they always have in the past, simply using their 'magic box' to provide a running cross-check on position. Relative newcomers, on the other hand, often take quickly to the available technology and it soon becomes the principal means of finding their way about. It is clearly important to strike a balance between getting the best out of these electronic devices and becoming too dependent on it. Nobody should wander far from land without being competent in basic navigational skills, even if their wheelhouse is bristling with equipment. Yet it is a pity not to take full advantage of a position-fixing system which is normally highly accurate. As with any other kind of navigational information, it is important to mark your Decca position or DP on the chart at regular intervals, just in case of breakdowns, along with the time and distance log readings.

It is a good idea to become reasonably fluent with your Decca or Loran before you need to use it on serious offshore passages. Start by experimenting with familiar waypoints in your home area and carry out trial runs between these marks. Fig 5.19, for example, shows the short coastal hop described earlier in this chapter, from a typical river estuary to the nearby harbour of Oldhaven. You could enter four waypoints for this passage, as follows:

(1) a position just W of the isolated danger beacon off the river mouth
(2) the position SE of the Mew Stone, at which you alter course W along the coast
(3) the Oldhaven Fairway buoy's latitude and longitude
(4) Oldhaven harbour entrance, a position right between the pierheads.

These waypoints should all be keyed in carefully and double-checked, following the sequence of operations laid down in your manual. Considering the strategy for the first leg, remember that your navigation program will be able to calculate a bearing and distance between WP1 and WP2. Most sets give this bearing in degrees True, but some have the

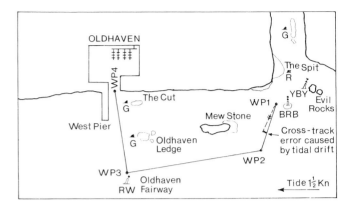

Fig 5.19 *Selecting the waypoints to use on a short coastal passage.*

facility to store compass variation, and sometimes even ship's deviation, so that any course displayed is a 'course to steer'. Now unless you have worked out a tide-correcting course for this leg beforehand, the unit's cross-track error display will soon indicate that you are being set to the west of the required track between WP1 and WP2.

Having reached this 'off-course' position, you now have three options for reaching WP2: (a) you can come hard-a-port and motor the shortest distance back to the required track until the CTE reads zero; (b) you can ask your set for a new course and distance to WP2, and set off on that course until another CTE is displayed; (c) having obtained this new course, you can make an impromptu tidal allowance and actually steer a shade east of the given heading until another CTE comes up.

In fact, on this short run, you ought not allow yourself to drift as much as 0.3 miles off track. Having left WP1 for WP2 on the given course, the trick is to make small helm adjustments as soon as a non-zero CTE is displayed. If the display shows a set to starboard, alter to port 10° say, until the CTE returns to zero. Then return to your original heading, perhaps steering a few degrees to port to counteract the tide. Continue making gradual course corrections whenever a CTE comes up. You are thus using your position fixer as a kind of on-track autopilot, steering

The Navstar 2000 Decca Navigator.

Fig 5.20 *Monitoring cross-track error.*

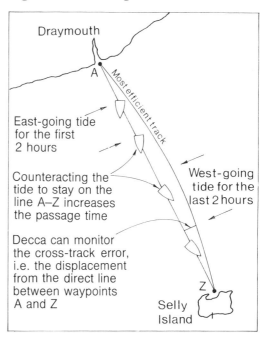

left when the CTE shows you have drifted right, and vice versa. On the second leg, between WP2 and WP3, the cross-set will be less pronounced with the tide almost astern. If WP3 is the Oldhaven Fairway, don't get so engrossed in the CTE that you collide with the buoy! On the third leg, you would only refer to the system in poor visibility. Keep your eyes ahead, be sure to leave the green buoys to starboard and watch out for traffic in the harbour approaches.

Using your radio position fixer like an autopilot, to stay on track between waypoints, is an ideal technique for short legs or where the tidal set is fairly constant. However, it is generally not the best way of navigating in tidal waters over longer distances. Fig 5.20 shows the passage from Draymouth to Selly Island which we looked at earlier in the chapter. This was a 4 hour trip at 15 knots, with an east-going tide for the first two hours and a west-going tide thereafter.

Now, from the point of view of minimising passage time and fuel consumption, the most efficient strategy is to work out a course to steer in the traditional way, taking account of the net tidal offset and allowing the stream to carry you eastwards off track for the first half of the passage and bring you back during the second half. Having defined waypoints A and Z in the system's memory, you can check the actual set and drift during the trip by monitoring the cross-track error. It should reach a maximum to port during the middle of the passage and then decrease to zero as you approach waypoint Z. Maintaining a direct track over the ground between A and Z would clearly involve steering a more westerly course for the first half of the passage and a more easterly course for the second half, counteracting the tide in both cases. Although this is perfectly feasible, it means a greater distance travelled through the water and a slightly longer passage time than the previous plan would involve.

Satellite navigation systems

The world's navies have been using satellite navigation systems for many years, but the first compact and moderately priced yacht receivers only came onto the market in the late 1970s. Unlike the Decca network, sat-nav offers almost world-wide position fixing. A set which you might buy in Europe and use in the English Channel or North Sea would operate in exactly the same way if you were cruising the Pacific, Australia or Canada. But whereas Decca gives practically continuous position updates, sat-nav can only provide a fix when a suitable satellite passes over your sea area.

Basic principle The system depends on various position-finding satellites that have been launched into orbit over the years, mostly by the USA. These have two important features: (1) they transmit a coded identification signal and a navigation signal of known frequency; (2) the path of their orbits is known precisely. When a satellite passes over the area in which you are sailing, your receiver decodes

the identification signal and then starts analysing the navigation signal. Since the software knows where each satellite should be tracking at any given time, it can work backwards to find out where the vessel must be in order to be receiving this particular pattern of frequencies.

The computer processing makes use of what is known as the Doppler effect, a phenomenon experienced when, for example, a moving fire-engine's siren changes pitch as it passes. Because the sound is being broadcast from a moving object, its frequency, as perceived by a stationary listener, is continuously changing. There will be a different shift in pitch (frequency) depending on whether you are standing in the same street as the fire-engine or a couple of blocks away. The satellite signals exhibit a similar kind of frequency change and this forms the basis of the position-fixing calculations.

The situation is complicated if the receiver itself is moving while it is picking up the satellite signals. A sat-nav therefore needs the boat's course and speed data in order to provide a really accurate fix. This information can be input either manually via the keyboard, or directly from a linked compass and log.

Yacht receivers Satellite navigators for yachts are just like Decca receivers to look at. In fact most manufacturers now use identical cases and facias for the two types of set, so the only visible difference is in the keyboards. A sat-nav aerial is similar, although not identical, to a Decca aerial and does not need mounting especially high up.

A sat-nav usually consumes more power than a Decca set, the popular models taking between 6 and 13 watts compared with 3 to 9 watts for Decca or Loran. Both types of receiver accept a range of voltages and can be used on either 12V or 24V. The most significant practical difference is that a sat-nav requires to be fed heading and speed information: this not only contributes to the accuracy of the satellite fixes, but also enables the software to maintain a DR or EP *between* fixes. The running position facility is important because the period between satellite fixes, although usually about $1–1\frac{1}{2}$ hours in European waters, can sometimes be as much as 3–4 hours in some parts of the world. Once a satellite pass does occur, the new fix replaces the EP on the position display.

The EP, of course, depends upon you keying in accurate tidal stream data, and a suitable electronic or gyro compass has to be installed if you would like heading information input automatically. Interfacing such compasses with sat-nav receivers is not always straightforward, so be sure to establish the compatibility of a particular compass before you are committed to purchasing. Most electronic logs can easily be interfaced with most sat-navs for automatic speed input.

A new form of satellite navigation is being developed, known as GPS or Global Positioning System. This also has its roots in defence technology and will eventually employ more sophisticated and better placed satellites for rapid and accurate position-fixing throughout the world—at sea, on land and in the air. GPS will be open to both commercial and pleasure users, but receivers are likely to be expensive initially.

Using a sat-nav

Because a satellite navigator can provide practically world-wide coverage but, unlike Decca, does not fix your position continuously, the system is generally more suitable for offshore navigation and distance cruising than for coasting. Yet you don't have to stray too far before sat-nav can begin to offer some advantages over Decca. Suppose, for example, that you are planning to cross the Bay of Biscay and cruise the north coast of Spain. On the direct passage across the Bay you can often experience a dead area for Decca, especially at night, when you begin to run out of accurate range of the SW British chain of transmitters before picking up the NW Spanish chain. However, a sat-nav makes an ideal electronic companion on this passage. In the open waters of Biscay there is no great problem even if you have to wait a few hours for a good satellite pass. When a satellite does come over, the signal will be strong and reliable and the resulting fix usually more accurate than one obtained from fading Decca trans-

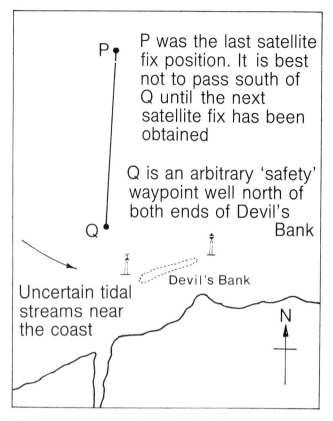

Fig 5.21 *Sat-nav assisted landfall.*

missions. When closing the land after a longish passage, though, it is important to keep your wits about you if sat-nav is your principal navigation aid. Although the NW Spanish coast is steep-to and free from off-lying dangers, you can experience some rather unpredictable currents and tidal streams which tend to make a protracted EP, even an automatic digital one, a mite uncertain.

When approaching a strange coast using sat-nav it is advisable to keep a careful note of when your last good satellite fix occurred, because that was when your displayed position was at its most credible. Your receiver will be able to predict the time of the next useful satellite pass, so try and arrange your landfall so that you obtain a reasonable fix before reaching the outer limits of any area which contains dangers to be avoided. In Fig 5.21, for example, the last satellite fix was position P at 1430. If the next pass is due 2hr 20min later, it would be preferable not to reach Q before 1650. You can regard Q as a kind of safety waypoint at which you'd like to establish your position before venturing too close to Devil's Bank. Having passed P, you should adjust your speed so that you don't arrive at Q too early.

Comparative accuracy of Decca, Loran and sat-nav

The quoted accuracy of different makes of receiver varies considerably, but under reasonable propagation conditions these systems are capable of fixing your position to within about 100m.

Decca signal reliability   In practice, most errors experienced on board yachts are due to either: poor aerial installation or connections; locally poor signal propagation conditions; operating at the limit of a Decca chain's range; or skywave interference, which can reduce effective night range.

Decca receivers have accuracy indicators which show the reliability of signals. Green, amber and red lights are the usual system. When the green light is showing, all is OK and you should be obtaining a good three-point fix; a red light means that you are *not* getting an accurate fix, either because the received signals are too weak or because the set has not been able to lock onto a Decca chain. An amber light indicates marginal reliability, generally because the fix is being derived using only two slave signals.

Loran-C signal reliability   One advantage of the Loran pulse transmission system is that, within a few hundred miles of a given chain, the reflected skywave component of a signal can be filtered out by the receiver, giving clean position-fixing within this 'home' area. The strength of the groundwave signal will obviously fall off as your distance from the transmitters increases and a point will be reached where the receiver has some difficulty in discriminating between the two. However, the range at which this happens is normally greater than the maximum effective range of a Decca chain.

Loran-C chains transmit a coded warning signal if there is any problem with or interruption in the master or secondary pulse transmissions. In this case, the receiver will display an appropriate alarm message.

Sat-nav signal reliability   A receiver 'grades' its own fixes, largely according to the angle at which satellites pass overhead. If the track is too far north or south of your position, the satellite signal will not only be that much weaker but, because of the geometry, there will also be relatively poor discrimination of the Doppler shifts by which a fix is calculated. A sat-nav receiver may decide not to compute a position if a particular satellite has too low a tracking angle, although the operator normally has the option of enforcing the fix and then using it at his discretion.

Radar

For motor yachts in particular, radar is probably one of the most widely useful of all electronic aids. The majority of boat owners don't actually do much real navigation in the course of a season, but accumulate their mileage in fairly short day trips; round to the next harbour for lunch and back, perhaps heading offshore for a mile or two to do some fishing, or hopping round the corner to anchor off a local beach for the afternoon. If a skipper does use a chart on such jaunts, it is apt to be in 'map-reading' fashion, to check on an entrance buoy maybe, or to identify some off-lying rocks as he edges into an anchorage. It is on such trips, however, that you can bless the day you had radar fitted. In anticyclonic summer weather, sea mists can creep in almost unnoticed. You may be basking comfortably at anchor with a good book and a cool beer to hand when, five minutes later, there is swirling grey vapour all around. In more turbulent frontal weather, rain squalls can reduce visibility surprisingly quickly, mischievously blotting out a river mouth just as you thought you were home and dry. Under such conditions, radar can be of great practical and psychological value by keeping you in touch, as it were, with terra firma.

A radar screen should be sited so that it can be easily read by the helmsman. The power supply has to be carefully specified and fused because even the smallest radar set can take up to about 60 watts.

If you cruise further afield, radar can soothe the process of making landfalls and take a great deal of stress out of crossing shipping lanes.

Compared with Decca, Loran and sat-nav though, radar demands rather more skill and attention from its operator. We have seen that both Decca and sat-nav essentially provide a very simple item of information—*their* estimate of *your* position—which you are free to put as much faith in as you choose. Radar, on the other hand, presents a more complex pattern of often ambiguous visual data. Despite the considerable technical advances of the last few years, a radar picture requires careful interpretation and this is a skill which improves with experience.

Basic principle Ultra-high-frequency pulses are transmitted radially from a revolving antenna or

scanner, and picked up again by the same antenna whenever they are reflected from a solid object. The time taken for this to happen depends on how far away the object is; the range and bearing information thus contained in these reflected signals is resolved digitally and presented on a screen. The scan represents a crude aerial view of your surroundings, normally with the boat at its centre, and this picture can include any nearby land, ships, buoys or beacons as long as they are reflective.

Yacht receivers Small radars have improved in leaps and bounds over the last few years: they consume less power, scanner units are much smaller and lighter, and screens are easier to read. Display software usually enables various 'markers' to be set up on the scan, or for the scan to be re-oriented from

An Ocean 37, built by Aquafibre Ltd in the late 1970s and powered by twin Perkins HT6354 diesels. The radar would give better reception if the scanner was mounted higher up. The present mounting would result in a lot of unnecessary sea clutter on the screen.

'head-up' to 'north-up'. When installing radar, the scanner (aerial) should be sited as high as possible for optimum performance. The mounting needs to be strong because even the lightest units weigh about 25lbs, and the higher they are the more stress on them as the boat rolls. Production boats often use a raised 'goal-post' over the flying bridge. The screen is best fitted in the wheelhouse where it can easily be seen by the helmsman: gone are the days when you had to peer into a flexible hood and only one person at a time could look at the scan. The power supply has to be carefully specified and fused because even the smallest radar set can take up to about 60 watts, which is 5 amps at 12 volts.

Using radar for navigation

Radar provides two distinct types of information. The first and most obvious is simply a graphic substitute aerial view for what you would otherwise be able to see, such as when the scan shows another vessel a mile away on your port bow, or land 9 miles off to the north. The second type of information has a more precise navigational value; if, for example, you can identify a particular seamark on the scan you can read off its range and bearing.

It is important to realize that most yacht radars use a *relative motion display*, in which your boat is always located at the centre of the screen and all other targets appear to move relative to you. This kind of scan is easy to visualize since it effectively mirrors the changes in perspective that occur as you look out of the wheelhouse window. It is possible to operate a radar set at various different ranges, so that the scan can either provide a large-scale picture of an area within a small radius of your position, or a smaller-scale picture within a larger radius.

The standard convention for a relative motion display has always been with the ship's head pointing towards the top of the screen, known as 'head-up' mode. But it is now possible to obtain sets which offer a 'north-up' facility, so that the scan is fixed with north at the top of the screen, and a central heading marker indicates changes in the boat's course. The north-up mode has the advantage that the scan remains stable, even in heavy seas when the boat is veering about; it is also easier to compare a north-up scan with information from a chart. This facility uses an interfaced electronic compass, and there will be increasing scope in the future for greater integration of individual items of marine electronic equipment, such as radars, position-fixers and autopilots.

When using radar to make a landfall it is important to appreciate the inherent limitations of the scan and to understand what your set will actually pick up. Bear in mind that radar can't see beyond the horizon, round corners or behind other targets. You will need to study the largest scale chart of your landfall carefully, to see what is likely to appear first on the screen.

Steep cliffs show up well, but when you are approaching a low coast the first echoes may come from high ground well inland. Slab-sided buildings give a strong return, but rounded structures such as lighthouses, chimneys or buoys can be elusive. Some lighthouses, lightships and buoys are equipped with Racon beacons, active pulse transmitters triggered by a vessel's radar signals, and they show up as very distinctive blips on the scan.

Fig 5.22 shows a close-quarters scan of a narrow passage between two spurs of land. This is a reasonably clear scan, but note the dark areas beyond the coastline to starboard. These probably don't indicate

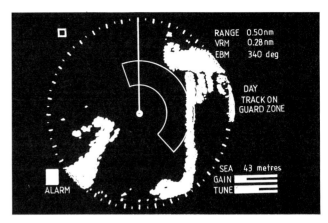

Fig 5.22 *A close-range scan of a narrow passage between two spurs of land.*

an absence of land (i.e. sea), but are simply gaps in the picture caused by relatively low ground which is shadowed behind the nearer targets. On the other hand, what appears to be a long, above-water rock about $1\frac{1}{2}$ cables on the port quarter is probably just that, since the radar should be able to detect the inlet between this target and the mainland.

Fig 5.23 *Using the same scan to fix a position.*

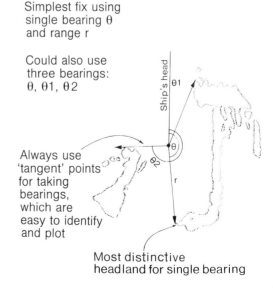

Simplest fix using single bearing θ and range r

Could also use three bearings: θ, θ1, θ2

Ship's head

θ1

θ

θ2

r

Always use 'tangent' points for taking bearings, which are easy to identify and plot

Most distinctive headland for single bearing

There is no need for any plotting on the chart in this case, because the passage is less than $\frac{1}{2}$ mile wide and you can easily gauge your position visually by reference to the headland close on your port side. However, if the land was further away you could usefully fix your position in one of two ways: (1) by reading the relative bearing and range of any single spur of land which could be clearly identified; or (2) by taking radar cross-bearings of two or three headlands. Fig 5.23 illustrates these methods of fixing. The first is normally preferable since the range readings on a radar set tend to be more accurate than its radial representation. In any case, taking a single bearing and distance is much quicker than taking several bearings.

When taking radar bearings it is best to maintain a constant heading and cruise fairly slowly. Older sets have a *bearing cursor*, which is physically rotated about the screen to obtain the relative bearing of a given target. Modern sets use an *electronic bearing marker* which is part of the radar graphics, and the latest sets with a 'north-up' mode can display the bearing of a selected target digitally. Distance off is read directly from the range rings on the scan, or by using a *variable range marker*. Bearings and distances obtained by radar are then plotted on the chart in the usual way to obtain a fix.

In the past, it was often easier and more accurate to use radar for measuring distance off but to take bearings with a hand-bearing compass. However, developing technology is greatly improving the facility of taking bearings by radar. As far as distance off is concerned, it is worth checking the range accuracy of your set from time to time. You can do this by passing close to a buoy whose position is known and marked on the chart, and then comparing the displayed range of identifiable landmarks with their charted distance off.

In recent years great advances have been made in the display of radar information and this trend towards 'user-friendliness' is likely to continue. Colour radar will probably become the norm and decrease in price. Some scanners will probably become yet lighter and more compact. We should also be seeing increasing integration of marine electronic systems.

For example, when a radar set is interfaced with a navigator and an electronic compass, a very wide range of facilities becomes possible. Position information and waypoints can be displayed on the radar screen, bearings of targets and between targets can be read off directly, and so on. It won't be too long before we can dial a harbour, send our boats off into the watery wastes, and sit comfortably at home with our feet up!

Choosing and Using Pilot Books

Pilot books are an important part of any seagoing craft's navigational equipment, so it is worth considering exactly what they contain, what they aim to tell us and what they can't tell us. The various types of publication seem to fall into the following categories:
—Pilots published by government or official national authorities. These are compiled with all mariners in mind, especially the masters and navigating officers of large ships;
—Yachtsmen's pilots for specific cruising areas, produced by commercial publishers and often written by yachtsmen;
—'Non-commercial' pilots, produced by yacht clubs or other boating organizations;
—Pilots or coast guides published locally and written in the language of the country covered;
—Guides to inland waterways;
—Commercially published guide books which, although not written with yachtsmen specially in mind, nevertheless contain information of value to anyone cruising in their area.

In the UK, Admiralty pilots are published by the Hydrographer of the Navy and are available for sea areas all over the world. Other maritime nations produce similar books. Although some yachtsmen believe that Admiralty pilots are suitable only for large ships, they are excellent references to have aboard any cruising boat. Provided that you use them in conjunction with up-to-date charts, they will earn their place on the bookshelf long after publication. While the Hydrographer rarely gives detailed entry directions, he excels on coastal topography and navigational hazards. Admiralty pilots are particularly valuable for providing a general impression of a landfall coastline, or helping to identify headlands, above-water rocks or other natural features which change little over the years. They also contain fascinating introductory sections on local buoyage, tides, currents, climate and weather—all good background reading when you are planning a route for your summer cruise and trying to work out a schedule.

Illustrations are largely confined to climatic maps and tables, buoyage diagrams, line drawings of principal lighthouses, and strip views of selected stretches of coast. These views are annotated with prominent landmarks such as church spires, lighthouses, mills or water-towers, such as the example in Fig 5.24. They need to be used with caution, though, since many are based on rather old originals.

Commercially published yachtsmen's pilots tend to be laid out less formally than Admiralty publications and illustrated with photographs and sketch charts. The more traditional books stick to black-and-white photos, some of which may be intended simply to give a flavour of the harbour concerned; others highlight particular dangers or features such as rocks, beacons and headlands, and some are landfall or pilotage views from seaward. More recently published pilots often employ colour to great advantage, both for charts and photographs. Good aerial shots can be effective for depicting harbour entrances, combining the realism of photography with the overall perspective of a chart.

It is important to remember that yachtsmen's pilots are not compiled by some august body like the Hydrographic Department, but are usually written by yachtsmen who have particular experience of the cruising area concerned. Although authors and publishers make every attempt to ensure that basic navigational data is accurate and up to date, you should always bear in mind that some directions will reflect only one person's view of what could, in practice, involve quite a complex set of decisions. Of course many aspects of pilotage will be fairly uncontro-

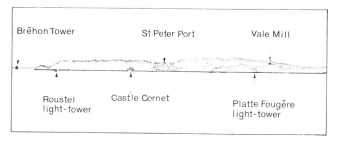

Fig 5.24 *Panoramic 'strip' views in Admiralty pilots are annotated with prominent landmarks.*

versial; for example, which entrance channels are navigable at a given state of tide, which harbours are safe to approach at night or which anchorages are secure in certain winds. Yet much advice is necessarily contingent upon the experience of the reader, the likely strength of his crew, the type, speed and seaworthiness of his boat, which navaids are carried aboard, and so on. Anyone compiling pilotage directions will find himself trying to steer a middle course between, on the one hand, freely offering advice which might be inappropriate in certain circumstances or, on the other hand, including so many provisos and caveats that what is being recommended will appear almost impossible to act upon under most normal conditions. In the end, navigators have to decide for themselves how appropriate any published directions are to their own situation. As part of this process, try to take into account the author's preferred *style* of cruising as well as his credentials as a seaman.

Sketch charts need interpreting with special care. Their main purpose is to give a clear idea of the layout of a harbour or anchorage, to indicate entrance channels and to show visitors' berths and facilities. They are normally drawn to an approximate scale only, and much of the detail which appears on a large-scale Admiralty chart is either omitted or greatly simplified. Patchy shoal areas or rocky dangers are often combined in a single depth contour. Soundings may be given where they seem relevant for a yacht of modest draught, and you will need to check whether they are in feet, fathoms or metres.

Approach routes are often drawn as ideal tracks with bearings marked against them, but they usually hand responsibility over to the skipper. An instruction such as 'make good 187°T for 3½ miles' really means 'navigate your boat safely so as to follow this line, allowing for any tidal set or leeway'. Some directions require on-the-spot assessment of weather, sea state or tide. For example, 'the estuary should only be entered in quiet offshore conditions'; or 'this channel is only passable in good visibility and within two hours of high water'.

There are many excellent pilotage publications produced on a more or less amateur basis by yacht clubs or other interested groups. Such pilots tend to be relatively inexpensive and often contain a great deal of local knowledge. Although most are carefully checked for factual accuracy, you will sometimes come across directions which are ambiguous or not very clearly expressed. Pilot books or coast guides published abroad can be extremely useful, although you obviously need a sound working knowledge of the language in which they are written.

Guides to inland waterways can be invaluable, especially for extensive networks of navigable rivers and canals. They are usually concerned with routes, distances and facilities, rather than with navigational dangers. You might think that one couldn't go far wrong on a peaceful canal, and yet it can sometimes be rather important to avoid taking a wrong turn. In the Netherlands, for example, there are countless canal routes throughout the country, but many are limited in headroom by fixed bridges. It is highly frustrating to have travelled a long day through a maze of waterways and swing bridges, only to find yourself dead-ended by a solid stone arch! On the French waterways it can be surprisingly easy to miss a critical junction, perhaps from a river into a canal. Unless you have a reliable route guide, you might only discover this mistake after several hours of pleasant progress in the wrong direction.

Finally, don't forget that various 'non-nautical' publications can earn their space on your boat's bookshelf when you are cruising. Michelin Guides, for example, contain useful town plans as well as clues to places of interest ashore. Ordinary road maps may come in handy if you enjoy making forays inland, or if you have to travel locally by taxi or public transport, perhaps to change crews or to track down a vital spare part.

The Fastnet lighthouse is probably one of the most famous navigation marks in the world. There is no more satisfying feeling than making a landfall after a longish open sea passage.

Chapter 6

Understanding Weather and Sea Conditions

The weather represents a major preoccupation for cruising yachtsmen, especially in the changeable maritime regions which are often popular. It has a direct effect upon anyone and everyone bound seawards, from the small outboard cruiser venturing into an apparently sheltered estuary, to much larger yachts making open-water passages.

For sailing yachtsmen, the weather provides three main areas of possible concern: (1) the actual force of the wind, present and forecast, because this will obviously affect how much sail can be carried and the rate of progress; (2) the sea conditions which are likely to result from a given strength and direction of wind; and (3) visibility, which has an important bearing on navigation and pilotage, and on a yacht's ability to negotiate other traffic safely.

For motor yachtsmen, the first of these factors—actual wind force—is not usually a prime consideration *in itself*, but is highly relevant to the extent that it determines the second factor—sea state. The third element, visibility, tends to be even more critical for power than for sailing boats, partly because they normally depend upon travelling at faster speeds, but also because the crew of a motor boat are often unable to employ their vital sense of hearing.

Understanding and predicting weather, and then assessing its probable effect on sea conditions, are distinct, albeit related skills acquired gradually with hard-earned experience. It is one thing to decide from national and local forecasts, and perhaps your own observations, that fine weather is on the cards for the next twelve hours or so, with good visibility and a northwesterly wind of force 4–5. It is another matter to be able to visualize this weather in the context of your planned passage, and to work out the practical implications for different sections of the trip.

There are three broad areas of knowledge involved. First, you need some appreciation of basic meteorology, in order to make informed sense out of forecasts and be able to relate them to your own observations of the weather. You should know what is meant by a depression and an anticyclone, a trough and a ridge, cold and warm fronts, and you ought to be aware of the kind of weather associated with each. The second significant area is an appreciation of the full range of forecast facilities available to yachtsmen, even those who don't have the benefit of VHF or other radio aids. Never before have weather forecasts been so widely and easily available, so comprehensive and up to date, and despite the flak occasionally dished out to the met men, so generally reliable. Finally, in order to put any forecast to practical use, you need to understand how wind strength and direction can combine with tidal streams and coastal geography to produce particular sea conditions, and how these conditions are likely to affect your own boat and crew.

Some Basic Meteorology

It is often difficult to separate cause and effect in weather, but all changes fundamentally derive from differences in atmospheric temperature. These are caused by the two facts that some parts of the earth are nearer to the sun than others at any given time, and that land and sea warm up and cool down at different rates. Once significant temperature differences exist, relatively warm air starts rising while relatively cool air starts falling. Thus you have the birth of depressions (areas of low atmospheric pressure) and anticyclones (areas of high atmospheric pressure).

Because the earth is spinning, depressions and anticyclones are not static masses of rising or falling air; they develop circulations which can vary in speed and intensity. Local temperature differences occur within these circulations, particularly within depressions, with warmer air trying to rise above cooler air. The boundaries between these areas give rise to warm and cold fronts.

Depressions or 'Lows'

Large circulating air masses of relatively low pressure are normally associated with changeable or unstable weather. It is not difficult to understand why, since depressions themselves are apt to be inherently unstable. Almost everything about them is on the move. For a start, they come into being from air which was moving upwards. Once the circulation of a depression begins to develop momentum, it is usually fed by air from outside the system which tumbles in from adjoining regions of higher pressure: this effect accelerates the vortex for a while until the depression begins to fill.

Local temperature differences within a depression

cause further instability. The circulation is likely to contain or pick up masses of warmer and colder air. Where faster-moving warm air overtakes a mass of cold, more sluggish air, it rises above it and forms a *warm front*. This warm air is cooled by being forced steadily above the cold and, as its ability to hold moisture is thereby reduced, cloud and continuous rain are often produced along a warm front. A *cold front* occurs when the main circulation forces a mass of cold air against a mass of warm air. The cold acts like a wedge under the warm, causing the latter to rise more rapidly but also more locally than it does along a warm front. This leads to heavy showers developing along a cold front.

Most depressions which track across Northern Europe, the English Channel and the North Sea start life way out over the Atlantic, somewhere on the long boundary between the extensive masses of predominantly warm tropical air to the south and the cold polar air to the north. 'Waves' can develop along this boundary, when some of the warm air penetrates into the cold air mass or vice versa. The thermal energy generated by these waves may then cause the formation of full, circulating depressions (Fig 6.1).

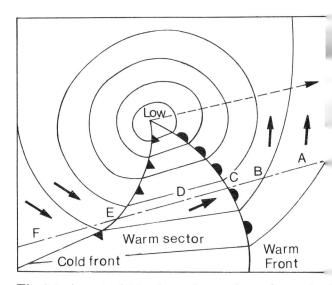

Fig 6.1 *A typical Northern hemisphere depression with associated fronts.*

A depression is represented on a weather map by a centre surrounded by roughly concentric *isobars*, which are lines of equal atmospheric pressure. Pressure will be lowest at the centre, with isobar readings increasing outwards. The closer the isobars, the greater the pressure gradient within the depression and the stronger the winds circulating around the system. Warm and cold fronts are shown by heavy lines which run approximately perpendicular to isobars; warm fronts are identified by solid semicircles and cold fronts by solid triangles.

Wind circulates anticlockwise about a depression in the Northern Hemisphere (clockwise in the Southern), following the general direction of the isobars but blowing slightly in towards the centre. The whole system will tend to progress in a direction parallel to that section of the isobars which links the warm and cold fronts; the smaller the depression, the faster it usually moves.

Imagine a normal Atlantic depression which moves into the Western Approaches of the English Channel, tracks across Southern England and then rolls on over the North Sea. Out in the English Channel you will soon experience winds shifting in strength and direction, as well as weather changes caused by the warm and cold fronts. The depression will be heralded by a falling barometer and a slowly backing wind from a broadly southerly quarter. As the warm front moves in, you can expect gradually thickening cloud and then rain, light and even intermittent at first, but becoming heavier and continuous in the main body of the warm sector. The wind will veer a little, settling down from between south and west and steadily increasing in strength, perhaps to gale force if the depression is sufficiently deep and active.

Here are the grim conditions which most yachtsmen keenly try to avoid by listening to weather forecasts. This period may last anywhere between three and twelve hours, depending on the size of the depression, how fast it is moving, and how far north it is passing. As the cold front approaches, the wind will decrease temporarily and you should see a lighter sky to windward as the cloud base lifts. When the cold front arrives, the barometer should begin to rise and the temperature fall. The wind will veer sharply and freshen again, becoming gusty with heavy showers. The frequency and intensity of these squalls will diminish as the cold front passes away, with the weather gradually improving.

There are several important practical questions to consider about particular depressions, whenever you are studying a met map or listening to a weather or shipping forecast.

How large, how deep, and how close? Large, spread-out lows move more slowly than smaller, compact ones. Deep lows have more *potential* for moving quickly, but a depression already travelling fast will not usually deepen unless it begins to slow down. Large, slow-moving depressions may drift at speeds of less than 15 knots, while a low which the shipping forecast has described as moving 'very rapidly' would be tracking at 45 knots or more, which is over 500 miles in twelve hours.

So one of the first points to establish about a low is how mobile it is likely to become. In practical terms, a rapidly approaching depression only 300 miles away has almost arrived from the yachtsman's point of view. Anyone at sea has but a few hours in which to make for shelter or prepare for a dusting; those in harbour should not be contemplating passage-making, except perhaps a short hop along a sheltered and familiar coast. On the other hand, apparently quite substantial depressions can remain more or less static for days on end, especially if a large area of high pressure is blocking progress.

What else lies around the system? A depression should never simply be considered in isolation, because its possible effects may depend on adjoining systems of either low or high pressure. If, for example, there is a large but moderate depression out in the Western Approaches to the English Channel, with an extensive area of high pressure over Northern Europe, you have the makings of a fairly static period of weather; the high preventing the low from tracking east, and the low unlikely either to deepen or fill appreciably for several days (Fig 6.2). The whole configuration might edge a little way east or

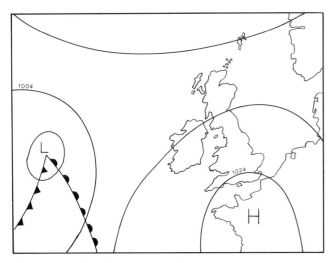

Fig 6.2 A *'blocking' anticyclone.*

Fig 6.3 A *typical secondary depression weather pattern.*

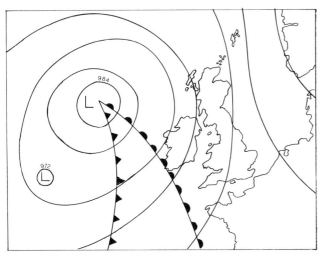

west, causing only minor changes for areas near the boundary between low and high. This kind of pattern will often generate a corridor of quite fresh winds between the low and the high, where the isobars are close together and the airflows around each system become merged and accentuated.

Fig 6.3 shows a deepish depression to the west of Ireland, with a smaller low caught up in the SW sector of the main circulation. This is the classic 'secondary low' pattern, which is potentially dangerous for shipping in the Western Approaches, the English Channel and, later on, the North Sea. Forecasters and seafarers will be monitoring this secondary closely, even though it seems further away than the main low. Secondaries may move very rapidly within the parent circulation, and the winds on a secondary's 'lower edge' can be especially vicious since they are effectively being accelerated by two separate depressions.

Anticyclones or 'Highs'

In those large areas of relatively high atmospheric pressure, air is tending to sink. Highs in our latitudes are associated with warm settled weather during summer months and cold, crisp weather during the winter. They are generally rather slow-moving systems and, once established, are reluctant to disappear. Motor yachtsmen are fond of highs because they usually presage light winds and calm seas, although they can also bring unwelcome fog. As with a depression, an anticyclone is represented on a weather map by a centre and surrounding rings of isobars. Pressure is highest at the centre and decreasing outwards, with the isobars further apart than for most lows and less likely to be concentric. Wind circulates clockwise round highs in the Northern Hemisphere (anticlockwise in the Southern), and yet anticyclones are not highly dynamic systems in the same way as depressions. You can visualize the circulation as being caused by air tumbling gently off the top and gathering a sedate momentum round its periphery.

When studying weather maps or listening to forecasts, it is important to consider what might be happening at the edges of an anticyclone. A low and a high together can generate fresh and sustained winds in the boundary area between them, but the edge of a high can also produce cloudy, unsettled weather, local rain or drizzle, and somewhat unpredictable winds. Such perturbations are usually caused by small waves of lower pressure encroaching into the high and running along its front. They are often not forecast, and may fizzle out before gathering enough energy to grow into anything more serious. However, when the weather is exceptionally warm for the time of year, thundery disturbances can develop at the edge of anticyclones and become unpleasantly active. As well as having the worry of thunder and lightning playing around while your boat is the highest object for miles, you can also experience quite savage squalls, locally heavy rain and violent wind shifts. If you are unlucky enough to run into lightning at sea, it may be some comfort to remember that the statistical risk of being struck is very slight, and is even less significant for low motor cruisers than for sailing yachts.

Troughs and ridges

These terms are commonly used in forecasting, although it can sometimes be difficult to see exactly what they mean. Troughs and ridges appear on met maps as kinks in the isobars around a depression or an anticyclone respectively, and a useful way to visualize them is by analogy with topographical maps. A trough of low pressure is rather like a valley of air sloping down towards the central dip of a depression, whereas a ridge of high pressure has a similar form to a mountain ridge falling away from a peak. Troughs often drift slowly around a shallow low, bringing cloudy weather, occasional rain and fluky winds. Frontal troughs can be more active since they contain both warm and cold air masses and so have the potential to generate heavier rain and fresher winds. However, troughs are more likely to provide low cloud and poor visibility than choppy seas.

Ridges of high pressure bring periods of quiet, settled weather. There are two types: those which travel and those which are more or less stationary. A trav-

elling ridge may provide a respite between depressions and can be used for passage-making before the next low starts moving in. A stationary ridge is usually a high-pressure spur extending from an anticyclone, such as might be described in a shipping forecast as 'High Azores, 1032, stationary, with ridge to Biscay persisting'.

Fog

In some respects, fog can be more nerve-racking than heavy weather, although well-equipped motor yachts will carry electronic aids which can take a lot of worry out of poor visibility. Sea fog occurs when the air dewpoint is higher or very near to the sea surface temperature—that is, when moisture-laden air is sinking towards a relatively cold sea. In European waters such conditions are common in spring and early summer when warm, maritime air arrives over water which is still cold from the winter. Extensive fog in the Western Approaches and English Channel is often associated with mild south or SW winds on the edge of an early summer anticyclone centred over Southern Europe. Fog in the North Sea can be caused by a similar system, but occasionally occurs when winds between south and east, which have travelled over the industrial Low Countries, emerge offshore and are prone to foggy condensation.

Coastal fog is usually land-formed fog which has drifted over the sea during the night. In fine summer weather coastal fog will burn off during the morning, as the air over and near the land is heated above dewpoint. Fog further offshore is not able to disperse in this way, because the sea does not absorb heat to anything like the same extent as the land. Such fog can only be 'blown' away, either by a straightforward weather wind picking up during the morning or by sea breezes setting in later in the day.

Fog of any kind is notoriously difficult to forecast, since its very existence hinges on a critical balance between air and sea temperature, or sometimes the temperatures of two adjoining air masses. Remember that poor visibility may also be caused by the low rain clouds associated with depressions and warm fronts. Such conditions can be even more unpleasant than calm weather fog, because you may have rough seas to contend with as well. Shallow depressions or troughs often bring murky visibility, but without the accompanying fresh winds of a more active low. One particular feature to watch out for on a weather map is when the cold front of one depression curves back to form the warm front of another depression coming along behind it. This can happen within a slow-moving, complex area of low pressure, for which the weather changes are apt to be difficult to predict.

Using Weather Forecasts

When you are cruising, especially under power, it can sometimes be tricky to decide whether to wait for weather and sea conditions to improve or to press on before they get worse; you may often need to strike a delicate compromise between prudence and opportunism. Of course life would be easier if we all had plenty of leisure, but boating time is limited for most of us and many enjoyable jaunts would never take place if we always made pessimistic assumptions about the weather.

We therefore tend to accept a certain risk of being delayed by the elements and, when this does happen, we gamely face the problems of rethinking deadlines, weighing up different forecasts, and trying to predict when conditions might be feasible for our intended passage. Of course the met men have their problems too, and the timing of weather remains a chancy and artful business. A four-hour 'window', for example, may be all that a fast motor cruiser needs to get back home safely from a weekend trip, but it can still be difficult for the forecasters to locate such a lull between two fast-moving depressions, even with the use of satellites.

It is preferable to draw upon as many sources of met information as possible, especially when you are trying to make 'marginal' passage decisions. The shipping forecasts broadcast on BBC long wave are invaluable and can be picked up all over NW Europe, although they are widely spaced throughout the day and use rather a broad brush on large sea

areas. You ignore their gale warnings at your peril but always bear in mind that motor boats are concerned primarily with sea state, and it is into such terms that any weather forecast should be translated. The proximity of land, the 'fetch' or distance over which waves can build up, the direction and rate of tidal streams, and the general depth of water can together have as much bearing on sea conditions as absolute wind strength.

If you listen to the Forecasts for Inshore Waters you'll often hear predicted wind forces a notch or two lower than the Shipping Forecast is giving for open sea areas. This is exactly what you would expect in most cases, but to hear such confirmation over the air can be encouraging if you are planning a coastal passage and are on the brink of deciding whether or not to go. Ordinary land forecasts are also helpful, because the general char can give a good idea of how and when particula depressions and frontal systems are likely to move Seemingly unspecific terms like fresh, breezy, unsettled, blustery, can all add perspective to a rather skeletal Shipping Forecast.

Local radio stations near the coast now broadcas frequent forecasts geared to the needs of boat owner: They include Small Craft Warnings during the summer months, whenever winds of force 6 or more ar expected within 12 hours. Telephone recorded forecasts are useful and can be dialled at any time. Yo can also phone local met offices and speak with th forecaster on duty, who should have up-to-date in formation on actual conditions at specified place around the coast; try to keep such enquiries brie and don't put any met officer in the difficult positio of being pressed for an opinion on whether or n you should sail.

Weather bulletins on marina and harbour offi noticeboards are often précis or straightforwar repeats of the Shipping Forecast for the relevant se areas, although some are compiled by local m offices. But if you are leaving for an offshore trip yo will run out of the scope of this forecast and need take account of what is predicted for the sea area a your destination.

HM Coastguards are very helpful on VHF and w

often provide the latest forecast on request. Coast Radio Station forecasts on VHF or MF are usually based on Shipping Forecasts, but are often broadcast at more civilized times. There is an extensive network of UK and Continental Coast Radio Stations whose VHF channels, working frequencies and broadcast times are listed in the almanacs. French stations broadcast in French, but quite slowly and clearly; Spanish stations broadcast in rather rapid Spanish; most Belgian, Dutch, German and Baltic stations give forecasts in English as well as the local language—Scheveningen is a particularly useful station for southern North Sea coasts, since it covers all the Dutch coast and its estuaries using various slave stations.

Although it makes good sense to use as many sources of met information as possible, there are times when one feels overloaded with forecasts and advice. Reconciling several forecasts can be difficult enough on your own, but when bad weather threatens, marinas soon fill up with other uncertain mariners keen to compare notes. Although a second opinion may help your decision-making, group discussions can easily flummox the whole business! Even if a skippers' gathering agrees about a forecast, the implications for each of them will be different. All have their own criteria to satisfy—different boats, experience and strength of crews, with different destinations and timetables. I have known such forums cause considerable stress for skippers who believe that it would be prudent to stay put, but who see other crews planning to set off. If you get involved in these pontoon debates, try and talk with people whose circumstances are similar to your own. Trust your own judgment if in doubt, and remember that 'having to be back at the office' is one of the most common causes of yachts getting into trouble in bad weather.

Having said all that, it can sometimes be helpful at least to poke your bow beyond the pierheads to get an idea of what is actually happening. Some sheltered harbours tend to convey an over-optimistic impression of conditions outside, but it is also possible to be kept at bay by a grim forecast when you cannot actually *see* that things are not so bad as they

Rather a hard looking sea off the Norwegian coast – not too bad when running before it, but life would be uncomfortable if you were going the other way. (Photo: Ron Dummer)

sound. In a marina, even quite a moderate wind will set rigging moaning and halyards tapping, instilling 'harbouritis' in the best of us! And if, having set off, you find that conditions really are hard and you decide to turn back, you can then relax and enjoy your enforced stay without the nagging doubt that it might just have been possible to get away.

Predicting Sea Conditions

Anyone confronted with a weather forecast when cruising under power will always try to translate predicted wind force into probable *sea state*, since it is the actual height, length and shape of waves or swell which will determine whether a passage is going to be enjoyable, exhilarating, uncomfortable, unpleasant or downright dangerous. Of course wind is the most significant determinant of sea state: the harder it blows, the rougher it gets, and when the wind dies away the sea usually quietens down soon afterwards. Yet geographical and tidal factors also play an important part and require careful consideration.

Working out what will be happening offshore is comparatively simple; one can hazard a pretty accurate guess at the kind of sea a given wind is likely to kick up, not forgetting that wind-over-tide is a sure recipe for rougher water. But things are more complicated when you are planning an inshore passage. Then you need to interpret forecasts with a close eye on the chart. You will be looking for lee and weather shores, deepish soundings where the seas should be regular in pattern, and shallows where they could be short and steep. Headlands or off-lying banks might have smooth patches under their lee, but some produce even rougher water. You will be trying to avoid areas of overfalls caused by shoals or tidal streams, and working out which parts of your passage would best be negotiated at slack water.

As an example of a coastal passage which ought to provide a varied set of sea conditions, consider the 'circumnavigation' shown in Fig 6.4. Suppose you are moored at Flathaven, in the protected upper reaches of the River Buckle. You have promised some friends a trip round Bear Island and the local forecast was giving SW winds force 4–5, with fair weather and good visibility. Your boat is not quite 30ft, has a semi-displacement hull and can cruise at 10 knots. It is nearly 40 miles round the island, HW at Flathaven is at 1030, and the main tidal streams start flowing broadly west about ½ hour afterwards.

The forecast falls into that tricky band of wind where conditions are probably going to be fresher than you would like, but not quite strong enough to make you call off. Force 4–5 waves in the open sea are beginning to seem rough, so you'd have been happier if the forecast had given 3–4. If they had talked about 5–6, you would probably have opted to stay in Flathaven.

However, the passage should be quite feasible provided you give some thought to the timing and choice of route. One of the first decisions is whether to go clockwise or anticlockwise round the island. Clockwise, you tackle most of the headwind at the beginning of the trip, when you can see what the weather is up to; going anticlockwise, you can carry the tide practically all the way.

Suppose that you decide on a clockwise route. The first tricky feature is the area of overfalls to the south of Sharpnose Head. The headland itself is steep-to but it juts into the tidal stream and is likely to churn up some rough water during the middle hours of both ebb and flood. You can imagine how these overfalls are caused. At half-ebb, say, the current coming out of the Buckle combines with the SW-going stream in Flathaven Bay to form quite a fast flow along the SE side of Sharpnose Point. Where this joins the main west-going stream a considerable turbulence will be set up. Add even a light wind against the tide and you have some rather nasty steep seas.

It will therefore be best if you can plan a departure time such that you'll be rounding Sharpnose Head near slack water high, while the stream is still trickling eastwards. Since the tide turns west-going half an hour after local HW, you would want to be rounding Sharpnose pretty much dead on HW, i.e. at 1030.

It is about 6 miles from your mooring to Sharpnose Head, so aim to cast off at about 0930. Pushing the last of the river flood will actually be an advantage given the forecast conditions: the wind will be blowing in the same direction as a weak tide, which should mean that the lower reaches of the river will not be too choppy, even in a full force 5. On the way out to Sharpnose Head you will still have a weak foul stream, but because this is lee-going it should help keep the sea quiet. The headland itself will provide a degree of shelter, especially if you tuck close into Flathaven Bay after leaving the river. Once round Sharpnose, you will have wind and regular sea on your port bow as you make for the channel between Kettle Stone and Kettle Point.

The tide will be starting to run NW through The Pass as you arrive, but with the wind across the stream the sea should not be too boisterous. You will find the calmest water by hugging the NE side of Kettle Stone, and this route also gives you a safe offing from Kettle Point. In a brisk northwester The Pass would be uncomfortable at any time during the ebb, the effect of the weather-going tide being amplified as the stream is accelerated in the narrows.

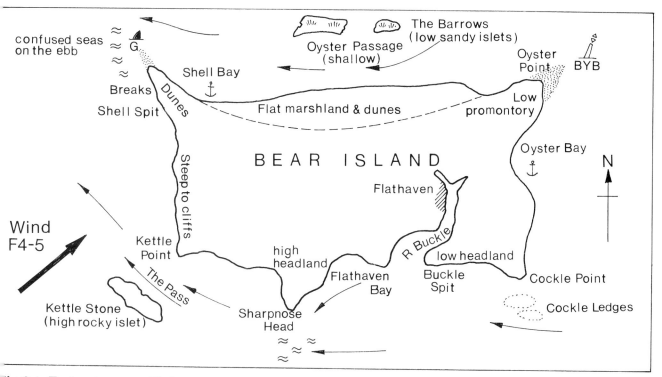

ig 6.4 *Trying to assess likely seastate.*

The west coast of Bear Island is steep-to, with cliffs
n the south giving way to a low, dune-covered pro-
iontory known as Shell Spit. In force 4–5 onshore
winds the sea and swell rolling in from the west will
e quite pronounced, although long and regular.
'ou'd be well advised to stay a safe distance off this
e shore, in case of machinery failure or problems
vith anything round the props. Shell Spit itself has
 narrow tongue of shoal water extending NW for
early ½ mile, and the sea in its vicinity will be rather
emperamental given the forecast wind. Steep waves
ay be breaking over and west of the shallows, as
e west-going tide gathers momentum along the
orth coast and meets the stream on the weather
de of the island. It would be wise to round the Spit
y a good margin and, as you turn landwards again,
void being set back towards the broken water.

On this occasion, Shell Bay just east of Shell Spit
ill probably make a good lunchtime anchorage.

You should find a calm spot by edging close in with
the echo-sounder, even though you will still feel the
wind coming across the promontory. The land may
afford better shelter as the tide falls. While the
stream is west-going, it will keep out any stray swell
which might otherwise filter round Shell Spit into
the anchorage. When the flood comes back, though,
it will be a different matter. Even though Shell Bay
is directly protected from the SW, the new east-going
tide will bring some uneasiness round the corner
from the open sea.

When negotiating the north coast of Bear Island,
you will have to decide whether to go outside the
Burrows or use Oyster Passage. In a southwesterly,
it would be better to stay as close as possible to the
shore. There are no navigational complications
about Oyster Passage, except that depths are fairly
shallow and the tide can run hard over the uneven
bottom. You could anticipate short steep seas during

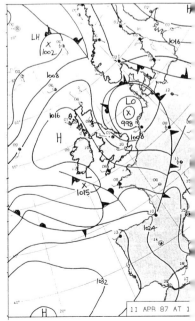

This satellite picture shows the swirl of a depression out across the North Sea. The met chart was drawn 9 hours before the photo was taken, and you can see how the centre of the low has moved south across the Netherlands. You could have predicted the general direction of this track, since the depression is on the east side of an area of high pressure which will have a broadly clockwise circulation. Note the area of clear skies where the ridge extends across Ireland and the west of England. (Courtesy University of Dundee)

the middle hours of a weather-going tide.

If you were to leave the Shell Bay anchorage after a leisurely lunch, you would arrive at the Burrows about an hour before LW. Although you'd meet the last dregs of the ebb, the worst of the tide would be over and Oyster Passage ought to be fairly smooth in the partly offshore wind. It is often surprising how tranquil life can be under a weather shore, even in quite a vicious blow.

Oyster Point has an area of shoals extending seawards for about $\frac{3}{4}$ mile and you need to keep outside the Oyster E-cardinal buoy, except near HW. Because this corner of the island is sheltered from the SW and you will be arriving there near slack water, Oyster Bank should be relatively quiet; however, you might deduce from the chart that confused and sometimes heavy breaking seas could accompany fresh winds from between NW through north to SE. Edge right into Oyster Bay for a quiet ride along the island's east coast, rounding Cockle Point close-to and thereby cutting inside Cockle Ledges. The last stretch home might be lively if the wind were in fact to pick up to a full force 5 during the day and stay there.

The more experience you obtain of different sea conditions in various cruising areas, the more accurately you should be able to peruse any chart and visualize what the sea state is likely to be along specific stretches of coast, at different stages of the tide, given a particular weather forecast. This is chart reading in its fullest sense and represents an important facet of seamanship. It is also a skill which one should be continually improving and refining in the light of new experiences. Whenever you get 'caught out' in unpleasant conditions along a strange coast, it is a good idea to have a short post-mortem when you are safely moored up somewhere, to see if you could reasonably have predicted a rough passage by carefully considering the forecast, the chart, and the tidal stream atlas in conjunction with each other.

Regional Weather

The Mediterranean

Surely there's not much to say about Mediterranean weather? Isn't the sun always shining, the sea calm and blue, and the winds light and balmy? Unfortunately not, although conditions are very pleasant for motor boating a good deal of the time during the summer, I have experienced some of my hardest blows down in the Med, early and late in the season.

Years ago we were on passage eastwards from Sète along the south coast of France and I recall being pounced on by a Mistral between Marseille and Toulon. The sky was clear and the barometer had hardly moved for a week, but a gentle northwesterly picked up to force 7 within half an hour and gave us a hard fight into the attractive shipbuilding town of La Ciotat. We were there for three days, while the wind howled down off the high slopes of Provence and screamed through the forest of masts in the marina. The locals were phlegmatic about this unseemly assault on their normally peaceful coastline. They remained dressed in fine weather clothes, shrugged their shoulders, and pointed knowingly at the long cigar-shaped clouds which were chasing each other out over the sea. These characteristic cloud formations were the key signs to watch for, apparently, but I was never able to predict a Mistral from looking at the sky.

The Mistral is partly a 'coastal slope' wind, a phenomenon typically found where you have respectable mountains rising back from the sea, and usually strongest if the peaks are covered with snow. Local depressions can develop without much warning over the Alps, and then the cold northerlies on the west side of these lows are accelerated down off the mountains and funnelled along the Rhône Valley to the sea. Because the depressions tend to form 'in situ' rather than tracking in from elsewhere, yachtsmen receive precious little help from their barometers. In fact the pressure on the coast often doesn't begin to fall until the Mistral is well under way and the airstream is already moving quickly. The sky is usually clear both before and during a Mistral, so it appears

The Mediterranean often looks blue and idyllic, but the Mistral or Tramontaña will bring hard conditions which are not to be trifled with.

that the infamous cigar-shaped clouds are not true portents of an approaching weather system but merely represent pockets of relatively moist air which happen to get caught up in the fast-moving stream.

The Mistral fans out when it reaches the sea, emerging as a northwesterly to the east of Marseille, a northerly opposite the Rhône delta and a north-northeasterly in the west part of the Golfe du Lion between Sète and the Spanish border. It is a hard, gusty wind and exhibits some of the savage qualities of our own cold front blows, albeit with mitigating sunshine.

The Spanish name for this wind is *Tramontaña*. To the west of Barcelona the Spanish coast is more or less sheltered from its worst effects, but the north coasts of Mallorca and Menorca are vulnerable early and late in the season, and during the winter. To the east, the French Côte d'Azur is pretty well protected, especially between St Tropez and Menton. Corsica can experience a stiff NW Mistral and the passage between mainland France and Corsica is very rough going under those conditions.

For some reason the Mediterranean is apt to produce very short, steep seas when the wind freshens, which are generally less manageable for motor boat than the longer rolling waves of the ocean. If you are cruising in a Mistral or Tramontaña area, you have always to bear in mind that the wind could increase significantly at short notice. Try to plan your passages so that you have a series of possible bolt-holes available which are well protected from the north. Many yachts suffer damage in Mediterranean marinas each year. If you are contemplating keeping your boat there, either permanently or perhaps just for a season or two, you will need to pick your winter haven carefully. Look for a harbour which is sheltered from the local version of the Mistral, where the marina has hardly any fetch from the north (even within the harbour), and where the actual pontoons are substantial and securely moored.

Further east in the Mediterranean, you will come across the *Bora* in the Adriatic, which is another coastal slope wind with similar characteristics to the Mistral and Tramontaña. Like them, the Bora is not a regular or predictable feature of the weather. It is a potentially severe north wind which only springs up from time to time, but when it does you know about it.

In the Aegean Sea the prevailing summer wind is the *Meltemi*, which usually begins in early July and continues into September. The Meltemi is driven by the area of low pressure which becomes established over Cyprus and the Middle East; it blows mainly from between NW and north and is at its strongest over the southern part of the Aegean. Its saving grace is that it is a diurnal wind with extremely regular habits, starting each day towards noon, reaching force 5 or 6 and sometimes 7 by afternoon, and dying away again in the evening. Sailing boats can plan their passages to use the Meltemi to advantage, but motor yachts will aim to travel early in the day before the wind gets up, or much later when things are falling quiet. If you are down in the Aegean for a whole summer, there is something to be said for cruising the south part of the area in May and June when, before the Meltemi starts, you can expect mainly light and variable winds. The trick is then to work north before the Meltemi gathers full momentum.

Southeast winds in the Mediterranean will often bring wet and windy weather, not unlike that associated with our own depressions and frontal systems but much warmer and more oppressive. The *Souróko* in the Aegean, or the *Sirocco* further west, originates over Africa and picks up moisture on its way over the sea. This is 'bad' weather for people ashore, although the wind strengths are generally less than a decent Mistral or Bora can generate.

Local wind	Type	Location
Mistral	Coastal slope	Golfe du Lion, originating over the Alps and blowing down the Rhône valley.
Tramontaña	Coastal slope	Spanish version of the Mistral which reaches the Balearics and the E end of the S Spanish coast.
Bora	Coastal slope	A sometimes severe N wind which occurs in the N part of the Adriatic.
Meltemi	Cyclonic with diurnal thermal effect	The prevailing summer wind of the Aegean, which blows from early July to the middle of September from between N and NW. Fresh to strong from noon to late afternoon.
Souróko or Sirocco	Cyclonic	Unsettled SE'ly originating over Africa and blowing across the Med towards southern Europe.

A popular area of the Mediterranean for European-owned motor boats is the south coast of Spain roughly between Estepona and Alicante. During the summer months you can expect fine sunny weather for most of the time, with quiet conditions in the morning and a sea breeze building up towards midday and lasting until early evening. If you are marina-hopping along this coast, there is much to be said for making an early start and arriving somewhere well before noon. This makes the most of the calm conditions and you can enjoy a leisurely lunch in a new harbour with a cooling sea breeze, take a siesta perhaps when the sun is at its hottest, and then stroll ashore in the late afternoon.

When the Mediterranean is nice it is very very nice, mostly during the normal summer holiday period between mid-May and early September. However, visiting boat owners who make early or late season delivery trips are often surprised by the severity of winds which the Med can deal out. It is worth keeping this in mind if you are planning to try and squeeze 12 months cruising out of a year by keeping your boat down in the sun for a while.

The Great Lakes of America

American and Canadian yachtsmen have access to the largest expanse of inland water in the world, the Great Lakes. Now the weather experienced over large lakes is often a rather complicated mixture of forecast weather and local thermal effects. For example, when there is very little gradient wind over the Great Lakes in the morning, you can expect a 'lake breeze' to spring up during the day. This is an inland version of the sea breeze and it can significantly shift the wind over a shoreline during fine summer days.

The lake breeze season over the Great Lakes generally runs from mid-April to mid-August. The maximum effect occurs in June and July, and there is very little chance of a lake breeze from September through to March. Suppose, on a fine summer morning in June and July, you were standing on the shore of one of the Great Lakes looking out over the water. If the 'real' wind was blowing along the coast from your left, you could expect a sudden veer of up to 40° when the lake breeze started up. If the real wind was blowing along the coast from your right, you could expect it to back very slowly to blow more onshore as the lake breeze began to take effect.

If the early morning wind was actually blowing more or less onshore, the effect of the lake breeze, as with a sea breeze, would be to increase the wind speed by mid-afternoon but leave the wind direction essentially unchanged. If the early morning wind happened to be blowing directly offshore, the lake breeze would eventually be acting in opposition to the gradient wind, so that the net wind would tend to calm down towards midday and then gradually pick up onshore during the afternoon.

Given a settled weather pattern, you can usually expect the wind to fall calm in the evening over the Great Lakes, with a light land breeze overnight whose direction may be deflected by hills or moun-

tains further inland. This nocturnal wind will tend to fall away near dawn, when you can expect another period of relative calm until the lake breeze gets going again.

East Coast of America

The huge eastern seaboard of the USA stretches for more than 1600 nautical miles from Miami, at the southern tip of Florida, right up to Grand Manan Island and the mouth of the Bay of Fundy. Another 600 miles of easting takes you past Nova Scotia and Newfoundland to the very eastern edge of Canada.

The summer weather on the southern mainland coast, between Florida and Cape Hatteras, is affected by the position and extent of the North Atlantic high. Down in Florida the climate is more or less tropical and the winds normally come off the Atlantic, from the E or SE in the summer and the NE during the winter. Hurricanes can hit this coast at any time in the summer, but are more likely to track north from the Caribbean towards the end of the season, the high risk period being September and October.

The weather becomes progressively more maritime the further north you go. Up towards Cape Hatteras you can expect variable summer winds with a slight predominance of south-westerlies. Between Cape Hatteras and Nantucket the winds are also rather variable during the summer, but the North Atlantic high tends to feed in south-westerlies for much of the time. You can experience fresh northerlies if the land mass anticyclone over North America slips east a bit, or more changeable weather associated with depressions and fronts moving broadly from west to east.

The Intracoastal Waterway stretches from Key West right up to the mouth of Chesapeake Bay. Anyone cruising this amazing network of canals, rivers, bays and swamps will find the hottest weather in the south, but the coasts of North Carolina and Virginia usually have excellent summer weather as well, especially in June and July.

Between Cape Hatteras and New York you will

often get coastal fog in the mornings when the weather is fine and settled. This usually clears towards midday, burned up by the sun and dispersed by sea breezes. Fog is even more prevalent further north, but this is usually a more persistent form of sea fog, caused by warm southerly or south-westerly winds arriving over the cold waters of the Labrador current.

Between Nantucket and Nova Scotia the weather is distinctly maritime. Depressions and fronts pass across the area from west to east, following the general airflow on the north edge of the North Atlantic high. You can expect south or south-westerly winds ahead of a depression, which veer to the north-west as the system moves through. There are very few gales during the summer months, but late August needs watching and April or September can turn up some nasty storms at sea.

The extreme north-eastern stretch of this great coastline, between Maine and Newfoundland, is extremely prone to sea fog if the wind is in the south-west, especially during the early part of the season. You can expect fog on more than 10 days a month in April and May. July tends to be the quietest month as far as winds are concerned, but the season finishes early as the North Atlantic depressions begin to track across more frequently in August. Along the whole of the Eastern Seaboard, but especially in the north, the winds are generally lighter and the seas quieter closer inshore. The US Coast Guard forecasts are reliable and it is particularly important to monitor them in the south for prior warning of the likely development of tropical storms.

The Bahamas

The luxurious Bahamas lie off the south-east tip of the East Coast, between Florida and the West Indies. The weather in these low-lying islands is undoubtedly congenial for tourists, and yet it can be tricky for boat owners at certain times of year. The hurricane season lasts from May to November, although most tropical disturbances pass safely south of the islands in mid-summer. The prevailing summer winds in the Bahamas are from the east or south-east, but the late season can often be very calm. Local troughs of low pressure, known as Easterly Waves, can interrupt fine periods of summer weather to bring temporarily unsettled conditions, with shifting winds and rain squalls.

West Coast of America

The Pacific seaboard of the USA stretches for over 1100 nautical miles, from Cape Flattery in the north down to the Mexican border near San Diego. The weather on the southern part of this coast is affected by the North Pacific high, whereas the area to the north of San Francisco is more subject to depressions which come in off the Pacific.

Off California, the winds tend to follow the line of the coast, with north-westerlies prevailing in the winter and southerlies or south-easterlies more common during the summer. There is a risk of tropical storms in August and September, but these North Pacific hurricanes usually hit the coast well south of San Diego. Thick fog is common between San Francisco and Los Angeles, caused by warm moist winds blowing over the cold California current.

Between San Francisco and Vancouver, the North Pacific high brings fine settled weather during the spring and summer, with the prevailing winds from between west and north. Boats cruising this coast can often benefit from travelling at night or very early in the morning, when calm conditions may allow good progress to be made. The season starts drawing to a close towards the end of September, when the North Pacific high is slipping southwards and allowing depressions to track in from the west.

This traditional West Country day cruiser has a delightful sheltered berth in Gannel Creek, near Newquay. The legs keep her nicely upright on the firm sand and she is securely moored 'all-fours'.

Chapter 7

Using your Boat

Day Cruising

The majority of boats are actually used for a surprisingly short total period each year, and most of that time often consists of day cruising from a home port and local pottering. In fact this can be one of the most pleasant and relaxing ways of boating, needing relatively little in the way of capital investment and avoiding many of the niggling stresses that longer passages can sometimes involve. 'The smaller the boat, the greater the fun' is a wise old saying, and anyone who is contemplating taking up boating from scratch would do well to think small for at least the first couple of years.

You can get away with having less gear aboard a boat used mostly for day cruising, although you still need all the basic safety equipment such as lifejackets, flares, fire extinguishers and a comprehensive tool kit. A reliable engine is a vital key to enjoyable boating, so however else you manage to economise, don't skimp on the main machinery, whether it be inboard or outboard. The navigation set-up need not be too sophisticated, but a good steering compass and echo-sounder should definitely be on the inventory. Opinions vary about VHF for day cruising, although it can be very handy for local

weather forecasts and strong wind warnings, and worth its weight in gold in an emergency. You should have an adequate main anchor and kedge, together with plenty of either chain or nylon warp with chain. Apart from the fact that the hook is an important item of safety equipment, anchoring is very much a part of day cruising as you will often be looking for somewhere interesting to stop for lunch and perhaps a short expedition ashore. A handy tender makes life easier and can be great fun for exploring in shallow water. A good quality inflatable is usually the most convenient type of dinghy to have, maybe with a small lightweight outboard.

Day cruising is an ideal way to introduce children to boats, because you can offer them plenty of different things to do and see. A short trip out to a beach and then rowing ashore for lunch and a swim; pottering about in the dinghy, climbing rocks, landing on uninhabited islands, venturing up narrow creeks—these are all the stuff of the long summer holidays that many of us remember. You don't need a large, expensive boat to enjoy this kind of messing about afloat. On the contrary, the owner of such craft often miss out on some of the simplest but most enjoyable aspects of boating. You can see examples of this syndrome in most marinas, where certain

The Natant 24 is an attractive small displacement cruiser which will appeal to anyone who simply enjoys being afloat and prefers their boating to be uncomplicated and relatively inexpensive. The standard engine installation is a single 50hp Perkins Prima H50 diesel, which gives a comfortable and economical cruising speed of 6-6½ knots. The accommodation is fine for two, especially if you fit a cockpit awning to make an extra 'porch' when you are in harbour.

owners of large new boats do not feel competent or experienced enough to take them away for a cruise, and yet they also find it too much of a business just to slip out for a short day trip. With a smaller boat they might find themselves able to cast off more readily.

The modern styles of 'sportsboat' are very versatile for local cruising and their fast speeds can greatly increase the range of options for varied day trips. Yet high speed is by no means essential for interesting day cruising. The sad truth is that fine summer weather in Northern Europe is not all that common and a slow, rather solid boat might well take you out and about in comfort and safety when the more flighty sports types are confined to their berths. If you like nosing up creeks and rivers, going alongside rough stone quays and exploring offbeat landing places, then there's a lot to be said for a boat which is heavily built, able to withstand a few knocks, and which can take the ground safely without the risk of punching a hole through her hull or damaging the sterngear.

Two Fairlines having fun off the Mediterranean coast of France. On the left of the picture is a Fairline 26 Sport Fury; on the right is a Fairline 24 Carrera.

Weekend Cruising

I have taken this to mean the stage that you reach when you begin to stay aboard your boat for a night or two, perhaps in a harbour or anchorage quite close to your home port. It might seem a small step from day cruising, but in practice there is a significant difference between making a short trip with the intention of leaving your boat again at the end of the day, and making the same trip in the knowledge that you will be living aboard overnight. Even if you stay on your own mooring, there is somehow an enhanced feeling of potential—a sense of being free, if you so decided, to set off on an expedition to unknown parts.

However, it is when you come to regard your boat as a home from home that the real magic of cruising can start to tantalize you with its possibilities. Weekend cruising is a gentle way to acquire this state of mind, even if you can only spare the time to drive down to your boat on a Saturday morning, return home on Sunday afternoon, and don't manage to go anywhere in between. As with a house, most people take a while to organize their boat so that they can live there comfortably. Even with a new boat, it may

145

This Fisher trawler yacht is heavily built and is definitely a 'going places' cruising boat.

take several seasons before things aboard are fully 'comfortized' and you have collected together the various homely items which make a night aboard a relaxing pleasure rather than an austere ordeal. Cruising is partly about getting to new places by boat, but is very much about living afloat once you get there.

Of course it can be tempting to 'make do' when weekending, not bothering to refine your accommodation when you know that you'll only be aboard for one or two nights at a time. You might get into the habit of slipping out to a pub or restaurant to eat rather than putting your galley into working shape; perhaps you will tend to rely on marina showers instead of organizing proper washing facilities aboard. Yet it is much more satisfying if your boat, whatever her size, can serve as a fully independent weekend cottage. Then you can sample some of the more secluded anchorages and really enjoy the pleasures of getting away from it all.

The weather can pose problems for weekend cruising folk who would prefer to make a passage to a different harbour for Saturday night, but who definitely need to be back at their home port on Sunday evening. In this respect, you should always keep Sunday's weather in mind when you are listening to the forecasts on Friday and trying to make your weekend plans. One of the great secrets of stress-free cruising is to cultivate a considerable flexibility in your attitude to destinations and schedules. Let the weather determine where you go and you will avoid a lot of the tension that some skippers can build up when the elements appear to conspire against their carefully laid timetables. Make a plan by all means, but have two more ready up your sleeve in case a depression moves more quickly than expected or a transient anticyclone seems to vanish into thin air overnight.

If you do a lot of weekend cruising it's a good idea to keep your boat well stored and fuelled so that you can get away on a Friday evening or early on Saturday. It is also wise to have a generous selection of charts aboard, covering the far fringes of areas you might possibly be able to reach. It can be frustrating if you've managed to get down to the boat in good time on a Friday afternoon, the weather looks set fair for a couple of days and seems just right for making a passage to somewhere a bit different, but you don't have the necessary charts to hand and your local chandler doesn't have them either.

Shortage of time is a problem for most of us who go cruising, and weekends can be especially tight if you have to travel some distance to your boat. Yet it is vital to keep on top of your maintenance during the season, so try and make a point of fitting in at least a couple of jobs whenever you are aboard, whether or not you actually go away anywhere. The engine routines are especially important and you will, in the end, pay a high premium for neglecting such small but necessary tasks as tightening a fan belt as soon as it needs attention, checking your fuel filters and water traps, cleaning cooling water inlet strainers, keeping grease reservoirs topped up, cleaning battery terminals and earth connections, and so on. Your auxiliary equipment will need a little attention now and again, so don't forget the anchor winch, the heads, your screen wipers or the bilge-pump strum boxes.

You also need to allow sufficient time on Sunday afternoon or evening to make sure that you leave everything aboard as it should be left. Every skipper has his own particular list of things to do, but most will include checking the moorings, turning off seacocks, turning off the gas, isolating the batteries and opening the cabin ventilators. There is nothing worse than having to dash to clear up late on a Sunday, then getting halfway up the motorway and feeling a niggling doubt about whether you did in fact check the gas or the heads.

One of the advantages of weekend cruising is that your boat and engine(s) are worked regularly. Most machinery likes nothing worse than lying idle, so provided you keep up with the maintenance, a boat which is being used nearly every weekend is likely to stay in better shape than one which lies at her moorings for weeks on end, waiting for her relatively brief annual cruise. Many people manage to get around a great deal by weekend cruising: given a fast cruising speed, settled weather and a fair degree of stamina, it can be quite feasible to consider weekend destinations up to about a hundred miles from your home port. If you are prepared to leave the boat away from your home port, you can sample a wide range of weekend venues and organize a surprisingly long cruise in weekend stages.

Extended Cruising

For many owners or would-be owners, this is the *raison d'être* of the whole business of boating—visiting new places in their own little ships and living aboard for several weeks at a time. For those relative novices who are lured into buying quite large cruising yachts at a glossy boat show, the reality of cruising can differ widely from both the initial dreams and from the expectations conjured up by a salesman's expansive spiel. But once you get used to the general pace of cruising, become attuned to the kinds of travelling schedule that are realistic in a smallish boat, and start to acquire some of the diverse skills that cruising requires, you will find that there is no finer way of spending your time.

One of the most attractive aspects of cruising is

that you can travel as quickly or slowly as you like. By far the majority of motor yachts cover the bulk of their mileage close to the coast, hopping from port to port and rarely making open sea or night passages. Yet once you get into a routine of making good about 30 or 40 miles each day, it's amazing how far you can travel without really noticing it. From the south coast of England, for example, any motor boat that you can live aboard, and which is capable of taking a bit of a pounding if you happen to misjudge the weather, will be able to cruise all the way up to the Baltic in short daytime hops by way of France, Belgium, the Netherlands, the German Friesian Islands and the Kiel Canal.

Given a seaworthy boat and a willing crew, the single most important constraint on any cruise is usually the time available. This is a perennial problem for most of us, although there are ways and means of stretching precious holidays to best advantage. It is difficult to generalize about how far one can expect to cruise in a given period, partly because of the vagaries of the weather, but also because different boats and different parties progress at very different rates. Some boats cut along at 20 knots, while others amble at more modest displacement speeds. This doesn't mean that the fastest boats travel the greatest distances, however. On the contrary, many high-speed motor yachts are only under way for a couple of hours each day when cruising, while the apparent tortoises are apt to rumble on for much longer periods. Some crews like to travel a certain distance each day, while others prefer to make a longish passage and then linger somewhere for a day or two before pressing on again.

Cruise Planning

When you plan a single week afloat, especially in Northern Europe, there is always a real risk that your schedule will be thrown out by a spell of bad weather. If that does happen, there is usually nothing for it but to be philosophical and make the best of a bad job. It is rare to be completely harbour-bound for a whole week; occasionally you can strike lucky

with a short cruise and have everything fall neatly into place! Having a fortnight at your disposal opens up more than twice the number of options that a week provides, and a further week adds a welcome element of leisure to the proceedings. Four weeks' cruising is verging on the luxurious, unless you are lucky enough to be retired or otherwise reasonably free of shoreside commitments.

There are various ways of organizing a limited holiday period so as to fit in as much cruising as possible and to extend your effective range to take in new areas. In deciding on a schedule, you sometimes choose where you would like to go and then work out how much time you need to get there, have a good look round, *and* get back. Often, though, it is more a question of deciding how much time you can afford and then selecting a cruising area which can be reached, explored and returned from in that period. As you begin to venture further afield, there is much to be said for trying to separate the travelling out and back from the main part of the cruise.

There is nothing worse, when cruising, than to find yourself tied to a strict timetable. It is both unrelaxing and potentially dangerous, since experience has shown time and again that 'having to get home' is one of the most common causes of boats being caught out by bad weather. One way of easing the timetable would be to cruise your boat towards the destination area over several weekends before your main holiday, making convenient hops between suitable marinas and 'commuting' home for the working week. This involves a certain amount of expense, but such delivery weekends can be good fun and you can always regard them as extra 'mini-cruises'. Then, when your main holiday comes along, you have the added interest of a trip out to join your boat and the undoubted advantage that you will be starting a foreign cruise almost from day one, regardless of what the weather is doing. This strategy can make efficient use of valuable holiday time and you are also likely to start the main cruise in a more relaxed frame of mind, not being faced with a long haul to your intended destination.

A variation on this theme is to leave your boat somewhere safe at the end of your holiday, coming

Two extremes, ancient and modern. In the days of sail, it might have taken two or three weeks to beat down-Channel against westerly weather. A motor yacht capable of cruising at 25 knots doesn't take quite so long.

149

home instead by public transport and then returning later in order to 'weekend' her back to base. I generally find this less attractive, because you still have that outward passage at the start of the cruise, and somehow the business of weekending home never has quite the same appeal to a crew as working the boat outwards.

If you are the joint owner of a boat you have the advantage of being able to organize one-way cruises with your partner(s), a facility which can greatly increase your cruising range and/or relax your schedule. But even if you are a sole owner, it is some-

times possible to come to a similar arrangement with someone whom you are able to trust with your boat. I have done this on many occasions, when old friends have been happy to take over the boat at the end of our holiday and cruise back in their own time.

If you decide to arrange your cruise in stages using any of these methods, it follows that an important part of your cruise planning will involve locating suitable transport routes and convenient ferry terminals, railway stations or airports. You will also be looking for a selection of secure and moderately priced harbours at which you can either leave your

When you are planning a cruise in stages, it makes sense to change crews at a comfortable marina which has good facilities close to hand.

boat unattended or make crew changeovers.

Where one particular port-of-call stands out as being both secure and well placed, it can be useful to go ahead and make a firm decision that this will be a key destination in your plan, weather and Acts of God permitting. It is a good idea to contact the Harbourmaster well in advance and explain when you would like a visitor's berth and when you would like to leave your boat unattended. You may have to pay a reservation fee, but at least you then have something definite to work to.

The timing of a cruise requires some careful thought. If you are tied to school holidays the choices are somewhat simplified, but that still leaves a six-week window in which to locate a period of two, three or four weeks. It is anyone's guess when to expect reasonable weather in Northern Europe, so it is worth perusing the tide tables to see if any specific period is more suitable than another.

If, for example, you were planning a fortnight's cruise to the Channel Islands, you might aim to arrive in the area as the tides are taking off from springs. The considerable local tidal streams would then be gradually slowing down during your first week, making inter-island navigation less stressful. Until dead neaps, each successive low tide would also be 'less low' than the last, allowing you to visit an increasing number of anchorages which might otherwise dry at low water springs. However, tide times may be relevant too. St Peter Port's Victoria Marina is accessible for about $2\frac{1}{2}$ hours either side of local HW and St Helier Marina for 3 hours either side. Morning HW springs are around 0700 GMT in the Islands, or 0800 BST, so three days after springs takes HW to 1000 BST or thereabouts. You'd then be able to leave Victoria Marina from about 0730 to 1230 BST, which would allow a civilized morning start, but as the days progress it would be later each evening before you could get into the marina.

It is useful to consider how much flexibility a given cruising ground can provide. Is it possible to make short coastal hops in case the weather is hostile, or if you have a young family and prefer to keep passage-making to a minimum? If the legs between interesting havens are rather long, are there still ports of refuge to tuck into if the weather turns foul? Is there scope for making a round tour within a given cruising area, so that you can plan a roughly circular cruise and don't have to retrace your steps? Some straight coastlines offer a similar facility, being so well endowed with frequent harbours and anchorages that you can cruise in both directions without calling at the same place twice.

Cruising with children brings its own special criteria, such as the availability of good beaches, perhaps a lively town or two for diversions ashore, the occasional launderette to keep the dirty washing at bay. It is usually preferable to plan a very modest itinerary, with relatively small hops, various expeditions up creeks and rivers, and plenty of shore leave.

Scope for chartering?

One way of overcoming tight time constraints and seeing new places is to charter a boat in a cruising area which you would like to visit. Hitherto, chartering motor boats has been largely restricted to either inland waterways or to expensive Mediterranean or Caribbean based super-yachts. However, this situation is gradually changing; we are beginning to see more frequent advertisements offering family sized motor yachts for both bareboat and skippered charter.

Even if you own a boat, it can sometimes be attractive to charter in an area that you are keen to cruise but which would take a while to reach under your own steam. Bear this possibility in mind if you find yourself trying to devise a complicated schedule of crew changes in order to reach a more distant cruising ground. Chartering locally may not only be more convenient, but may also work out to be less expensive, once you have taken the total cost of fuel and travelling into account.

These two sports boats (above and facing page) are nice examples of the genre, capable of fast cruising speeds so long as the sea is only 'choppy' rather than 'rough'. Accommodation is usually rather limited, but can be quite comfortable for two for a weekend.

Coping with Heavy Weather

This curiously fuzzy term can mean very different things to different crews in different boats under different circumstances. Most mariners would class gale or near-gale winds as heavy weather, and yet every season many yachtsmen and their families take a dusting in winds and seas which are nowhere near force 7 or 8. If you have children aboard, the level at which you define conditions as heavy will be much reduced. Tidal streams have a malevolent effect on sea state and can turn an apparently

innocuous breeze into something more serious. There is a great difference between open water passage-making and coasting and, for the latter, whether the wind is onshore or offshore.

The size and type of boat is obviously a significant factor in coping with heavy weather, but all yachts seem small when the going gets really nasty; then the experience and stamina of the crew will count for more than the size and shape of their container. Fast planing boats can get you out of trouble more quickly than a displacement boat, but their range and endurance at sea is generally more limited.

Because of their gently contoured 'wine-glass' sections, comparatively deep draught and heavier weight of hull, displacement boats are traditionally reckoned to be more seaworthy and comfortable in heavy weather than planing boats. The classic example is the genuine MFV type yacht, with her long straight stem, broad beam aft for stability and tucked-in canoe stern to minimize wash and help make the hull more easily driven. Yet the displacement/planing debate is less clearcut than it used to be, as modern hull design is now so advanced that some of the larger production planing yachts can hang onto full cruising power in surprisingly severe conditions. They need to, of course, because their Vee hulls depend mainly on lift for stability at sea and general ease of handling. Once a planing boat is forced to slow down to displacement speed in heavy weather, she will be at a disadvantage compared with a boat which has been designed to travel *through* the water rather than partly across it.

However, planing hulls vary considerably in their ability to stand up to real waves, and you need to be aware of that critical sea state which will force your own boat off the plane. Much depends on the length

153

The 85ft Gitala *was designed by Laurent Giles and built in aluminium alloy by Whisstocks of Woodbridge. She displaces 50 tonnes, has an aerodynamic profile and is powered by two GM Detroit 650hp diesels. Luxurious as well as seaworthy, Gitala's facilities include a swimming pool and an internal telephone system.*

Never take the sea for granted. Small motor boats are vulnerable to freshening winds and rising seas, even in partially sheltered waters.

and steepness of the waves and your direction of travel across them. A boat which can keep flying at force 5 with wind and tide together, may have to slow down if the tide turns against the wind and the waves steepen. The force 4–5 notch on the Beaufort Scale is often a critical turning point between acceptable and stressful conditions. Once the wind touches force 6 away from the shelter of land, it won't be long before the waves start becoming large and distinctly threatening. Whereas a steady force 4 will generally give you a sea which is lively rather than rough, a true force 5–6 in open water is invariably

hostile and will soon undermine the morale of an inexperienced crew.

Small-boat heavy weather Although the categories tend to blur at the edges, most of us can distinguish between a day cruiser and a more substantial boat capable of venturing offshore. The modern style of sports cruiser is perhaps rather tricky to place, since many have an impressive turn of speed and can easily make a quick 60 mile passage when the weather is quiet and the forecast favourable. By and large, though, I would describe most

155

FORCE	Mean Velocity	Description	Open Sea State	Possible Implications for Motor Boats
4	11–16 knots	Moderate breeze	Small waves, becoming longer. Fairly frequent white horses.	Smaller planing boats begin to slam in the open sea and may need to reduce speed.
5	17–21 knots	Fresh breeze	Moderate waves, taking a more pronounced long form. Many white horses are formed, with the chance of some spray.	Heavy weather for smaller motor boats. Conditions seem hostile in the open sea, especially with rain and poor visibility. A long passage turns into an ordeal. Many production planing boats will start to slam and may have to slow down or alter course.
6	22–27 knots	Strong breeze	Large waves begin to form. The white foam crests are more extensive everywhere. Probably some spray.	Heavy weather for family crews in the open sea, or near headlands where tidal streams can kick up dangerous overfalls. Larger planing boats start to slam and may have to reduce speed. Life is even unpleasant aboard genuine MFVs. Most motor yachtsmen wish they were at home mowing the lawn.
7	28–33 knots	Near-gale	Sea heaps up and the white foam from breaking waves begins to be blown in streaks along the direction of the wind.	Heavy weather for all motor yachts. Shelter should be sought as soon as safely possible. To inexperienced crews in the open sea, conditions seem to be at a survival level. A considerable effort is needed to maintain a sense of order aboard, cope with steering and navigation, and keep up morale. The end of the world is nigh for anyone suffering from seasickness. Even MFVs may heave-to.
8	34–40 knots	Gale	Moderately high waves of greater length. Crests begin to break into spindrift. The foam is blown in streaks in the direction of the wind.	A nightmare for any family caught in the open sea. Much discipline and will-power needed to stay in control of events. Only cast-iron stomachs immune from seasickness.

Fig 7.1 *The Beaufort Scale, with implications for motor yachts.*

motor boats under 25ft as 'small' for the purposes of discussing heavy weather, because they seem particularly vulnerable to freshening winds and rising seas, even in partially sheltered waters. The majority of boats which cruise regularly are over 30ft, but a large in-between group includes a good proportion of basically seaworthy boats whose skippers nonetheless have to keep a close eye on the weather.

Small boats are affected by quite modest waves, especially when planing. A force 3 wind may seem more or less negligible close inshore or in a sheltered stretch of water; yet out in the open sea, a steady force 3 will produce waves of quite pronounced form, insidious embryos of something more dangerous. Remember the Beaufort Scale description of the sea state associated with a gentle breeze: 'Large wavelets. Crests begin to break, foam of glassy appearance. Perhaps scattered white horses.'

Force 4 is usually described as a moderate breeze.

Away from the shelter of land, though, a steady force 4 gives rise to a sea which is definitely on the move. The rather languid atmosphere of force 3 is replaced by an altogether more active scene: 'Small waves, becoming longer. Fairly frequent horses.' If the forecast is for strengthening winds, force 4 waves should start making a small-boat skipper edgy, especially if he is out where he knows he really shouldn't be. In a weather-going tide, an occasional steepish sea will provide a foretaste of what may lie in store.

Out in open water, or in areas of strongish tidal streams, force 5 represents heavy weather for a small boat. There is some weight in the wind now, enough to send plenty of spray aft if you are heading into it. When the sun goes in, you begin to sense that the elements are quite indifferent to your presence.

The Beaufort description looks somewhat less light-hearted at force 5: 'Moderate waves, taking a more pronounced long form. Many white horses are formed. Chance of some spray.' Life aboard a small boat is becoming distinctly unpleasant, especially if you are out of sight of land with the prospect of several hours' passage-making ahead of you. An inexperienced crew will now be vulnerable to a selection of possible mishaps or crises which, if they start occurring together and are allowed to get out of hand, can easily escalate into an emergency.

Preparations

Seasickness Of course seasickness can strike at any time, even on calm summer days, but when the first victim succumbs to *mal de mer* in a rising sea, morale on board usually plummets and the general level of tension will increase significantly. In a family crew, the mother may become especially worried if one of the children is seasick, and her increased anxiety can accentuate the stress felt by everyone else. If the skipper becomes seasick first, which is not uncommon if he or she is apprehensive about deteriorating weather, things can go from bad to worse very quickly. In any adverse conditions the crew of a small boat need to feel that there is someone in effective control. They will be looking for an outwardly calm and collected skipper, one who seems to appreciate what is happening and can take the necessary steps to navigate the boat to safety.

It is an important part of heavy weather routine for the skipper to anticipate and try to forestall seasickness if possible. In a crew of four, say, it's highly likely that at least one person is going to feel queasy if things start getting rough. Prevention is better than cure, since the only infallible remedy I know is for the sufferer to stand under a green tree! There are various measures to minimize the risk of serious seasickness. A full night's sleep before a passage is advisable, and so is a good unhurried breakfast before you set off (but try to avoid fried foods or orange juice). The navigator should do his homework in advance, so that he will not need to spend too much time at the chart table under way. Prepare sandwiches, Thermos flasks and various nibbles for the trip, so that nobody has to linger in the galley. Distribute seasick pills the night before a passage and

at least two hours before you set off. Make sure that everyone is warmly dressed, and try to keep one of the wheelhouse windows open when under way to allow fresh air to circulate.

If any of the crew become chronically seasick, they will usually be better off tucked up below in a sleeping bag with a bucket handy. At least you know that they are keeping warm and dry and are not in a position to take risks by going out on deck to be ill over the side.

Stow carefully to avoid chaos It is vital to maintain a sense of control in heavy weather, but you will soon feel it slipping if loose items start crashing about below. Anything that *can* move *will* move in a rough sea, so spend half an hour before you leave carefully securing and stowing, especially in the galley. The sound of breaking crockery is not at all uplifting at sea, particularly if something else is going wrong at the same time.

Dirty fuel filters In calm conditions you might get away with skipping your routine engine maintenance 'just for today', but heavy weather will exact the price with interest. Engines need clean fuel above all else, and if you haven't checked your water traps and other filters for some time, a stiff force 5 against a moderate tide is likely to cause heart-stopping hesitations in engine revs just when you really need reliable power.

Navigational uncertainty Rough weather brings its own stresses and can also be accompanied by deteriorating visibility. A skipper should do his utmost to have the navigation completely under control, using all facilities at his disposal. If you have Decca you should enter your passage waypoints *before* setting off, preferably the previous evening. Be sure to check the stored latitudes and longitudes for accuracy, and make a habit of listing each waypoint on a planning sheet for easy reference.

Radar can be a boon in heavy weather, but a prudent navigator will have studied the large-scale charts of his possible landfall coasts at leisure before leaving, to form a mental picture of what is likely to come up first on the scan. You don't want to be doing this homework on passage when the weather

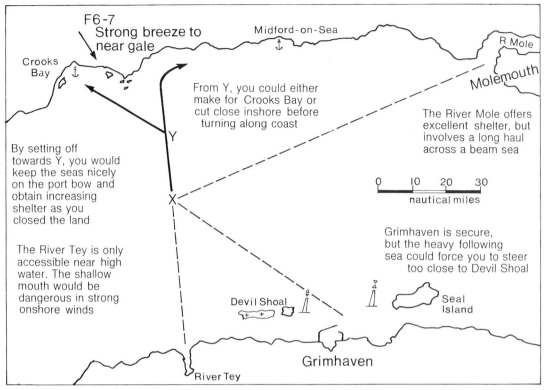

F6-7
Strong breeze to near gale

Midford-on-Sea

R Mole

Crooks Bay

Molemouth

From Y, you could either make for Crooks Bay or cut close inshore before turning along coast

The River Mole offers excellent shelter, but involves a long haul across a beam sea

By setting off towards Y, you would keep the seas nicely on the port bow and obtain increasing shelter as you closed the land

0   10   20   30
nautical miles

The River Tey is only accessible near high water. The shallow mouth would be dangerous in strong onshore winds

Grimhaven is secure, but the heavy following sea could force you to steer too close to Devil Shoal

Devil Shoal

Seal Island

Grimhaven

River Tey

Fig 7.2 *Deciding on a port of refuge. You are at* X, *wishing you weren't.*

is getting worse and there may be other problems demanding your attention.

Weather forecasts and small craft

One reason for relatively inexperienced crews becoming caught out at sea is that small-boat heavy weather is not at all exceptional. A fresh wind may not excite much more than a passing comment during a general weather forecast, or perhaps a rather throwaway 'locally 5' in the course of a shipping forecast. What might be 'a bit breezy' to the Met. man could be a real struggle for a family crew in a light 20ft boat off a tide-troubled headland. You need to appreciate that force 5 is a significant wind in open or tidal waters before your ears will automatically prick up and warning bells begin to sound.

Small-boat heavy weather doesn't always go hand

in hand with 'bad' weather. Land forecasters may be waxing lyrical about long summer days and large anticyclones, but it only takes a high pressure system to shift a hundred miles and for a shallow low to form on its edge to give you fresh winds blowing out of a clear blue sky. It may be all strawberries and cream at Wimbledon, but pretty wild offshore in a full force 5 easterly.

The more you accumulate experience at sea, the easier it becomes to visualize the kind of condition to expect on a given stretch of water if a forecast turns out to be accurate. You can sometimes 'finesse' the forecast and make short coastal hops just before or just after a period of heavy weather. Psychologically, as well as in reality, there is a world of difference between a short rough spell along a straightforward coast and a heavy weather passage of indeterminate length out in open water.

Fringe forecasts

Whatever their shoreside commitments, most cruising skippers feel fairly relaxed about staying tucked up in harbour when a gale is in full swing and it is quite clear that no-one in his right mind would poke his nose beyond the pierheads until things quieten down. When the forecast is giving force 7 or more there is rarely any doubt about whether to go or to stay. But the most difficult forecasts to react to are those that mention stronger winds than you would like, yet not necessarily strong enough to make you feel completely at ease about postponing your passage. Marginal forecasts are especially tricky if you are running out of time at the end of a cruise and waiting for a weather window which will let you return to your home port. The pressure to set off is intensified if there are several crew members who need to be home by a certain date. There is also the argument that if you hang about too long after a blow, you may not get away before the next low starts tracking in and making its mark on the forecast.

This kind of situation is one of the most common causes of yachts getting caught out in heavy weather, so there are several points to bear in mind when you find yourself toying with going to sea when your instinct is telling you to stay put.

—Trust your own judgment. If you are feeling edgy about the risk of running into heavy weather by giving a marginal forecast the benefit of the doubt, you probably have good reason. Remember the old adage 'It's better to be in harbour wishing you were at sea than to be at sea wishing you were in harbour.'

—If in doubt, wait and see. If you are uncertain about whether the strong winds associated with a passing depression are really on the decrease, stay put for another couple of hours, keep an eye on the barometer, and watch how conditions develop. Motor yachts generally have plenty of flexibility about when they set off on an open-water passage.

—Go and have a look. If you think that a depression is safely past but you are still concerned about sea state, there's usually nothing to be lost by setting off and giving it a try, with the intention of turning back if conditions are too hard.

Heavy weather tactics

However cautious you are about interpreting forecasts, and however much scope you have to linger in harbour until the weather seems settled, a time will come when you find yourself out in rough water, wishing that you'd never taken up boating at all and wondering why you are not playing golf somewhere instead of being tossed about on an ugly grey sea.

Various important calculations should be running through your mind at this stage, aided by a strategic study of the small-scale chart of your sea area. How much fuel do you have and how long can you stay at sea at various cruising speeds? A selection of possible ports of refuge may lie within safe range, although some will be easier to reach than others in the present conditions, or in the weather likely to develop during the forecast period.

Choosing between these options is not a simple matter of comparing straight distances on the chart. 50 miles dead to windward is a much harder objective than 50 miles at an angle to the sea or downwind. In heavy weather, most motor yachts handle best by taking the seas 'on the shoulder', i.e. at about 20–30° on either bow. The risk of slamming is reduced and part of the wave energy is absorbed by the boat's rolling. Your best bet may be a port of refuge whose course takes you across the weather at this sort of angle, so long as it's not too distant and there is no problem about getting in safely when you finally arrive.

Some harbours can be entered at any state of tide, whereas others are only accessible for a limited period either side of high water. Is it likely to be dark by the time you arrive and is your selected haven easy to navigate into at night? Will your route take you near shoal water or close to a tricky headland where the seas may be much steeper than out in the open?

A heavy beam sea is potentially the most dangerous for a motor boat, because of the ultimate risk of capsize. Unlike sailing yachts, power craft are generally unstable *in extremis*; if heeled beyond a certain critical angle they can roll right over rather than return to a level keel. Even the MFV type of hull is vulnerable in really serious weather, as the number of fishing boat losses each winter testifies. So when you are trying to decide on a haven of refuge, it is wise to avoid a course which takes you across a beam sea, or a possible beam sea if the wind should shift and freshen.

Running before the weather is a common strategy under sail, but most power boats handle very uneasily with large seas rearing astern. As conditions deteriorate, a point will be reached when you find yourself surfing down the fronts of steep waves, with the consequent risk of your stern overtaking the bow and the boat being swung round beam-on to the seas, or 'broaching-to'. In heavy weather which is unpleasant rather than dangerous, the attraction of running before the seas is that there is usually much less strain on the boat and crew. Things don't seem so bad when the elements are behind you and there is none of that vicious slamming which is so wearing on the nerves. Yet this easing of tension can bring its own dangers, lulling you into a false sense of security and leading you gently towards a trap.

When running before heavy weather, it is all too easy for the wind to freshen and the seas to build up further without you really noticing. When it finally dawns on you that to carry on is becoming dangerous, the waves may be too severe to allow you to round up safely and face the music. The other edge to this trap is the classic mistake of careering towards a lee shore, pinning your hopes on making a safe landfall and somehow reaching a port of refuge. This is probably the most common cause of shipwreck and loss of life in heavy weather, mainly because of the numerous hazards associated with proximity to the coast. Negotiating rocks and shoals is often tricky enough in quiet conditions, but a gale or near-gale will put your navigation under great stress and can also tempt you to take chances in your haste to get in somewhere.

If you make an inaccurate landfall, ending up even a mile or two along from your intended destination, the seas may prevent you from being able to alter course safely and make good your error. Inshore waters usually mean shallower surroundings and stronger tides, both of which can have a dramatic steepening effect on waves which might be savage enough already. Poor visibility can intensify this danger, delaying the point at which you discover your dodgy landfall and thus making it that much more difficult to recover the situation.

Making for a weather shore   The opposite of running towards a lee shore is to make for a weather shore, even if there is no actual harbour of refuge available. There is nothing so welcome as the natural shelter of land after a worrying spell out in heavy seas; nothing quite as blissful as cruising in calm water, half a mile or so off an attractive coast after long hours spent battling with the helm and the elements. Keep this in mind when considering the options for seeking shelter. If it is not too far to work directly up to windward and tuck under the lee of some land, you may be able to find a snug anchorage until conditions improve, or at least coast along in protected water to a secure harbour of refuge. An obvious advantage of heading for a weather shore is that the sea should become progressively quieter as you approach; with a lee shore, the converse is true.

Heaving-to   In certain circumstances you could decide to sit things out at sea until conditions improve. This strategy is often forced upon fishing boats and sometimes emulated by displacement motor yachts on a longish passage. The trouble with heaving-to under power is that you are continually burning fuel while making virtually no progress towards harbour. You need a generous range and a fair idea of how long the worst of the weather is likely to last.

To make the conscious decision to stay at sea in heavy weather, you also have to be reasonably confident that you and your crew can withstand the strain, and will be able to snatch sufficient food and rest to remain in good shape and therefore in effective control of the boat. Life after force 6 goes on much as normal for professional mariners, albeit in greater discomfort. For most yachtsmen, though, and especially for family crews, being out in heavy weather is an ordeal rather than an inconvenience, and energy reserves can soon drop to a dangerous low.

Heavy weather at night There are various complications about coping with heavy weather at night. The first is largely psychological but can be vital, in that the whole mood of a rough sea often seems much more hostile and lonely in darkness. More practically, it is difficult to steer a safe course at night in heavy weather, when the helmsman is liable to be caught off guard by invisible waves. Navigation may be more tricky, since there is a real danger of mis-identifying lights in a rough sea. Distant flashes can be partially obscured as the boat falls into deep troughs. Fatigue will relentlessly take its toll, especially in the small hours; you can easily find yourself staring blankly at the chart, your eyes unable to focus properly and your faculties dulled from worry, queasiness and lack of sleep.

The skipper should set regular watches, sharing the burdens of steering and navigation as far as possible. It is important that he himself doesn't get too tired and that any navigational slips have a chance of being picked up by someone else. Full participation will also help to keep everyone motivated, reasonably alert, and fully interested in their joint fate.

Cruising Inland

There is a special kind of contrast in making an open water passage to an unknown area, negotiating a safe landfall and then penetrating the very heart of the country by meandering up a river or locking into a canal. I can think of no finer way to see France or the Netherlands than by exploring their fascinating networks of waterways; to have had a good dousing of salt spray *en route* adds a certain piquancy to your travelling. By the same token, most cruising folk feel a definite excitement at that first sniff of sea air after a spell among green fields, and the boat herself almost seems to relish the slightly uneasy sensation of real waves after a few days of being land-locked. There is a kind of schizophrenia about the whole business, because coastal and inland cruising have such disparate characters. When you are slicing through a steep chop a couple of miles off a bleak, wind-swept headland, it can be strange to recall that, an hour or two ago perhaps, you were idling past herds of cows with a tractor overtaking you on the towpath. Coming in the other direction, how blissful to be tucked alongside a rustic canal quay after the tension of trying to identify an enigmatic harbour entrance in a rising sea and deteriorating visibility.

To get the best out of both worlds, you really have to get used to thinking in two distinct modes. Factors which are critical at sea, such as gale warnings, accurate navigation or careful stowage, become less relevant inland. On a canal, you can set off in the morning without listening to a weather forecast or worrying about the tide. Down in the galley it is easy to make coffee or lunch on the move, and you can leave things lying around in the saloon just as you might in your own living room. Yet there are various tricks of the trade to inland cruising, especially on the Continental waterways. (French and Netherlands cruise planning are covered in the last section of this book.)

Tidal streams, currents and sea state are still important in large rivers. When you enter the River Seine, for example, catching a fair or a foul tide will make a considerable difference over the 70 miles up to Rouen. The same is true for the Gironde estuary and the trip to Bordeaux. Along the North Sea coast you have the Westerschelde and the passage up to Antwerp, the Nieuwe Maas to Rotterdam, the Eems between Borkum and Delfzijl, and the Elbe up to Cuxhaven, Brunsbuttel or Hamburg. In all these estuaries streams run up to 5 knots, especially on the ebb, so your time of arrival at the mouth should be worked out carefully. A weather-going current will also kick up nasty steep seas which can be more unpleasant and harder going than open water. As far as anchoring is concerned, fast currents and the threat of wash from passing traffic can make the lower stretches of a large river rather hostile. Neither are you likely to find any spots where it is safe to lie alongside. There may be quays or wharves for coasters or barges, but these are often private and, in any case, somewhat 'heavy duty' for yachts.

The Channel Islands 32 is built by Silva Yates of Jersey and designed by Alan Buchanan and Partners f
both the pleasure and workboat markets. Her sea-kindly semi-displacement hull has a fine Vee entry, roun
bilges forward and flat aft sections. She can be fitted with single or twin engines and the usual options a
Mermaid or Volvo Penta diesels.

A French motor cruiser moored in the attractive upper reaches of the Vilaine River. There is a special satisfacti
in negotiating a safe landfall and then penetrating the very heart of a country by meandering up a ru
waterway.

Further upstream, the bank itself will rarely be safe for berthing alongside, with shoal water and lurking underwater hazards such as rocks, piling or old tree roots. You can sometimes cope with these on a canal or in the peaceful upper reaches of a river, so long as it's possible to edge in gingerly and moor in still water. In a strong current though, going aground or hitting an obstruction is a different matter altogether and can easily result in serious damage to your hull, props or rudders.

Anchoring can be an uneasy business in a fast-flowing river, with the boat inclined to sheer from side to side and a significant risk of dragging when the tide turns. It may be worth trying to find a bay or inlet where you can tuck out of the stream, so keep an eye out for those swirling eddy lines which often separate areas of quieter water from the main current. Many small creeks shoal quite quickly beyond their mouth and you will usually need to anchor just inside the 'shelf' scoured out by the river (see Fig 7.3).

Mooring to two anchors is sound practice in a narrow river, especially if there is any chance of swinging out across a busy fairway. By setting two anchors in line with the tide you greatly reduce your swinging circle, lying to one anchor on the ebb and the other on the flood. I usually find that the most reliable method of mooring is to settle down to the main anchor first and then use the dinghy to carry out the kedge. It is thus fairly easy to place your second anchor accurately and ensure that it has plenty of scope. Alternatively, you can carry out a 'standing' or a 'running' moor (see Chapter 4).

Two likely reasons for wanting to anchor in the lower reaches of a large river are either to wait for a fair tide or because you have run out of daylight. If you arrive off the mouth of an estuary in the late afternoon, you may decide to make a couple of hours' progress upstream before it gets too dark for safe navigation. Strangely enough, it can often be quite difficult to find a safe spot for the night in a large river, especially if the current is fast and you are out in the wilds between towns. Try to anchor in good time if you see somewhere suitable, rather than be forced to stop later by the gathering dusk. Once you

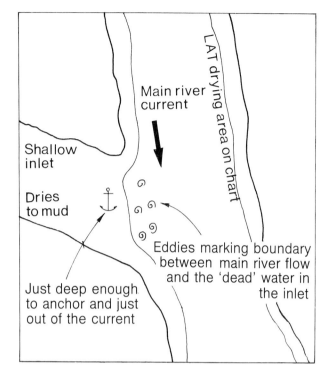

Fig 7.3 *Anchoring near the mouth of a shallow creek.*

are safely anchored, set a bright white riding light for the benefit of any ships or barges on the move in the small hours. Life becomes less hectic once you lock through into non-tidal water, and yet suitable overnight berths can still be widely spaced. In my experience, it is easier to pull up at short notice on the Dutch canals than on the French. The latter are generally more rural and are mainly geared to the needs of commercial traffic, whereas pleasure boats are very much part of the waterways scene in the Netherlands.

One of the hazards of mooring alongside in a narrow canal is having laden barges pass by, however slowly, causing a formidable surge of water which can wrench at your warps and even put you aground. Fig 7.4 illustrates this effect, which is essentially that of a piston moving loosely in a cylinder of fluid. A full barge displaces a huge volume of water, some of which heaps up to form a bow wave and then rushes along either side of her from stem to stern. A yacht lying alongside will first be lifted bodily on this wave, sometimes by well over a foot; she will

Yacht moored in wider part of the canal suffers less surge

Water rushes between barge and canal bank

Piston-in-cylinder effect. Laden barge pushes a large bow wave ahead of her

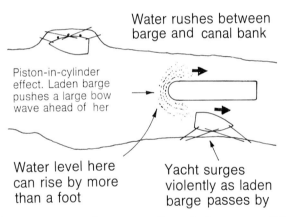

Water level here can rise by more than a foot

Yacht surges violently as laden barge passes by

Fig 7.4 *The displacement effect of a barge travelling in a narrow canal.*

then dip into the trough and be forced in the direction from which the barge has come as the piled-up water tries to find a way through between the ship's side and the bank. Finally there will be a suck-back as the barge moves away, and the yacht will surge in the opposite direction, straining her warps once again. It is possible to sustain considerable damage in this way, especially if moored against a shallow, uneven bank or a rough stone quay.

The risks can be reduced by selecting a comparatively wide stretch in which to moor, making sure that you have a good couple of feet of water under the keel and checking that there are no nasty obstructions nearby. It is a good idea to use springs rather than just a bow and stern line, if any barge traffic is expected. I like to use fairly long warps on a canal, so that the surge restraint acts more or less parallel to the bank. You need to rig plenty of substantial fenders, not just amidships but also right forward on the turn of the bow and well aft on the quarter.

The powerful bow wave surge can be tricky when you meet a laden barge face to face in a narrow canal. You should pass port to port, just as at sea, but the trick is for both vessels to stay near the middle of the canal for as long as possible. Fig 7.5 illustrates the standard technique, which involves heading straight for the bow of an approaching barge until you are very close. The bargee may edge over to his right, but you should only steer to *your* right at the last moment, slipping down the barge's bow wave and close along her port side. If you come to starboard too soon, you'll probably be forced too close to the bank and risk going aground or damaging your

1. Barge edges to the right of centre, but needs to stay in deep water if she is fully laden

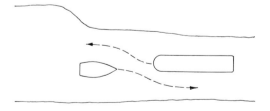

2. Approaching yacht heads straight for the barge's bow until almost the last moment

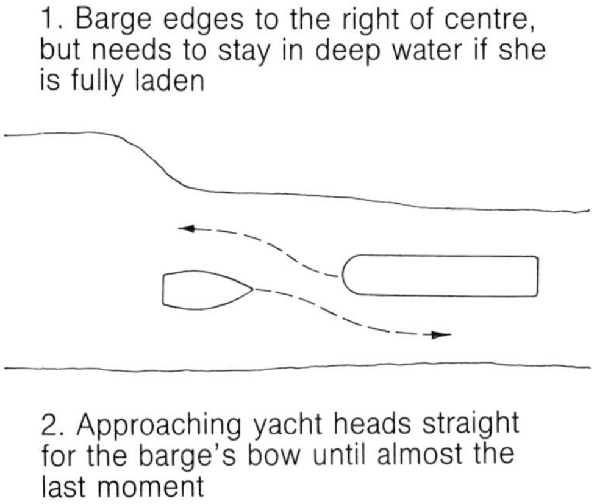

Fig 7.5 *A yacht and a barge passing in a narrow canal.*

he waterways of the Netherlands provide some of the finest cruising grounds in Europe. This boat has found
quiet berth on one of the Friesland canals, tucked well away from the madding crowd.

erngear in the shallow water. As you clear the
arge's stern, come to port towards the centre of the
anal, but be prepared to be pushed off course by the
arbulent thrust of her prop.

On the French rural canals you often come across
ther attractive lay-bys, complete with apparently
nvenient stretches of quay and several handy bol-
rds. You should be circumspect about turning into
ese 'ports', because many are badly silted up once
u leave the main line of the canal (Fig 7.6). Unless
u edge alongside very gently, you can easily push
ell into the soft silt before you realize that you've
n out of water. In fact it may only be when you try
leave that you find yourself stuck fast, especially
the water level in your pound has fallen overnight.
I once nosed alongside an idyllic old quay in one
these basins, way out in the heart of Burgundy.
memorable dinner, a quiet night, but next morn-
g we were absolutely hard aground. The weather
as set fair and I could see us remaining in this
arming spot until the next autumn rains arrived.

1. Tempting looking spot for an
overnight berth. Good quay with
bollards?

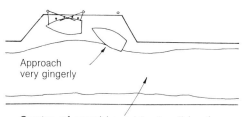

Approach
very gingerly

Centre of canal kept 'dredged' by the
passage of laden barges

2. But many canal 'lay-bys' are
heavily silted up

3. Yacht may be well aground before
her skipper realizes it

Fig 7.6 *Beware of shallow lay-bys when mooring in*
a canal.

165

The eastern sea-lock of the Crinan Canal, on the west coast of Scotland. Sea-locks have an atmosphere of thei own, transitional oases between the unforgiving elements and quieter inland waterways. Some yachtsmen fin canals frustrating, but I have always found them relaxing places, which can provide a welcome interlude fror the harsh milieu of the sea. The Crinan Canal eases the route between the Firth of Clyde and the Western Isle by cutting out the arduous passage round the Mull of Kintyre. The canal has 15 locks and 7 swing bridges.

Our attempts to escape were to no avail. Even an ingenious system of blocks and tackles to a distant elm threatened to uproot the tree rather than pull us clear. In the end, we were rescued with great panache by a passing farmer who kindly towed us off with his tractor.

Locks are very much part and parcel of inland cruising, but it is important to appreciate that negotiating them can be a ponderous and time-consuming business. The wise skipper will do his best to cultivate realistic expectations about the likely daily mileage. Personally, I find locks relaxing places, offering agreeable social interludes in that slow pace of travel which is unique to inland waterways. In the more remote parts of France, lock-keepers' cottages are often picturesque and immaculately kept. The *éclusier* or his wife are usually pleased to pass the time of day with yachtsmen a though, understandably, they do not respond well you are impatient and expect to go charging throug their lock at rally speed or during the lunch brea

In the Netherlands, most locks are automated ai fairly large, but they are still gregarious meetir points where boating people on passage come t gether for half an hour or so before going their se arate ways. If you can savour the whole rigmaro of locking as an entertaining bonus to your cruisir so much the better for your blood pressure. After a if you were to take the Burgundy route throug France from Le Havre to Marseille, you'd have pass through about 240 locks. If you are prone fuming at delays, the chances of reaching the sun Mediterranean in a relaxed frame of mind would pretty slim.

Chapter 8

Incidents and Emergencies

Man Overboard

I will always remember a true story I was once told, by someone who had experienced one of the most alarming of possible boating incidents: falling overboard. Now it can be quite a shock even for a strong swimmer to accidentally slip into a canal on a hot summer afternoon. To lose someone overside at sea is a frightening business that demands considerable discipline if you are to stay calm and make the right sequence of manoeuvres to maximise the chances of recovery. In this case, a Fairline Corniche 31 was cruising at 18 knots a couple of miles off Beachy Head; she was bound for Newhaven, with just the owner and his brother aboard. The owner was helming and his brother, coming out of the wheelhouse into the cockpit, noticed that one of the davit falls was trailing over the stern. He stood on the aft bench-seat to coil in the rope, a rogue wave gave the boat an unexpected lurch, and the conscientious crew suddenly found himself plunged into cold water and engulfed by turbulence. When he came to the surface, luckily unhurt, the Fairline was already some distance away, cutting a relentless track towards Newhaven. The helmsman was unaware of what had happened.

A black moment. Shouting was useless, but the man in the sea yelled loud and long. The Fairline seemed almost hull-down before she eventually began to turn and retrace her path. It felt like an hour, although it was only five minutes, before the familiar hull nosed alongside and the owner's brother was able to climb to safety up the stern ladder. It could, he said, have happened to anyone. A momentary lapse of attention and suddenly his continued existence was hanging by a thread. Since this incident, the Fairline's owner has made a point of practising man-overboard drill for half an hour each month, and he also goes through the routine with every new crew he takes out.

Man-overboard drill seems to be taken more seriously by owners of sailing boats than by motor cruising folk. Perhaps it's because there are more obvious problems in close-quarters manoeuvring under sail, whereas the handling of motor boats is generally assumed to be straightforward, particularly if you have twin engines. Yet there are plenty of traps for the unwary and it is worth giving careful thought to exactly what you would do if *you* lost someone over the side. In fact the first steps are common to both motor and sailing boats: the person who first sees the incident should immediately shout 'Man overboard!' and then throw a lifebuoy towards, but not straight at, the casualty. It is important that one or two lifebuoys should be on the flying bridge, in case only the helmsman is left aboard.

The skipper should, if possible, detail a crew member whose sole duty is to watch the victim and point continually in his direction. The helmsman should note the boat's compass heading as soon as he hears the cry of 'man overboard', mentally working out a reciprocal course which will take the boat back to the casualty. Now comes the area of debate. What is the best kind of manoeuvre to take you back quickly and safely? In sailing, the current vogue is the 'crash stop', which involves coming about immediately, heaving-to, starting the engine and then lowering the headsail to facilitate handling under power. A kind of crash stop might be thought the obvious plan for a motor boat, but going hard astern isn't necessarily the surest way of maintaining full control.

Big-ship practice traditionally involves something called the Williamson Turn (Fig 8.1), designed to bring a vessel onto a reciprocal heading along the line of her original track. If a coxswain received the report 'man overboard to starboard', he would immediately apply full helm to turn to starboard, thus swinging the stern clear of the victim bobbing alongside. Once the heading had come off by 60°, full port helm would be applied until the ship reached the reciprocal of her original heading.

Although a Williamson Turn takes into account the likely rudder response of large ships and their considerable side-slip when turning at speed, there is much to recommend the basic idea for smaller motor boats, whether of heavy or light displacement. In their case the direction of the first swing usually has less to do with which side the casualty went overboard (he will probably be well astern anyway before the helmsman can react) than with the prevailing sea conditions (see Figs 8.2 and 8.3).

What about crash-stopping for motor boats? By going hard astern soon after someone falls overboard, you do at least stay close to them; however this strategy is not much use if, as in the case of the Fairline, the incident is only discovered some time after it happened: then the accuracy of the turn is the most important factor. But the crash-stop has inherent disadvantages even if the helmsman actually sees the man go overboard. It always takes a little while to lose way completely, particularly with a displacement hull, and you still have the problem of getting safely alongside your man. The transverse thrust of a single prop, or the hasty use of two en-

gines, will almost certainly throw the stern askew leaving you awkwardly placed for manoeuvring. There is also the risk that an over-zealous helpsman may bring propeller(s) and casualty perilously close together.

Isn't it preferable to combine turning and coming alongside in one smooth operation, since most boats are best handled when travelling forwards under a reasonable amount of power, with the rudder biting well. My own drill is to carry out the important first steps of throwing out a lifebuoy, appointing a lookout and noting the compass heading. I then throttle back to half-ahead, whether I am in a single or twin-screw boat, and make a standard Williamson Turn. With a twin-screw boat, I might shift the inner engine into neutral—but not astern—for the second part of the turn. Having reached the reciprocal course and sighted the person in the water, I would head back towards him and prepare to come alongside.

Skippers of twin-engine boats might argue that this procedure doesn't make the best use of equipment. Surely you can turn a modern planing hull on a sixpence by running one engine ahead and the other astern? Well, yes and no. In calm weather you can, especially when carrying out a manoeuvre you are prepared for. Pivoting with a sea running is by no means so quick, and if you were running before the sea to start with, you are quite likely to get a wave breaking over your stern in the process. Also, pulling out of a pivot turn accurately is not always easy. You need considerable anticipation, orientation and familiarity with your boat in order to 'get off the roundabout' at the right place. A turn which is too rapid can disorient both helmsman and lookout, and waste valuable time by overshooting.

Of course, getting back to your victim is only the start of your problems. You then have to manoeuvre alongside safely, make contact and somehow have him aboard. Easy enough to say quickly, but verging on the impossible if your casualty has been knocked unconscious or is stupefied with shock and cold. Going alongside poses two distinct questions: do you approach upwind or downwind, and where do you aim to bring him in relation to the boat? Except in gentle conditions, it is usually best to make your

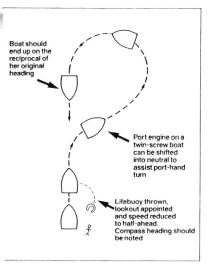

Boat should end up on the reciprocal of her original heading

Port engine on a twin-screw boat can be shifted into neutral to assist port-hand turn

Lifebuoy thrown, lookout appointed and speed reduced to half-ahead. Compass heading should be noted

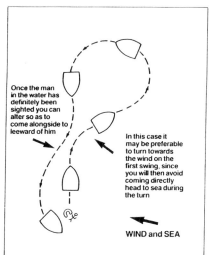

Once the man in the water has definitely been sighted you can alter so as to come alongside to leeward of him

In this case it may be preferable to turn towards the wind on the first swing, since you will then avoid coming directly head to sea during the turn

WIND and SEA

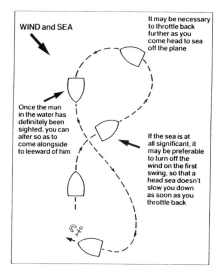

WIND and SEA

It may be necessary to throttle back further as you come head to sea off the plane

Once the man in the water has definitely been sighted, you can alter so as to come alongside to leeward of him

If the sea is at all significant, it may be preferable to turn off the wind on the first swing, so that a head sea doesn't slow you down as soon as you throttle back

Fig 8.1 *The standard Williamson Turn, recommended even for twin-crew boats.*

Fig 8.2 *A modified Williamson Turn, bringing the boat to leeward.*

Fig 8.3 *Another modified Williamson Turn for use when the casualty is downwind.*

final approach with the wind nicely on one bow, so that you stay to leeward of the casualty (see Figs 8.2 and 8.3) avoiding the risk of being blown over him while you are trying to make contact. You then have the flexibility to close with or sheer off your target by using the wind as a controlling force.

I would aim to fetch the casualty alongside the cockpit if you have one, or somewhere amidships if you don't. Sending what remains of your crew right forward is an added risk—one man in the water is quite enough—and the motion amidships is usually easier for working. But don't let the casualty come too far aft until you have made contact and finished with the engines. Your props will pose a threat, especially if there is any sea running.

The important next step is to get the casualty permanently attached to the boat so that you don't lose him again. A bowline round the armpits and chest is usually the best plan: pass him a line if he is able to tie the knot himself, or else somehow reach over and make fast for him. Secure the other end of the safety line aboard. It is sound practice to keep a suitable heaving line hung up somewhere handy in the cockpit for just this eventuality, a line which is light enough to throw, strong enough to take a man's weight, and thick enough not to bite into him too much when the strain comes on.

Now to get your man back aboard. Many modern boats have a stern ladder or boarding platform, so this is the obvious place to manoeuvre him for lifting out. It is important to turn the engines off, rather than keep them idling in neutral. But you need to be very careful when using a stern ladder or platform at sea, because it doesn't take much pitching to turn these structures into lethal weapons. If you don't have a permanent stern ladder, try using a swimming or a harbour ladder. All boats ought to have some system by which you can climb aboard from the water but, if you've never quite got around to fixing something up, other tricks will have to be employed. At all times keep the safety line attached to the yacht.

Launching the dinghy is one option so long as there is not too much sea running, because it's comparatively easy to haul someone into an inflatable and transfer him aboard from there. You might even consider inflating your liferaft for this purpose if your dinghy isn't handy and the casualty is showing

signs of losing consciousness or becoming danger-
ously cold. Dinghy davits, if they are sturdy enough,
can be used to lift a man bodily over the side. A
decent-sized anchor winch could also save the day if
you were short-handed, particularly if your victim
was able to help himself and get a foothold in a
bowline. A block and tackle rigged from a strong
point on the wheelhouse roof is another possible
makeshift.

People often ask if you should ever send someone
else into the water to help a man overboard. I would
generally caution against this, except as a last resort
if the casualty is injured or starting to lose strength
and you can't otherwise get a line round him. Even
then, you need to have a foolproof way of getting
both crew members back on board. One person in
the water is one problem—two down there is a hell
of a situation of more than twice the proportions.

When I was talking to the owner of the Fairline
and his brother, I couldn't decide who'd had the
greatest shock—the brother in the sea, watching the
boat disappearing at 18 knots, or the owner on suddenly discovering that he was the only person
aboard. The incident had certainly made them both
more cautious. It is rather a strange paradox that,
to the landsman, falling overboard probably seems
the most obvious danger in going afloat, but most
boating people hardly ever contemplate the possibility.

Opinions on man-overboard drill differ widely and
there are arguments for and against most procedures. However, three practical points seem to me
to be quite clear.
—It is important to devise some sort of drill with
  which you feel comfortable, and to practise it regularly. The existence of a familiar routine will help
  crews stay calm in an emergency.
—It is vital that your boat has an effective boarding
  ladder or platform of some kind that can be used
  from the water, even if it isn't permanently
  mounted.
—Every skipper should work out how he would lift
  the dead weight of a soggy, exhausted man from
  the sea if he ever had to. He should also make sure
  that each of his crew understands exactly what

the procedure would be and where any necessary
equipment is stowed.

Fire on board

This is one of the most frightening accidents a
yachtsman can experience. Fortunately, the
thoughtful design of most modern galley and engine
installations helps keep the risks to a minimum,
but it is vital to be well prepared to fight a blaze
should the worst happen. The three most common
causes of fire are flare-ups in the galley, bottled gas
leaks and petrol (gasoline) leaks. Galley fires are
usually best tackled with a large fire blanket, which
should be mounted near and to one side of the stove
(rather than behind or over it) so that a flare-up is
unlikely to prevent access to the blanket. Lacking a
proper fire blanket, you can improvise with a large
towel or similar heavy cloth soaked in water.

Fire extinguishers should be as large and numerous as you can reasonably accommodate. If you have
ever attended a fire-fighting demonstration, one of
the first things that will have struck you is how
quickly an ordinary household fire extinguisher can
run out and how puny it seems in the face of any
blaze which is well alight. The dry powder type is
the most versatile and each separate compartment
in the boat should have its own, with a total of at
least two except in very small boats. The minimum
capacity of any extinguisher aboard a boat should
be $1\frac{1}{2}$kg although one of at least $2\frac{1}{2}$kg should be readily accessible from the cockpit, so that anyone out-
side can begin to fight a fire which has started inside.

Avoid throwing water on burning liquids (especially fuel or cooking oil) or on electrical fires. Aboard
larger motor yachts there is much to be said for fitting an automatic extinguishing system in the engine compartment; these systems generally use
either CO_2 or BCF gas, so that the engines and machinery do not suffer more damage from the extinguisher than from the actual fire. It is important to
appreciate that BCF gives off toxic fumes which can
be dangerous in a confined space, and for the accommodation areas this kind of extinguisher is therefore
less suitable than the dry powder or foam types. The

boat should be allowed to ventilate once the fire is out.

Burns represent one of the most serious classes of injury for anyone unable to obtain medical assistance quickly. Any burns should be cooled instantly by the liberal application of cold water. Limbs can be immersed in a bucket of cold water and kept there for at least ten minutes, while burns to the head or body can be cooled by applying a large thick pad kept soaked in cold water. Because the shock reaction to apparently quite minor burns can be surprisingly severe, anti-shock precautions should be taken with anyone who has experienced burns. Lay the patient down with his head low and feet raised, and then move him as little as possible. Loosen any tight clothing and keep him warm by laying a blanket or sleeping bag quilt loosely over him. Give nothing by mouth in the first instance, particularly not alcohol. In the case of anything more than a minor burn, try and reach medical assistance as soon as possible.

The prevention of fire is clearly a vital aspect of safety at sea and every skipper should always be aware of the risks associated with the various fuels used aboard his boat. Bottled gas and petrol are the high-risk contenders, although diesel fuel is obviously flammable if it reaches a sufficiently high temperature, or is feeding a fire. All fuel supply piping needs to be impeccably installed and checked regularly for signs of strain, leaks or fatigue. Gas bottles must be stowed in their own vented locker outside the accommodation and you should always switch off at the bottle whenever the galley is not in use, especially at sea.

Even diesel powered boats may carry an outboard motor with its own supply of petrol. You need to take great care when filling an outboard fuel tank from a jerrycan, and the best place to do this is with the motor clamped to a stowage bracket which is permanently fixed to your guard-rail or stern. Any spillage will then drain over the side and petrol fumes will be prevented from escaping below, where they can lurk for a surprisingly long time. It always amazes me that more boats are not fitted with gas detectors, which can usually pick up very small traces of butane, propane or petrol. Gas detectors are comparatively inexpensive compared with the numerous other pieces of sophisticated electronic equipment which are installed nowadays as a matter of course. Ideally, you should fit a separate detector head in each bilge compartment and one in the engine space.

Seasickness

Despite the sophistication of modern production boats, safe passage-making still depends largely upon the good seamanship and sound judgment of skipper and crew. Hardware can be undermined at a stroke if its operators are below par. Seasickness remains a significant contributory factor to many boating incidents, and it is for this reason that I have included some thoughts on the subject. Anyone who has suffered from *mal de mer*, and that includes most of us at one time or another, will know how debilitating the symptoms can be and how quickly a sufferer ceases to take any real interest in what is happening around him.

Any skipper planning to go to sea should seriously consider the possible implications of seasickness, because even the early symptoms can turn an apparently efficient crew into a liability in a very short time. It is also important to realize that it is more 'normal' to experience queasiness than it is to be immune, so it's odds-on that a certain proportion of any crew will be subject to *mal de mer*, especially if conditions start to get lively.

There are various old wives' cures, new drugs are developed and tried out, and several homoeopathic and pressure-point remedies are now on the market. Yet, like much of medicine, the treatment of seasickness is partly a hit-and-miss affair, with any given remedy effective for some individuals and seemingly useless for others. Prevention is the vital object in most cases, and this is what most of the proprietary drugs aim to do. In my experience, anyone who is badly seasick is most unlikely to start feeling better until the boat arrives in the calm waters of a harbour and the prospect of dry land is reassuringly imminent. Exceptions sometimes occur on long passages, say of three or four days, when the sufferer may become accustomed to the motion after a day or two and acquire 'sea legs'. Several key factors seem to have an important bearing on most people's susceptibility.

Balance and orientation

One of the surest methods of making inexperienced crew feel seasick is to ask them to go below when under way, to make a cup of coffee, prepare lunch or simply to look at the chart. Exactly what triggers the sensation of nausea is difficult to say, but sufferers usually complain that, having lost sight of the horizon, they cannot then orientate themselves as the boat pitches and rolls. There is an apparent conflict between what the inner ear balance mechanism is telling them, i.e. that they are definitely on the move, and what their eyes deduce from the immediate surroundings down below. This conflict is gradually reduced as one becomes acclimatized to the motion of a particular boat. The brain and sense of balance begin to untangle the complex pattern of pitching and rolling and can therefore attempt to predict what will happen next. Anyone new to boating will be starting from scratch in this respect and may need some while to get their sea legs. Even quite seasoned crew are apt to feel uncertain for the first day or two of a cruise. Someone who is very familiar with the motion of one particular boat and normally not prone to seasickness, may feel queasy in a different boat for the first time.

Preventives

A skipper should do everything possible to reduce the risk of seasickness by making careful preparations before a passage, so that nobody has to spend any longer than necessary at the chart table or in the galley. For relatively short passages the bulk of the navigation should be worked out before leaving. Lunch should also be prepared beforehand.

A stuffy wheelhouse or cabin, permeated with just a hint of diesel, greatly increases the risk of queasiness. It is a good idea to keep ports or windows open

wherever possible, especially if anyone does need to linger below for any reason. In choppy weather, keep a close eye on anyone who has to go outside for fresh air. Someone who is beginning to feel definitely seasick will probably become careless about holding on as they move about the boat. The pervasive lethargy and state of lassitude associated with *mal de mer* can make crew more vulnerable to dangers such as falling overboard.

Seeking fresh air introduces the problem of keeping warm. It is all too easy to become cold at sea, and this in itself will increase one's susceptibility to seasickness. It is quite normal for someone who is feeling queasy to go outside for a breath of air, but make sure that they don't become chilled by sitting for too long in a spray-drenched cockpit. If seasickness takes a real hold, it is important to keep the patient warm, tucked up in a bunk with a bucket close to hand, and taking small quantities of fluid from time to time.

Be careful about what you eat and drink before a longish passage. If possible, avoid fatty or acidic foods for several days before going to sea. It makes sense to have a good breakfast before setting off, although cooking a big fry-up is a reliable way to seal your crew's fate. Cereals are quite safe, and so is hot porridge if you like it. Boiled eggs and toast make a fairly innocuous combination, but orange juice can be risky. Alcohol the evening before substantially increases the risk of seasickness next day. Red wine tends to be the worst offender, but I have much sympathy for the argument that a cheerless dinner is a high price to pay for 'shaving the chances of the morrow'. Once on passage, frequent nibbles of food are usually easier on the digestion than full-scale meals.

There is evidence that, for some sufferers, seasickness can be wholly or partially psychosomatic i.e. real physical symptoms are induced by psychological factors such as stress. It is an unfortunate vicious circle that newcomers to boating are sometimes stressed by the very idea of becoming seasick and therefore increase their chances of succumbing. A relatively inexperienced skipper, with only his family aboard, will be aware of plenty of potential for stress, so it is especially important that such a crew should only undertake passages which are well within their joint competence. Successful and enjoyable passages, however modest, will bolster confidence and help reduce stress for the next time out.

Remedies

If you find a remedy which works for you, the best thing to do is use it early and stick to it. Stugeron℗ has now established a good reputation, but some people respond well to antihistamines such as Dramamine℗ or Marzine℗. Any of the anti-seasickness pills should be taken well before you go to sea, while you are feeling on top form. If possible, start the dose the evening before a passage, then keep taking it at the recommended intervals. Some people have had great success with those behind-the-ear stick-on pads. Heaven knows how they work, but try and get hold of some if you've had no success with pills.

Coping with Fog

Many yachtsmen, if asked about the kind of conditions they like least at sea, will reply unhesitatingly 'fog'—dryly referred to by the Collision Regulations as 'restricted visibility'. I recall one very murky trip across the English Channel when we had set out expecting occasional fog patches and found one which followed us all the way across. Somewhere in mid-Channel, having turned the engine off for a few minutes to listen for ships, we were overtaken by another motor yacht. We couldn't see anything, only hear the hiss of a bow wave and the rumble of exhausts. She was close, less than 200 yards probably, and seemed to be travelling fast. She was not sounding a fog signal and I wondered whether her navigator had seen us as a blip on a radar screen. It appeared to be a case of traditional seamen's lore being disregarded, unless the passer-by was out in clear sunshine while we were smothered in our own personal gloom.

Slow down at once is the cardinal rule in fog, and yet how slow is slow? A planing boat which normally slips along at 15 or 20 knots may *feel* to be

dawdling when forced to travel at 8 knots. Yet this is pretty brisk in absolute terms and represents a respectable cruising speed for a displacement boat. The important figure is the speed at which you and another vessel may be coming close together. Given a real pea-souper, you might need to throttle back to less than 3 knots before you could be said, in the words of Regulation 19, to be 'proceeding at a safe speed adapted to the prevailing circumstances and conditions of restricted visibility'.

Here is an exact parallel to the Highway Code, i.e. go slowly enough to be able to pull up within the distance you can see to be clear. Potential targets are ships and other boats, land, buoys and beacons, lobster-pot markers and miscellaneous floating debris. If you are out in open water, clear of shipping routes, the last two items probably represent the most significant hazard, and you need to be moving slowly enough either to take avoiding action or to minimize the risk of hull or prop damage if you do hit something. There is also a certain psychological benefit in travelling gingerly: somehow the situation seems less tense and more under control.

Even if you have an apparently reliable radar, you should still use the circle-of-vision criterion to determine your speed. Radar will not pick up a large baulk of timber or a submerged packing case, common enough chunks of litter at sea and both able to inflict considerable damage if struck at speed. Remember to hoist your radar reflector if it's not a permanent fixture, making sure that it hangs in the 'rain-catching' position and not point up. If the visibility is very poor and the sea calm, get one of your crew togged up in oilskins and onto the foredeck as a lookout. It's a good idea to prearrange some hand signals for steering clear of debris and for indicating the direction of ships' foghorns. Don't forget to keep an eye out back over your shoulder as well as ahead.

Make sure that you sound the appropriate fog signals—one long blast at least every two minutes for a motor vessel under way, two long blasts if stopped. A sailing vessel sounds one long blast followed by two shorts, at least every two minutes (see Collision Regulation 35). The aerosol type of horn is generally the most effective, but you need to have a good supply of spare canisters: they run down quickly when used in anger. While you are listening for fog signals, bear in mind that even a light breeze has a marked effect on the direction of audibility.

If you do hear a ship's foghorn getting closer, stop the engines and listen carefully over a number of blasts. Use the hand compass to take rough bearings of the ship—I say rough, because sound can travel in peculiar ways in fog and you can't always pinpoint its origin. If the ship seems very close, keep sounding your own horn, try to stay cool and don't take avoiding action unless you are sure of making a safe move. Statistically, in the absence of information to the contrary, you are just as safe where you are as somewhere else nearby, and there's always a chance that you are being watched on a radar screen. If you feel like a sitting duck and can't keep still, there is something to be said for motoring away from the signal at a good speed, while still trying to work out in which direction the other ship is moving.

In extremis, if you find yourself among really heavy traffic in fog, you must be prepared for sudden collision, however statistically unlikely this can be shown to be! Have the liferaft or dinghy clear for launching and see that everyone is wearing warm clothes, oilskins and lifejackets. A waterproof 'panic bag' is a wise precaution, packed ready with red flares, easy food such as chocolate and fruit, plastic bottles of drinking water, and an emergency radio if you have one. If you suddenly see a huge steel bow slicing out of the murk, there won't be much time for gathering useful items of gear together.

A key rule in fog is to take special care with navigation. Note the time and position at which you reduce speed and keep your reckoning worked up every half hour thereafter, calculating new courses to steer as necessary. Carefully record and plot any sustained alterations to avoid ships, and don't forget that a cross-tide of 1 knot has considerable significance if you are only making 3 or 4. I always find it useful to pencil likely shipping tracks on the chart. *Lanes* as such don't exist offshore, but Separation Zones do—in congested areas or off certain 'waypoint' headlands. Often it is reasonable to join up two Zones on the chart, assuming that ships will travel in straight lines between them. There is a good example in the west part of the English Channel; if you connect the Ushant Separation Zones with those near the Channel Light Vessel, the resulting 'lanes' give a fair idea of where to expect shipping and from what direction.

Fog is apt to induce a curious sense of unreality. Your imagination can easily start playing tricks and it often takes a determined discipline to accept that nothing has changed navigationally—you just can't see anything. At night the eeriness seems ten times worse, even though the lack of light makes precious little difference in a thick fog. But never forget that your best estimate of position comes from your workings on the chart, and from your Decca, Loran or sat-nav if you have one. Don't alter course for ghostly dangers without a rational reason. Most navigators have had the experience of 'feeling' that they were being set too close to a headland, or of 'hearing' waves breaking against cliffs when their boat was clearly miles offshore.

Your echo-sounder can provide useful information near a shelving coast, or it can simply confirm that you have plenty of water under the keel when you imagine that you are just about to run aground. However, don't try to use an echo-sounder too precisely at sea. Soundings figures are often well spaced on the chart and depth gradients fairly slight. In any case, moderately priced echo-sounders are not always very accurate in deep water, and you've got that tricky problem of reducing readings to chart datum using an uncertain rise of tide.

The visibility information in shipping forecasts is often given less attention than it deserves, and the full implications of that short phrase 'moderate becoming poor later' can be overlooked in the scramble to take note of lows and highs and wind forces. Yet fog can be far more harrowing than a stiff blow, especially where you are enclosed in a wheelhouse and the engine noise prevents you from listening out effectively. It might have been Dr Johnson who said that the surest way of avoiding marital argument was to stay single. By the same token, the best advice for dealing with fog is to keep out of it wherever possible.

Appendix 1

Terms of Agreement for Construction of a New Craft

Specification

1. The Builders will build and the Purchaser will buy the craft ("the craft") described in the specification and drawings ("the specification") annexed to this agreement. The Builders will construct the craft in compliance with the specification. The Purchaser and/or his authorised agent shall have the right to reject all workmanship, materials and/or equipment which is not in compliance with the requirements set out in the specification. Such rejection shall be ineffective unless confirmed promptly to the Builders in writing in accordance with clause 15.

Modifications or additions

2. Any modification or additions to the specification shall not form part of this agreement until confirmed by both parties in writing.

Price and instalments

3.1 The price of the craft, and the stages at which it shall be paid by the Purchaser to the Builders, shall be as stated at the commencement of this agreement.

Price variation clause

3.2 If so required by the Builders, the price stated shall be increased by the addition thereto of such percentage of each instalment (other than the first) as is equal to the percentage increase in the figure at which the Index of Retail Prices stands at the date upon which the instalment falls due over the figure at which the index stood at the date of this agreement. Further, the Builders may require the Purchaser to pay any increased costs resulting from a change in law or regulation occurring or announced between the date of this agreement and the final instalment falling due. However:

(a) no account shall be taken of increases in the price which would not have been chargeable but for the failure of the Builders to proceed with the construction of the craft with reasonable despatch;

(b) if there is a material change in the basis of compiling the Index of Retail Prices published by the Department of Employment (or by any government department upon which duties in connection with the Index shall have devolved) or if that Index is discontinued, price adjustments shall be based on some other index to be agreed from time to time by the SBBNF and the RYA;

(c) to the extent that the Builders do not make an increase when demanding an earlier instalment, the entire amount of the increase shall be payable with the final instalment.

Delivery date and place

4.1 The Builders shall deliver the craft, completed in compliance with the specification, to the Purchaser or his agent by the date and at the place stated in this agreement, but subject to prior signature of the satisfaction note herein. This delivery date shall be deferred if completion is delayed due to modifications or additions to the specification or any cause whatsoever (including delay by suppliers in delivering equipment) outside the control of the Builders.

4.2 If all or any of the materials or equipment built in to the craft or appropriated to this agreement shall be seriously damaged by any cause whatever, the delivery date stated herein shall be deferred for such time as is necessary for the Builders to reinstate the work and to purchase and obtain delivery of materials or equipment in substitution for those damaged.

Builders' failure to proceed

5. If the Builders fail without reasonable cause to proceed with the construction of the craft with reasonable despatch, the Purchaser shall be at liberty to remove the craft and such materials and equipment as have been purchased or appropriated by the Builders for construction of the craft, provided that payments made or tendered by the Purchaser to the Builders are at least equivalent to the cost to the Builders of the goods to be removed (including the Builders' current profit margins). If the craft is at such stage of construction that it is impracticable to remove it, the Purchaser shall be entitled to employ alternative labour and materials to proceed with the construction of the craft (and to exercise all necessary rights of access to the Builders' premises during their normal business hours), but only as far as is necessary to enable the craft to be removed. Such rights shall be without prejudice to any other rights that the Purchaser may have.

Access to craft and Builders' premises

6. Subject to the prior consent of the Builders, the Purchaser and/or his authorised agent shall have free and reasonable access to the craft and to the materials and equipment to be used in the craft, for the purpose of inspection at any time during the normal business hours of the Builders' establishment. Such consent shall not be unreasonably withheld but may be granted on terms that the Purchaser or his agent is accompanied by a representative of the Builders. Such right of access shall extend only to those parts of the Builders' premises necessary for the purpose of such inspection. If the Purchaser or his agent shall for that or any other purpose use any part of the Builders' premises and/or facilities, and whether by invitation or otherwise, he shall do so at his own risk, unless any injury or damage to person or property is caused by or results from the negligence or any deliberate act of the Builders or of those for whom they are responsible.

Acceptance trial

7.1 Not less than 28 days in advance (unless a shorter time be agreed by the parties), the Builders shall notify the Purchaser in writing that the craft will be ready for an acceptance trial on a stated date. The Purchaser or his authorised agent shall present himself within 7 days after that date, at an agreed time, to accompany the Builders or their representative upon an acceptance trial lasting not more than the duration stated in this agreement (such acceptance trial to be at the Builders' expense). If the Purchaser or his authorised agent shall fail to so present himself, then at the end of such 7 day period, the acceptance trial shall be deemed to have taken place.

7.2. It at the end of such acceptance trial the Purchaser or his agent shall for good cause refuse to accept the craft until faults have been rectified, then the Builders shall rectify the same, and if necessary a second trial shall be held in accordance with the provisions of sub-clause 7.1.

7.3. At the satisfactory conclusion of the acceptance trial or, as the case may be, after satisfactory rectification of any faults, the Purchaser or his agent shall sign the satisfaction note contained in this agreement. The final instalment shall become payable immediately upon signature of such note or upon unreasonable failure or refusal to sign. If the Purchaser or his agent shall fail to present himself within the 7 day period mentioned in sub-clause 7.1, the final instalment shall become payable at the end of such period.

7.4. If the Purchaser shall fail to take delivery of the craft within 28 days of the final instalment falling due, the Builders may thereafter require him to pay reasonable mooring or storage charges until he does so.

Statutory rights of Purchaser
8. The craft and all materials and equipment are supplied with the benefit of the undertakings (particularly as to conformity of goods with description or sample, and as to their quality or fitness for a particular purpose) which are implied by the Sale of Goods Act 1893 as amended. Nothing in this agreement shall affect those statutory rights.

Insurance
9. The craft and all materials and equipment supplied or installed by the Builders which are from time to time intended for the craft and within the premises of the Builders shall be insured by them. Such insurance shall be at Lloyds or with an insurance company belonging to the British Insurance Association, against all Builders' Risks in accordance with "Institute Clauses for Builders' Risks amended for Yacht and Motor Boat" until delivery. In the event of the craft, equipment or materials sustaining damage at any time before delivery, any monies received in respect of the insurance shall be applied by the Builders in making good the damage during ordinary working hours in a reasonable and workmanlike manner. However, if the Builders cannot reasonably be expected to make good such damage, then unless this agreement is determined under sub-clause 10.1 or 10.2 they shall pay to the Purchaser the monies so received (but not so as to exceed the instalments then paid by the Purchaser). The Purchaser shall not on account of the said damage or repair be entitled to reject or to make any objection to the craft, equipment or materials, or to make any claim in respect of any resultant depreciation in its or their value or utility.
   The insurance liability of the Builders under this clause shall cease upon delivery of the craft to the Purchaser.

Termination of agreement in event of damage
10.1. Notwithstanding the foregoing, the Builders may in their discretion elect either to fulfil or to determine this agreement if from any cause (other than the negligence or any deliberate act of the Builders or of those for whom they are responsible) and at any time:
(a) the craft shall become a total loss or be deemed to be a constructive, arranged or compromised total loss, or
(b) the Builders' premises, plant, machinery, equipment or any of them shall be seriously damaged so as to make it impracticable for the Builders to complete the craft.

If the Builders shall elect to determine this agreement, they shall forthwith refund to the Purchaser any instalments of the purchase price received by them. This agreement will thereupon be determined in all respects as if it had been duly completed and the Purchaser shall have no further right to claim on the Builders.

10.2. If by reason of serious damage to the Builders' premises, plant or machinery, or to the craft, its equipment or the materials intended for it, the craft cannot be delivered within a reasonable time after the delivery date stated herein (as deferred under sub-clause 4.2 where necessary), the Purchaser may determine this agreement. The Builders shall thereupon refund to the Purchaser any instalments of the purchase price received by them and thereupon this agreement will be determined in all respects and neither party shall have any further right to claim on the other.

Passing of property in craft etc.
11. The craft and/or all materials and equipment purchased or appropriated from time to time by the Builders specifically for its construction (whether in their premises, water or elsewhere) shall become the property of the Purchaser upon the payment of the first instalment under this agreement or (if it be later) upon the date of the said purchase or appropriation. The Builders shall, however, have a lien upon the craft, materials and equipment for recovery of all sums due (whether invoiced or not) under the terms of this agreement or any variation or modification thereof. Any materials or equipment rejected by the Purchaser shall forthwith re-vest in the Builders.

Unpaid instalments
12. If any instalment shall remain unpaid for 28 days after notice has been given to the Purchaser by registered or recorded delivery post, the Builders shall be entitled to interest at 3% above the Bank of England's minimum lending rate for the time being (calculated from the date when the Builders first issued an invoice or other written request for payment of the instalment). After a further period of 28 days the Builders shall be at liberty to sell the craft as it then lies, or may complete and sell the craft after completion. On such re-sale the Purchaser shall be refunded any instalments previously paid, subject to deduction therefrom of any loss suffered by the Builders on the re-sale.

Copyright etc.
13. Any copyright or similar protection in all drawings, specifications and plans prepared by the Builders or their architects shall remain the property of the Builders.

Bankruptcy etc. of Purchaser
14. The Builders shall have the right to terminate this agreement by notice in writing in the event of the Purchaser becoming bankrupt or entering into any composition or arrangement with his creditors or if, being a company, it shall enter into liquidation (otherwise than for the purpose of amalgamation or reconstruction) or any arrangement with its creditors, or shall have a receiver appointed of the whole or any part of its property.

Arbitration
16. All disputes arising out of or in connection with this agreement shall be submitted to a single arbitrator to be appointed, in default of agreement, by the President of the SBBNF and the Chairman of the Council of the RYA and the provisions of the Arbitration Act 1950 shall apply.

Appendix 2

Foreign Cruise Planning

The Netherlands

The Netherlands offer some of the most varied and fascinating cruising in Europe, especially for motor yachts. Because the whole country is geared to travelling by water the needs of boating people are provided for as a matter of course, yet in a delightfully low-key way. Dutch yacht havens are friendly, clean and tidy, moderately priced, and administered without fuss. The buoyage is excellent both along the coast and in the estuaries and rivers. Locks and canal bridges are operated with great efficiency and a minimum of delay.

If you study the chart of the southern North Sea, you will see that the Dutch coastline extends for about 200 miles, from the Westerschelde estuary in the southwest to the mouth of the River Ems in the northeast. The whole frontage is flat, featureless and low-lying, and can be extremely enigmatic from seaward, although the inshore shipping buoys provide useful clues for those making a direct landfall. There are comparatively few coastal harbours and points of entry, so the natural pattern of cruising is to penetrate the Dutch sea defences at one of these strategic gates and then to meander inland for a while before emerging into the North Sea again further along. In fact you need not emerge at all, since it is quite possible to traverse the Netherlands by a selection of waterways routes, from Flushing all the way up to Delfzijl.

One of the great advantages of waterways cruising is that you are not too constrained by weather. Progress can usually be made even in the foulest conditions, although the wider sections of the canalized rivers can be pretty choppy in fresh winds. You don't really need any special equipment other than plenty of large fenders and a good selection of warps. If you can manage to find room for a couple of folding bikes, so much the better. Holland's flat landscape is ideal

for cycling and it is interesting to be able to explore some of the interior on two wheels.

The Dutch cost of living is now on a par with Britain's, so there is no longer the incentive to load up to the gunwales with stores. Eurocheques provide the easiest method of obtaining currency and are readily accepted. There are plenty of alongside fuelling stations on the busier canals, although in the more rural areas it is wise to top up whenever a convenient opportunity arises.

We have always found early July a good time for cruising the Netherlands. It is sufficiently well into the season for a chance of some reasonable weather on the outward passage, but early enough to avoid the main European summer holiday period. Returning, July is often a better month than August for working back down the English Channel.

A one-week cruise

Such a trip is feasible from the East Coast ports between say Great Yarmouth and Dover. From Yarmouth or Lowestoft it is a little over 100 miles to IJmuiden, from where the Noordzee Canal will take you the 18 miles or so to Amsterdam. With a couple of days in Amsterdam and a day allowed for bad weather, you should just have time for a quick foray into the southern part of the IJsselmeer, maybe to one of the rather quaint harbours on the west side— Volendam, Edam, or Hoorn. For boats based further into the Thames Estuary, say between Harwich and the River Crouch, IJmuiden involves a somewhat longer passage, nearly 130 miles ENE from Harwich and 145 miles from the Crouch. For a one-week cruise it would therefore be easier to head across to Vlissingen (Flushing), on the north shore of the Westerschelde, which lies a more modest 95 miles ESE from Harwich and about 105 miles from the Crouch.

At Flushing you enter the attractive canal which cuts across Walcheren to Veere, via the old market town of Middelburg. You can traverse this short waterway in an afternoon, and the yacht haven at Veere is a delightful spot in which to spend a couple of lazy days. Then you might explore some of the anchorages and small harbours of the Veerse Meer, a picturesque man-made lake some 10 miles long formed by the construction of the Veersedam.

From Dover or Ramsgate you can just reach Veere in a week's cruise by crossing to Calais or Dunkirk and then making a coastal leg along to Flushing, possibly via Ostend. It is about 75 miles from Calais to Flushing and 55 miles from Dunkirk. The coastline is rather bleak and has various off-lying banks and shoals, but the shipping channel is well buoyed and the pilotage straightforward in reasonable visibility.

When planning a landfall on the southern part of the Dutch coast, note that the only feasible points of entry between IJmuiden and Flushing are at the Hook of Holland, which is a major shipping route for Europoort and Rotterdam, and via the Haringvliet-sluizen between Goeree and Voorne, a much shallower approach which is not recommended in fresh west or northwest winds. Although there is a lock through the Oosterschelde storm barrage at Roompotsluis, the whole area either side of this massive construction is pretty hostile for yachts, with fast currents and submerged dangers associated with the building works.

Yachts based a little way up the south side of the Thames estuary, below the Isle of Sheppey say, can just about fit in a cruise to Middelburg in a week, provided that the weather stays fair. From the Solent it takes at least 10 days to visit Dutch waters, although a fortnight is a more realistic minimum.

Two- or three-week cruises

Solent yachts with two or three weeks to spare can realistically plan a cruise to Holland, but much will depend on how quickly you can press on up-Channel and through the Dover Straits. By making longish day passages with a reasonable cruising speed, you could reach Veere in three days, weather permitting. The first leg might be from the Solent to Dover, or maybe to Boulogne, either of which would take about $7\frac{1}{2}$ hours at 15 knots. You could break this haul into two days by calling at Brighton or Newhaven. The choice between Dover or Boulogne is really a question of where you would rather negotiate the shipping lanes, and my own preference is usually the short hop across from Dover to a position about $2\frac{1}{2}$ miles off Cap Blanc-Nez. From here, whether you have come from Dover or Boulogne, it is a little over 50 miles along the French and Belgian coasts to Ostend, so that Dover or Boulogne to Ostend would take about 5 hours at 15 knots.

From Ostend to Flushing is not quite 30 miles, a pleasant morning run, so that you could lock into the Walcheren Canal and reach Veere on the afternoon of the third day. If you assume a similar schedule for the return trip, and take out two days for bad weather, you will have set aside eight days for getting to Veere and back. This means that you can enjoy six days in Dutch waters during a fortnight's holiday, and 13 days with three weeks. It would be a pity to miss a day in Veere, so a fortnight's holiday effectively leaves you five days' onward cruising, and three weeks allows you 12 days. In five days, by pressing on steadily, you can get to Rotterdam or Dordrecht and back with a day in hand. Your first inland passage might be Veere to Willemstad via the Veerse Meer, Oosterschelde, Keeten, Mastgat Krammer and Volkerak. Willemstad is a charming spot and worth a morning stroll before you carry on for Dordrecht by way of Hollandsch Diep and Dordtsche Kil. From Dordrecht you can continue towards Rotterdam via the Noord and the Nieuwe Maas.

There is a pleasant yacht haven on the outskirts of Rotterdam at IJsselmonde, opposite the entrance to the Hollandsche IJssel waterway. This quiet basin is sheltered from the river wash and has a friendly yacht club with a bar and good facilities. Further down the Nieuwe Maas, $\frac{3}{4}$ mile below the Willemsbrug, there is another yacht basin on the north bank known as the Veerhaven. This is not quite so peace-

The waterways of the Netherlands provide some of the finest cruising grounds in Europe. There are countless hideaways for a boat owner to explore, whether out in the country or in the backwaters of towns and cities.

ful as the IJsselmonde, but it is handy for the centre of Rotterdam. An alternative to returning to Veere by the same route is to continue down the Nieuwe Maas through Rotterdam and then to emerge into the North Sea at the Hook of Holland. This is an interesting trip if, like me, you are fascinated by large ports, docklands and all the associated bustle of activity.

Solent yachts will need three weeks to cruise as far as Amsterdam and back. There are various ways to reach this intriguing city and you can save time, weather permitting, by making either the outward or the return trip by sea. There is an interesting inland route from Rotterdam which, like the trip from Veere mentioned above, can be taken by masted yachts.

From IJsselmonde yacht haven you cross the Nieuwe Maas and enter the narrower Hollandsche IJssel, following this to Gouda and bearing left into the Gouwe Canal. It is important to turn left again at a 'crossroads' at Gouwsluis, passing through Alphen a.d. Rijn and turning right into the short Heimanswetering. Then cross the broad expanse of Braassemermeer and turn right to follow the Ringvaart as far as the two large bridges at Vast

Ged. You are now on the outskirts of Amsterdam, but the last dozen kilometres involve negotiating several city bridges which only open late at night. The Vast Ged bridges let you through at around 2000 local time, and you then cross a small lake known as Het Nieuwe Meer, mooring for a few hours at the yacht berths at the east end. Quite a sizeable convoy gathers here, waiting for the Nieuwe Meer road and rail bridges to open at 2320, and it proceeds very slowly through a lock and several bridges, emerging into the Nordzee Canal at about 3am. This route may sound a bit of a trial, but the scenery is attractive and varied and at least you can do Rotterdam to Amsterdam in a long day. The night convoy through Amsterdam's city centre has a rather special atmosphere.

There are various places to moor in Amsterdam, but the most agreeable and convenient is the Sixhaven, on the north bank of the Nordzee Canal immediately opposite the main line station. This is a tranquil basin with good pontoon berths, set nicely clear of the city centre and yet only 20 minutes' walk and ferry ride away. The free ferry runs continuously across the Nordzee Canal, from near the Sixhaven to the station slip.

From the East Coast, between Great Yarmouth and Harwich, yachts can reach Amsterdam in a week's holiday, and so two or three weeks offers considerable scope for onward cruising. One interesting possibility is a roughly circular route across to the Hook of Holland, up the Nieuwe Maas to Rotterdam, and then via the waterways to Amsterdam as described above. A day or two in Amsterdam, and then you could lock out into the IJsselmeer and sample a few of its fascinating little harbours on the way up to the northwest entrance at Den Oever lock. From there, a short passage across the southwest Waddenzee takes you to Den Helder or the island of Texel, whence you can emerge into the North Sea again via the Zeegat van Texel.

Yachts from the upper part of the Thames estuary can embark on a Dutch cruise given two or three weeks, and their most likely route will be across to Calais or Dunkirk from the North Foreland and then along the coast to the Westerschelde and Flushing.

I have only mentioned a handful of the main Netherlands waterways, but there are countless canals and rivers to explore, enough for almost a lifetime of annual cruises. Fixed bridges limit the headroom along some of the canals, especially those in the area south of Amsterdam and near Utrecht. Anyone planning an excursion into this amazing network will benefit greatly by obtaining one of the guide books listed near the end of this section.

Longer cruises

With a month's holiday one can plan for up to three weeks in Holland, depending on how quickly Flushing is reached. Quite a varied cruise is possible with this amount of time, perhaps taking in the Dutch Friesian islands and some of the Friesland canals. One possibility might look something like this. To Veere and return, 8 days; to Amsterdam via Willemstad, Dordrecht, Rotterdam and the Hollandsche IJssel, 3 days; Amsterdam, 2 days; harbours on the west side of the IJsselmeer, 4 days; the Waddenzee 3 days, perhaps calling at Oudeschild harbour on Texel, NE Vlieland, or West Terschelling harbour; to Harlingen and thence to Leeuwarden via the Van Harinxmakanaal, 2 days; to Lemmer via the Prinses Margriet Canal, 1 day; back across the IJsselmeer to Amsterdam, 2 days, allowing for weather or a stop en route; to Rotterdam via the Nordzee Canal, IJmuiden, and a 35 mile coastal passage to the Hook of Holland, 2 days, allowing for weather; from Rotterdam to Veere inland, 2 days; and finally a day in Veere to relax before setting off for home.

This adds up to 30 days and would provide an interesting introduction to different parts of the Netherlands—the polders of the southwest, Amsterdam and Rotterdam, the quaint old harbours of the IJsselmeer, the rather bleak but fascinating Friesian islands, and mainland Friesland. Up in the wild north, Friesland was once a separate province and even now remains a quite distinct and individual part of the Netherlands, much as Wales does within the UK. It has its own language, which a large proportion of the population still speaks. Friesland is sparsely populated and its rural waterways are among the most attractive in the Netherlands.

There is basically only one route through Friesland which has no constraints on headroom, although it can be joined at Lemmer, Stavoren or Harlingen. From any of these points of entry you make your way to Leeuwarden, the charming old capital of Friesland, famous for its cattle and its gin. On then via Dokkum to Lauwersmeer, where there is access to the sea by way of Lauwersoog lock. The Reitdiep continues to Groningen and then 25 straight kilometres of the Ems Canal take you to Delfzijl, from where you can glimpse the low coast of Germany, three miles across the turbid waters of the River Ems.

Few yachts manage to get as far east as Delfzijl, even with a month's holiday, and most English boats using the Friesland waterways are bound to or from the Baltic as part of a much longer cruise. However, East Coast yachtsmen who cross direct to IJmuiden or Den Helder can do justice to Friesland in four weeks, so long as those who turn inland at IJmuiden don't linger in Amsterdam or the IJsselmeer harbours.

Timing and flexibility

Although a cruise to the Netherlands may involve rather an eastward haul, the whole network of Dutch waterways opens up once you have reached Flushing, regardless of weather. You can enjoy coastal cruising when conditions permit, but have the option of ducking inland if things start brisking up. On the canals, there is the great advantage of being able either to press on or pull in somewhere as the mood takes you, and this flexibility gives plenty of scope to modify your broad timetable.

There is much to be said for planning a Dutch cruise for the end of June and early July, when you should miss the main period of Dutch summer holidays but can expect reasonable weather for both the outward and return passages. If you are tied to cruising in August, it is prudent to allow plenty of margin for your return trip in case you are unlucky enough

Barges and yachts rub shoulders very amicably on the Dutch waterways, but you should always give priority to commercial traffic.

o strike a patch of summer depressions to confound our progress back home. On the other hand, you should be ambitious about your outward schedule, especially if you are based west of the Solent. Try to cover mileage whenever conditions allow, since you never know when a spell of northeasterlies might set in to keep you in Dover, Calais or Dunkirk.

Leaving your boat

A Dutch cruise lends itself well to 'staging', since there are plenty of safe havens within Holland and, at least for south coast yachtsmen, on the way out.

Ferries are frequent and moderately priced. Calais or Ostend are possible bases from which to start a holiday in the Netherlands, perhaps having worked up-Channel over two or three weekends beforehand. Both ports have secure marinas and friendly yacht clubs in whose charge you can leave a boat with fair peace of mind.

Amsterdam is a convenient place to change crews, being strategically located near the centre of the Dutch cruising area. The Sixhaven is an agreeable spot to linger for a day or two and is close to the main railway station, which has good connections with the Hook of Holland ferry terminal. Rotterdam is feasible as a changeover port, although it is not so pleasant as Amsterdam for the shopping and pottering about which generally accompanies the start of a stage in a cruise.

Because marina charges and harbour dues are more modest in Holland and Belgium than in England, a staging operation need not be savagely expensive. The ferries provide the usual means of travelling to and from England, and Amsterdam (Schipol) has good connections with Heathrow and with some provincial airports.

Charts and waterway guides

It is definitely worth investing in a set of the excellent Dutch *Hydrografische Kaart*. It is cheaper to buy these in Holland and there is a convenient agent in Middelburg: Handelsonderneming Jos Boone, WS *Helena Maria*, Maisbaai, 4331 HJ Middelburg. You can also order in advance through Kelvin Hughes Ltd, 145 The Minories, London EC3N 1NH (tel 01-709 9076). The following are probably the most useful.

1803 Westerschelde, which covers the approaches to Flushing and the southern part of the Walcheren Canal.

1805 Oosterschelde and Veerse Meer, which takes you as far east as Krammer.

1807 Grevelingenmeer, Krammer, Volkerak and Haringvliet, Hollandsch Diep and as far as Willemstad.

1809 Nieuwe Waterweg, Nieuwe and Oude Maas, Spui and Noord, Dordtsche Kil, Brielse Meer; it covers Willemstad to Dordrecht, Rotterdam and the Hook of Holland.

1810 IJsselmeer, which covers from Amsterdam to Den Oever and the Waddenzee.

1811 Waddenzee (west), covering the Dutch Friesian Islands from Texel to Ameland.

1812 Waddenzee (east), which covers the Dutch and German Friesian Islands from Ameland to the west end of Norderney.

A new pilot, *Dutch Inland Sailing Guide* by H. Levison, is comprehensive and includes numerous maps, as is *Through the Dutch and Belgian Canals*

by Philip Bristow and published by Nautical Books. Also useful are two of the guides (in Dutch) from W H den Ouden NV, published by De Boer Maritiem and available from Dutch chandlers or through Kelvin Hughes Ltd: *Vetus Vaarkaart No.4 (Noord-Nederland)*, which covers the Friesland canals; and *Vetus Vaarkaart No.6 (Hollandse en Utrechtse Plassen)*, which covers all the canals in the old province of 'Holland', between Rotterdam and Den Helder. Recommended for the inland passage from Rotterdam to Amsterdam.

Chartering in the Netherlands

Various Dutch and English companies offer motor boats for charter on the waterways, and the following addresses may be useful. Blakes Holidays, Wroxham, Norfolk NR12 8DH (tel 06053 3224); Friesland Boating, De Tille 5, 8723 ER Koudum, Netherlands (tel 05142 2607); Holiday Charter Boats AB, PO Box 194, S-681 01 Kristinehamn, Sweden (tel 0550 82211); Hoseasons Holidays, Sunway House, Lowestoft, Suffolk NR32 3LT (tel 0502 62211); Muider Yacht Charter Station, MF Sachs, Naarderstraat 10, 1398 XR Muiden, Netherlands (tel 02942 1413); Netherlands National Tourist Office, 25-28 Buckingham Gate, London SW1 (tel 01-630 0451).

Queuing for a lifting bridge on the Dutch canals. The bridges in the Netherlands are very efficient, but bottle-necks sometimes occur in high season.

Which way now? The Dutch canals can be surprisingly intricate and it is important not to take a wrong turn.

French Inland Cruising

There are something like 8,000km of navigable waterways in France, and it is always fascinating to remember that you can travel the length of this grandly spacious country by river and canal, from the familiar grey wastes of the English Channel right down to the sunny warmth of Provence and the Mediterranean.

The French canals are much wider and deeper than our own, largely owing to the foresight and diligence of Charles Louis de Freycinet, the Minister of Public Works in the late 1870s. In his short term of office Freycinet established an improved specification and set of minimum dimensions for the waterways. His ambitious programme of deepening canals, increasing lock capacities and raising bridges has meant that much of the French network is still used commercially today. The present 'standard' barges or *peniches* are 38m overall with a capacity of about 350 tonnes and drawing up to 1.8m laden: these efficient vessels are a far cry from the English working narrow boats.

Most French waterways comply with the Freycinet formula and are of generous size for the majority of pleasure craft, although modern motor yachts with flying bridges and bristling aerials are apt to run into headroom problems. The official navigable draft on the Freycinet canals is 1.8m and they have at least overhead clearance of 3.4m. The minimum lock size is 38.5m by 5.1m, into which a *peniche* fits with only inches to spare. Some of the smaller waterways are now used mainly for pleasure and their dimensions are much more critical for yacht owners. The Brittany route between the Rance estuary and the Biscay coast falls into this category, with the Canal d'Ille et Rance and the upper reaches of the Vilaine River claiming a navigable draft of 1.3m and least headroom of 2.4m. In practice, you can probably only count on a metre of water during a dry summer spell. It is a great pity that this delightful navigation missed out on the Freycinet treatment, because many yachtsmen bound for the Bay of Biscay would be only too pleased to take an inland 'short-cut' and so avoid the rocky northwest corner of Brittany.

The popular Canal du Midi is one of the oldest waterways in France and forms the eastern half of the route between the Gironde estuary and the Mediterranean. The navigable draught is currently 1.6m, but a substantial improvement programme is under way to modernize most of the locks and bring the minimum depth up to 1.8m. The quaint stone bridges provide a least headroom of 3.25m under the centre of the arches and 3.0m at the sides. A considerable number of hire fleets now operate on the Midi and yachtsmen planning to explore this attractive canal with their own boats would do well to avoid July and August.

The Canal du Nivernais is one of the most restricted, with a least depth of 1.2m and a minimum headroom of 2.7m. It runs for 174km between Auxerre and Decize, offering a picturesque view of west Burgundy. If you are bound between Paris and the Rhone, the Nivernais has much to recommend it if your draught and height allow. Rarely used by barges, the canal forms the base for at least half a dozen hire-boat fleets.

Many yachtsmen, if they consider the French waterways at all, tend to think of them in terms of routes through to the Mediterranean. Yet you need not be heading way down south to enjoy the delights of meandering through rural France. Even the northern canals and rivers can provide unique cruising and a varied flavour within a normal summer holiday.

The main gateway to the system from the English Channel is undoubtedly the majestic River Seine, the longest and busiest waterway in France. The Seine is tidal as far as the first lock at Amfreville-Poses, 22 miles above Rouen. From Le Havre up to Rouen is about 70 miles and most boats can make this passage on one tide. Between Amfreville-Poses and Paris there are another five locks, large enough to accommodate several barges and yachts together.

Once you leave tidal waters you have to get used to thinking in kilometres rather than nautical miles. The various reference books and the French *Carte Guides de Navigation Fluviale* are so marked, and there are kilometre posts along the banks of the larger waterways. From Amfreville-Poses to Paris is only 100km as the crow flies but just over 200km by river: the course of the Seine is extremely tortuous below the capital.

About 70km short of Paris, the bustling barge port of Conflans-Sainte-Honorine lies at the confluence between the Seine and the River Oise. This is an important crossroads, because the Oise connects with the Canal lateral a l'Oise at Janville, some 100km NE of Conflans. Thence you can join the Canal du Nord at Pont-l'Eveque and reach St Valery-sur-Somme via the Canal de la Somme, or travel on to Calais, Gravelines or Dunkerque via the canalized River Aa. This northern network of waterways provides an interesting circuit in either direction between Le Havre and the Straits of Dover.

Paris itself is a natural high-spot on any trip up the Seine. The industrial outskirts are as grim as you will find on the approach to any large city and the barge traffic is particularly heavy, and yet that first glimpse of the Eiffel Tower from the deck of your own boat is an exciting moment.

It is important to obey the one-way system past the islands and through the numerous city bridges. Watch out for navigation signs on the banks and over the bridge arches, and follow the clear directions given in the *Carte Guide*. There are two possible berths in the centre of Paris for visiting yachts: the Touring Club de France jetty, on the north bank of the river next to Pont Alexandre III; and Paris-Arsenal marina, just off the Seine at the south end of the Canal Saint-Martin. Until the marina was opened in 1983, the Touring Club de France jetty was really the only secure place to moor in Paris. The Pont Alexandre is certainly well situated for sight-seeing, close to Place de la Concorde and the Champs Elysees and only 20 minutes' stroll from the Louvre. The main drawback is the considerable and persistent wash from passing barges and *vedettes*; it is not only uncomfortable, but likely to cause damage to topsides or guardrails unless you are extremely well fendered (as you will need to be for travelling further into the canal system).

The marina is the best bet, 4km further upstream. Entry is by way of a lock just below Pont d'Austerlitz on the north bank. The pontoon berths in the Bassin de l'Arsenal are quiet and sheltered and all the usual facilities are laid on; you are close to the Place de la Bastille and a short walk from Ile de la Cite and Notre Dame.

The River Marne joins the Seine on its north side, 5km upstream from the marina at the beginning of a fascinating vein of waterways through the heart of Champagne country and then either north towards Calais and the Low Countries, east to Germany or Strasbourg, or south into the Saone valley via the Canal de la Marne a la Saone. This last route is often used by yachts bound between Calais and the Med.

The two principal routes linking the Seine and the Saone are the Bourbonnais Canals and the Canal de Bourgogne. To reach the latter, you leave the Seine at Montereau and travel 85km up the River Yonne to La Roche. The Bourgogne is the shortest route through to the Mediterranean, but usually the slowest on account of the large number of locks: from Paris to Lyon is 629km and 219 locks. There is hardly any commercial traffic, though, and the spectacular climb through Burgundy makes all the hard work on the sluices worthwhile. At Pouilly-en-Auxois, the summit level, there is an eerie $3\frac{1}{2}$km tunnel to negotiate. Overhead conductors reduce the headroom to 3.1m, although boats with an air draught between 3.1m and the maximum of 3.4m may be towed through by the ingenious *bac transporteur*.

The Bourbonnais route is slightly longer than the Bourgogne but has fewer locks. You turn off the Seine 14km below Montereau at St Mammes, and then follow canals Loing, Briare, lateral a la Loire, and Centre to Chalon-sur-Saone. From Paris to Lyon this way is 643km and only 157 locks; the scenery is not so dramatic as on the Bourgogne and you are likely to meet a good many barges. Both the Bourbonnais and the Bourgogne are Freycinet waterways, although the former is less subject to local silting because of its heavier traffic. The Bourbonnais canals therefore offer a safer route if your draught is near the 1.8m official limit. They also carry a minimum headroom of 3.7m, except that you need to be careful when passing through the arched bridge at St-Leger-sur-Dheune. On the Canal du

Centre, most of the locks on the Saone side of the summit are automatic and self-operating. There are three fine aqueducts on the Canal lateral a la Loire, and the one over the Loire at Briare is particularly impressive.

Once you reach the River Saone you are back in wide water and can begin to make more rapid progress southwards. It is not quite 200km to Lyon from the Bourgogne junction at St Jean de Losne, with only five locks. Watch out for the traffic, since this lower part of the Saone is a busy commercial route, navigable by barges and large push-tows from all over Europe.

Lyon is an impressive city to arrive at by boat. The Saone passes under several historic bridges, overlooked by the tall and somewhat forbidding facades of Renaissance town houses which seem precariously perched on the steep sides of the valley. When the river is in flood, one-way navigation is enforced through the city centre, for $2\frac{1}{2}$ hour periods in each direction. There is no really secure place to berth in the centre; the best option is alongside the old *port de plaisance* quay, on the east bank between Pont Marechal-Juin and Pont Bonaparte. Make sure that you are well fendered and don't leave the boat unattended for too long.

Four kilometres downstream from this quay is the large lock at La Mulatiere, just below the confluence between the Rivers Saone and Rhone. The Rhone valley has been the subject of some amazing engineering over the last 50 years and this once wild river is now tamed into a huge waterway with a considerable hydro-electric generating capacity. In his book *The Inland Waterways of France* David Edwards-May observes that: 'The works completed by the Compagnie Nationale du Rhone between Lyon and the Mediterranean, have not only made the river navigable throughout the year by 1,500 tonne barges and 4,500 tonne push-tows; the 12 hydroelectric plants, with a total head of 162m, also produce 13,000GWh of electricity annually'. Because of its grand proportions, the Rhone has somehow managed to absorb these substantial changes without serious detriment to its natural beauty; because the river passage has been smoothed, yachtsmen are now able to appreciate this fine valley to the full, as they cruise southwards in bright sunshine between the Alps and the foothills of the Massif Central.

The actual mouth of the Rhone is not navigable, as it forms a broad shallow delta which encloses the extensive marshlands of the Camargue. There are two possible exits from the river for pleasure craft: one leading off to the west, via the Petit Rhone and the Canal du Rhone a Sete; and one to the east at Port-St-Louis—the Canal Maritime Saint-Louis, which lets you out into the Gulf of Foz.

A one-week cruise

In many ways, it is as difficult to offer sensible guidance about cruising schedules for inland waterways as it is for coastal passages. The Channel crossings may be subject to unpredictable weather delays, yet the inland part of the trip is equally tricky to plan, mainly because it is absolutely vital not to set too frantic a timetable. On this question, I agree wholeheartedly with Hugh McKnight's view, aptly expressed in his book *Cruising French Waterways*: 'There can be no more peaceful way to explore this beautiful land, seeking out ancient towns and villages, drinking local wines and eating in waterside *auberges*. The key to fullest enjoyment is to avoid being hurried; 30km and 10 locks each day is a target ambitious enough for anyone. Yachtsmen's stories of dawn to dusk navigation, through flights of tiring locks leaving a mob of angry canal staff astern of their wash, all too often suggest a totally wrong approach.'

Bearing these criteria in mind, a one-week cruise starting from the south coast of England would allow you just a brief taste of inland France, enough to whet the appetite for a longer visit. From the Solent, it is feasible to plan a short foray to the River Seine and back, although you won't have time to reach Paris. Even if the weather co-operates and you use no more than a day each way for the crossing, you still have only five clear cruising days to play with. The passage up to Rouen makes an interesting day and the old city is worth exploring. Above Rouen, you could perhaps meander gently up the last reaches of the tidal Seine. There is an excellent quay-side mooring at Elbeuf, on the south bank between Pont Jean Jaures and Pont Guynemer.

Having reached Calais, a one-week cruise could take you inland to sample some of the flat but rather evocative landscape of the Pas-de-Calais region. The Canal de Calais is entered via the Avant Port and the Bassin Carnot, leading SE for 30km to the canalized River Aa. If you turn left along the Aa, 14km of straight waterway take you back to the sea at Gravelines. About halfway along this stretch you have the option of turning right into the Canal de Bourbourg, once an important link between Dunkerque and its hinterland. Much of this area between Calais and Dunkerque is industrial and hardly picturesque, but it is interesting to see as you pass through.

A network of large-scale canals between Dunkerque and Valenciennes is designed to carry massive European barges. Known as the Dunkerque to Escaut Waterway or La Liaison au Grand Gabarit, this busy commercial route takes in the east end of the Canal de Bourbourg, the Canal de la Colme, part of the River Aa between Watten and St Omer, the Canal de Neuffosse, the Canal d'Aire, the Canal de la Deule, and the Canal de la Sensee. Yachts on a week's cruise might join the Aa from Calais, venture up La Liaison to Flandres lock, and turn back down the original Canal de Neuffosse to visit the fine old city of St Omer. Three short branches lead southwards off the Canal de Calais to the small towns of Guines, Ardres and Audruicq. These quiet *culs-de-sac* make interesting diversions on a short cruise inland from Calais.

The Canal de la Somme offers an inland route closest to yachts based between Brighton and Dover. Strangers should only make a landfall on St Valery-sur-Somme in reasonable weather. This broad estuary dries for nearly 2 miles out from the low shore-line, and it is important to pick up the Bale de Somme N-cardinal buoy about 2 hours before local HW before you start closing the coast to find the outer pair of channel buoys. The fairway is well marked thereafter, but you need good visibility and

nothing more than force 4 conditions. St Valery has a small marina and the canal entrance lies close to the east of the town. David Edwards-May observes that the canal is 'one of the most attractive waterways of northern France, passing through a marshy valley dotted with lakes and gravel pits'. It is 156km to St Quentin from the sea lock at St Valery, the lower 15km to Abbeville comprising the Canal Maritime. Maximum navigable draught is 3.2m between St Valery and Abbeville, but 1.8m otherwise. The Canal Maritime provides unlimited headroom, with four swing bridges and a lifting bridge. Maximum air draught between Abbeville and St Quentin is 3.4m.

It's nearly 75 miles to St Valery from Newhaven and about 65 miles from Dover. Given luck with the weather, a week's holiday could leave you with a day in St Valery and four days for meandering inland. Given two days each way on the canal, you might aim to stop the first night at Picquigny, 48km and five locks from St Valery, and the second night at Sailly-Laurette, another 43km and seven locks inland. Coming back, you stop at Ailly-sur-Somme, maybe pausing at Amiens during the afternoon.

Further down-Channel, boats with a brisk cruising speed crossing from the West Country can make for the River Rance during a one-week cruise, but the schedule will be very vulnerable to weather. A day to Guernsey, another to St Malo, and an optimistic forecast, may leave enough clear time to potter up the Rance and visit the restful medieval town of Dinan. The first lock takes you through the power station barrage, a little way above St Malo. Check the tide times with the *éclusier* to make sure it's safe to continue upstream to the next lock at Le Chatelier. Rance tides are controlled by the power station engineers, who open the turbine sluices according to a timetable. Le Chatelier lock normally operates between 0600 and 2100 during the season, so long as there is at least 8.5m of tide outside the gates.

Between the Rance Barrage and Dinan you can look forward to 25 peaceful kilometres of splendid scenery. The river is buoyed above St Suliac and the very narrow stretch immediately before Le Chatelier is marked by port and starboard-hand posts. Above Chatelier you are in the Canal d'Ille-et-Rance, which is supposed to have a least depth of 1.2m, but don't be surprised to come across shallower patches where the silt is gaining ground. There is unlimited headroom between St Malo and Dinan, but the fixed bridges above Dinan allow you only 2.75m in the centre of the arches and 2.3m at the sides.

Yachts from Falmouth can just reach the pastoral upper reaches of the Aulne River in a one-week trip. Given fair weather and a 10 knot cruising speed, you can make Falmouth to L'Abervrac'h in a long day, carrying on next day through the Chenal du Four to the Brest estuary. You are then well placed for exploring the 40km of the Aulne up to Chateaulin, a delightful town situated about 4km above the tidal lock at Guly-Glas. It is important to arrive there about half an hour before HW: if you are still in the shallow upper reaches of the tidal river when the ebb sets in, there is a real risk of going aground in unsavoury mud.

Two- or three-week cruises

With more time to spare, the scope opens up. From Calais one can make good progress south via La Liaison and then either the Nord or the St Quentin. So long as you reach Calais quickly, it is feasible to plan a circuit down to Peronne on the Canal du Nord and then back to the sea via the Canal de la Somme.

On the northern canals, Paris only comes within reach during a three-week holiday; the route from Calais to the capital via the Canal du Nord and the Oise tots up to 425km and 37 locks. However, Solent based boats can reach Paris on a fairly active two-week cruise, allowing a *minimum* of four days each way between Le Havre and Paris. Three weeks is preferable, giving breathing space to do justice to the inimitable River Seine and to Paris itself. Alternatively, with three weeks in hand, Solent boats can keep up a steady pace and carry on beyond Paris into the delightful upper Seine. If the weather co-operates on the Channel crossings, you might have time for three days each way above Paris, taking you

up to St Mammes perhaps or even just into the River Yonne.

Three weeks would also allow either Solent or Kent coast boats to make an interesting circuit either way between Le Havre and St-Valery-sur-Somme via: the Seine between Le Havre and Conflans-St-Honorine, the Oise to Janville, the Canal lateral a l'Oise to Pont-l'Eveque, the Canal du Nord to Peronne, and the Canal de la Somme to St Valery.

Down at the west end of the Channel, a moderately active three weeks would allow you to make a circuit of the Brittany canals, draught and headroom permitting. A day from Dartmouth to Guernsey say, a day in St Peter Port and a day to St Malo, and then you could afford to take seven or eight pleasant days to negotiate the Rance, the Canal d'Ille-et-Rance, and the Vilaine River to La Roche Bernard. You would still have ten days for cruising back along the Biscay coast of Brittany, round to L'Abervrac'h and back to the West Country.

With a more ambitious cruise in mind, three weeks would be enough to take a West Country boat down to the Gironde estuary, upstream to Bordeaux, and thence onto the Canal lateral a la Garonne—but you wouldn't have time to come back as well! One way to make this trip is to arrange two adjoining three-week periods, with one skipper and crew taking the boat out and the other bringing her home again. There is a fast rail service between Toulouse and Paris.

Four weeks or more

Because of the gentle pace of life on the more rural waterways, the more time you can make available the more you will be able to relax and savour the whole experience to the full. This is almost a truism for all cruising, but it seems especially germane to inland cruising.

In four weeks most South Coast boats can hope to penetrate well into central France, perhaps making for the Marne waterways or the Canal de Bourgogne, or maybe the Canal du Nivernais. Yachtsmen from further north can also begin to contemplate a worthwhile cruise in four weeks, based on one of the nearer routes mentioned in the last section.

People often ask how long it takes to travel right across France to the Mediterranean. I usually reply that it takes at least twice as long as you think, so long as everything goes according to plan. Even then, you'll soon wish you had more weeks to spare for lingering in the many charming spots along the way. But even if you are constrained to get down south as quickly as possible, you still need to allow an absolute minimum of 21 travelling days from Le Havre to Marseille or Sete via the Bourbonnais canals, and 24 days if you are coming from Calais. Add a 'weekend' or two, and various fuelling or provisioning stops, and you can hardly get away with less than a month.

Timing and flexibility

Progress along the inland waterways will not be greatly affected by weather; May and June are good months, but there is a lot to be said for off-peak cruising in April or September/October. The peak months of July and August are best avoided, especially on the Canal du Midi and the Canal du Nivernais. Some routes allow the flexibility to amend your plans if time runs short, but others are rather constraining once you have travelled a certain distance or perhaps passed a critical junction. Avoid carrying on too far along a waterway which is also your return route. For a first trip it is best to plan a very modest schedule and see how you get on. For the canals, I would use Hugh McKnight's yardstick of 30km and ten locks a day. The larger river waterways allow you to make faster progress, especially where locks are well spaced.

Leaving your boat inland is not as easy as you might think, unless you have someone staying aboard. An apparently secure canalside mooring can often be vulnerable to barge traffic or break-ins. The Paris-Arsenal marina is really the safest bet and

provides a convenient and interesting base for changing crews.

Waterway guides

The two books already referred to are both highly recommended: *Cruising French Waterways* by Hugh McKnight, pub. Stanford Maritime; and *Inland Waterways of France* by David Edwards-May, pub. Imrays. They complement each other perfectly. *Inland Waterways of France* is based on the classic work by E. E. Benest and contains concise and invaluable data such as route-planning charts, distance tables, and details of locks and bridges. Hugh McKnight's book provides a fascinating description of all the rivers and canals, and contains some fine photographs and useful maps. He paints an authentic picture of what to expect, blended with historical background about the whole network.

Other useful references are: *A Cruising Guide to the Lower Seine* by E. L. Howells, pub. Imrays, and good value for anyone planning a trip to Paris; *Through the French Canals* by Philip Bristow, pub. Nautical; the *'Small Boat...'* series by Roger Pilkington, pub. Macmillan; *Through France to the Med* by Mike Harper, pub. Cadogan.

Highly recommended are the French waterways strip maps, the *Carte Guides de Navigation Fluviale*, pub. Editions Cartographiques Maritimes, 56 rue de l'Universite, 75007 Paris. They are more costly if obtained in the UK, but should be available from chandlers in arrival ports. Their main use is for navigation while the guides are better for cruise planning.

Chartering

Hire companies operating on the French canals are too numerous to list here, but see the first two guides.

Index

Useful Addresses

Yacht Brokers, Designers & Surveyors Association, Wheel House, 5 Station Road, Liphook, Hants, GU30 7DW
Royal Yachting Association, RYA House, Romsey Road, Eastleigh, Hants, SO5 4YA
British Marine Industries Federation, Vale Road, Oatlands, Weybridge, Surrey